MEMOIRS

OF

ONSIEUR D'ARTAGNAN

CAPTAIN-LIEUTENANT OF THE 1st COMPANY
OF THE KING'S MUSKETEERS

W FOR THE FIRST TIME TRANSLATED INTO ENGLISH

BY

RALPH NEVILL

PART II.—THE LIEUTENANT

H. S. NICHOLS Ltd.

3 SOHO SQUARE AND 62A PICCADILLY

LONDON W.

1899

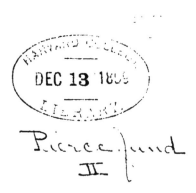
H. S. NICHOLS, LTD., PRINTERS, 3 SOHO SQUARE.

TRANSLATOR'S NOTE

In accordance with many suggestions, I have, in the second volume of these "Memoirs" ventured to compress certain portions of the text which deal with matters quite extraneous to the career of M. d'Artagnan, but the book has not been bowdlerised in any way whatever. The reader will find the last section of this volume, which describes D'Artagnan's adventures in London, especially worthy of his attention. The whole of it, however, is full of interest, and should it fail to meet with the flattering reception accorded to its predecessor, the fault will lie rather with the translator than with the work itself.

RALPH NEVILL.

MEMOIRS OF M. D'ARTAGNAN,

"CAPTAIN-LIEUTENANT OF THE 1st COMPANY OF THE KING'S MUSKETEERS."

I

PEACE having been made in the way I have described, a number of flatterers, who, on account of the great deeds M. le Prince had performed in the war, lauded everything else he did to the skies (as if his good points in this respect could wipe out all the bad ones he might possess), by so doing made him so vain that many people found difficulty in putting up with him.

The Cardinal, especially, could not reconcile himself to the airs with which he began to treat him. His Eminence, perceiving that he wanted to sell the help he had just given him against the Parisians at such a price that there would be no further favours he could dare to refuse him, made complaint of this to the Queen, who, for her part, was not too well pleased at a number of things which M. le Prince was every day asking for his dependents. M. le Prince had even wanted her Majesty to give the right of entry to her councils to the Prince de Conti, a proof that, when the latter had gone to offer his services to the Parlement, the matter had either been arranged between the two brothers, or, at all events, that they had since joined forces together, so as to make themselves more re- doubtable. This favour, as well as a number of others which he exacted for the Duc de Longueville, who had married his sister, very much displeased the Queen. It was her opinion that the revolt, with which the Prince de Conti and M. le Prince had associated themselves, deserved nothing less than rewards. Indeed this was all they might have hoped for, had they shown their fidelity instead of their rebelliousness. Anyhow, as at Court one looks just as pleasant when one wants to ruin a person, as when one intends to do him good, not only did the Cardinal conceal his resentment under the guise of civility and confidence, but also under that of a cordiality as great as might ever exist between two friends. He invited M. le Prince to come and feast with him four or five times in less than a month, and as this prince loved dissipation and plunged freely into it of his own accord, when once he was at it, his Eminence pretended to drink, so as to excite him to do the same. This minister knew that it was on occasions of this kind that a man loses control over himself, and that thus he might get his secret out of him without his noticing it. He succeeded none too badly. M. le Prince, who suspected nothing, having partaken pretty freely of wine, asked him in the presence of the Duc d'Orléans, who was at this banquet, if without his assistance the Parisians would not have terrified him a good deal. Were he to speak the truth, he must own to having trembled more than once on the day of the barricades, or at least to having turned pale ; so much

so, that if one had not known the cause, one could not
have failed to think that some accident had happened
to him !

He made besides other jokes, stronger even than
this, which causing the minister to fear that, if he
allowed himself to be attacked on such doubtful ground,
the prince would not be long in going even further, he
spoke of it to the Queen as being the only person able
to devise a remedy. The Queen decided not to
neglect his advice. She observed with pain that M. le
Prince, far from being satisfied with the favours which
he daily received from her Majesty, had again started
his old claims as to the Admiralty. This he haughtily
demanded again as something belonging to him by
right, and, on the Cardinal answering that, even were
this office his property, the recompenses he had already
received should make him abandon his pretensions, he
dared to tell him straight out that the services he had
just rendered spoke so much in his favour that, if there
was one of the two who could be called ungrateful,
such a term was much more applicable to the one
than the other.

Such haughty behaviour settled the matter of causing
his Eminence to nurture some extraordinary schemes
against him. As he was from a country where there is
a proverb which says,

"passato pericolo il gabbato del santo,"

that is, in good French, that "One thinks no longer of
the saint to whom one has vowed oneself, the minute
there seems no further use for him," he resolved on his
ruin, desiring to lower him to such a point as to make
him entirely dependent on his own will. The Queen

who began to place such confidence in this minister that she, so to speak, "saw only with his eyes," soon shared his ideas. The ruin of M. le Prince was sworn between the two and never had any hatred been seen to follow so quickly on trust; for, just as much as before both had relied upon this prince, so did they now think it a matter of their own safety to place him in a condition in which he could do them no harm. Perhaps their resentment would only have fallen upon him, if they had not been afraid that his relatives and friends would take his part, when they should perceive him in misfortune; but I must not say "perhaps;" this would actually have happened, at least there was every appearance of it. Indeed there was no one who did not know that the peace which had been made with the Parisians was not so well assured as not to be ripe for being broken at every moment and, as it was necessary to take away from them the leaders whom they might have made use of to recommence their agitation with, it was not a bad move for the Council to have decreed the arrest of the Prince de Conti and the Duc de Longueville at the same time as the Prince de Condé was arrested.

The governorships which both held, which were in the neighbourhood of Paris, further hastened their ruin. One was Governor of Champagne and Brie, and the other of the richest province of the whole kingdom, I mean Normandy, a province which was the more to be feared from being oppressed with a thousand taxes, and in consequence there was reason for fearing that the inhabitants, who loudly complained of the present government, would avail themselves of the first opportunity to show their discontent. Not that these two

governors were personally much to be dreaded; one
was a man much to be despised as a mere individual,
except for his birth, and on account of the alliance he
had contracted with two princesses of the blood; he
had no sense, and although the other did not resemble
him in this respect, but, on the contrary, had a good
deal, as he had been brought up for the church, it
was only the priests who were on his side. Not one
person of rank had thought of paying him court, but
the Queen and her minister were afraid, and with much
reason, that the friends and parasites of the Prince de
Condé, who were as numerous as those of his brother
were few, would soon rally to him, when they should
perceive his fall, and further, that his rank of prince of
the blood (which takes the place of worth among
people of quality) would produce its effect when least
expected. Accordingly, they thought that, to guard
themselves against all this, and against a quantity of
other things, which I suppress, because one can easily
picture them to oneself, it was urgent that his ruin
should be sworn at the same time as that of his
brother and his brother-in-law.

As it was difficult enough for a matter of such consequence, and one which required that several people
should be in the secret, to be carried out with certainty,
that is to say, without those against whom it was aimed
becoming aware of it, the Court deemed itself obliged to
win over some members of the Parlement, so that they
might restrain the people when the blow fell. As a
rule this body was ready enough to wish harm to M. le
Prince, because the side he had taken against it to
support the wishes of the Cardinal had made him forfeit the esteem and friendship which his great deeds

might have won for him.   Nevertheless, among its
members, as among the great number of people of
which it was composed, there were some greatly
attached to his person, and who thought much less of
the public weal than of their own private interests.
The President de Maisons, who was of the number, no
sooner got wind of what was going on than he confided it to M. le Prince.   The Prince de Condé who,
besides not imagining that the Cardinal would sully himself with such great ingratitude to him, thought enough
of the reputation of himself and of his friends to
imagine that he would never undertake a stroke of this
kind without thinking twice over it, made reply to
this magistrate, that he knew not whence this warning
came, but he was much deceived if it was not absolutely false.   Doubtless it had been given him only to
cause him to take some false step from stupid credulity:
but as, thanks to God, he had sense to discern truth
from falsehood, he would take good care not to fall
into the trap so clumsily set for him.   He spoke just
what he thought, and he would have even entertained
the idea (had not this magistrate been strongly attached
to his interests) that he was only speaking as he did to
be the first to hasten his fall, so firmly was he persuaded that it could not be true, that the Cardinal
would dare to think of such a stroke as this.   Be this
as it may, having neglected to take the precautions
which this president advised, he continued to go on in
the same way and was not long before repenting of so
doing.

The King had returned to Paris, after having granted
peace to the Parisians, and as it is much more difficult
to hide one's faults from those on the look out for them,

when one is near, than when one is far away, all the
Court and all Paris retained so little esteem for his
Eminence on account of a hundred things he was
observed to do, that it was only his servants or his
private parasites who kept quiet about it. Further,
his word was worth as little as if there had been dis-
honour in keeping it. What he promised to-day he
forgot to-morrow; for some sordid piece of self-interest
he would break with his best friend, and he had become so used to doing this, that it was constantly
happening to him. The principal cause of the hatred
M. le Prince bore him was that, after the reconciliation
with the Parisians had been effected, he had refused
him the governorship of Pont de l'Arche for his brother-
in-law. His Eminence had given as a reason that the
honour and interest of the State required that favours
should not be showered upon a rebel such as he; not
only would it be setting a bad example, but further, it
would make an evil impression upon the populace.
Besides, even had the Duc de Longueville been a man
who had remained faithful, it would not be politic to
make him so powerful. Already he possessed the
greatest number of the ports in Normandy, and to
give him this one would be to want to make him a
sort of king of the whole province. It was there that
the greater part of his estates lay, and as he raised
from it a number of gentlemen and persons of great
distinction, it was quite clear that one could not further
increase his authority without grave danger. M. de
Matignon, a near relative of this prince, who was
lieutenant-general of the province, served as another
pretext for the minister to support his contention with.
He said, with reference to him, that it was another

cause of the duc's power being increased.   This, indeed,
might have had some sense, had the Comte de Matignon been a man like anyone else, but his was such a
feeble intelligence, that all the prestige he might obtain
from the support of the prince and his own rank was
destroyed by the little he himself personally possessed.
He never said anything which was not pitiable, and it
was but a short time before that he had maintained in
very good company, that he had never partaken of
such good olive-oil as that which is made in Poitou.
Someone answered him that none was made there, and
that it must have come from Provence or Languedoc.
However, he again repeated what he had before said
and maintained that quite as much was made there as
in the two provinces just mentioned, and that he himself had seen the walnut-trees from which it came;
they yielded, he continued, as good oil as he had ever
tasted in Italy or anywhere else, and there was nothing
to be said against his statement, since he spoke not
from hearsay, but from the testimony of his own eyes.
Nobody would contradict him further, and, satisfying
themselves with admiring his great cleverness, they
agreed to what he wanted, that is to say, that the
walnut-trees of Poitou produced the best olive-oil in
the world.

Yet this gentleman was from the district known as
the clever district, and where, indeed, intellects are a
good deal more subtle than in any other; however, if
there are some which deserve this reputation, there
are as well others just as dull as can be found anywhere.   It even seems at present as if whatever part
of the country the Matignons hail from (for formerly
they lived in Brittany, since it is there that the family

arose) makes an effort to distinguish itself from other
parts by the simplicity, not to call it the stupidity,
which is to be observed there. It is of these people
that it is commonly said that, when they speak of
their seigneur, they declare he is just as great as the
King or at least very nearly so; and, indeed, I have
heard a gentleman who was not a man to amuse himself with fairy-tales say that, being one day at M. de
Matignon's, his peasants looked upon his praying to
God, just as they themselves did, as being something
worthy of admiration. This gentleman repeated this
to the curé so that he might reprove them, for they
thought him just as great as the King or very near:
they also thought that he was humbling himself a
good deal to do just as they did, when he bowed himself before God. But this curé, either because he
shared their obtuseness, although that is unlikely, or
because he was afraid of displeasing his seigneur by
disabusing these people of the great estimation they
had of him, contented himself with telling them that,
if the comte abased himself so much as to bow the
knee to God, it was because he wished to set them a
good example: this was very edifying in such a great
lord as he, and they must take good care to imitate
him.

However, to return to my subject. The Cardinal,
who was trying to render M. le Prince odious to all
the populace, was delighted at his asking him for the
governorship of Pont de l'Arche for his brother-in-law.
For, as he was afraid that, if he arrested him, he would
be accused of ingratitude, he looked upon it as being
a thing very lucky for himself that he should thus give
him a reason for so doing, without his being obliged to

resort to any pretext. He was aware that the one
course must break down sooner or later, even should he
be clever enough to well disguise it, whereas the other
would impress itself the more on his mind as he would
have reason on his side. Such a stroke as this could
not be the work of one day; for although it was but a
question of demanding his sword, not a very difficult
thing, since he came to the King's every day, as he
must not be taken alone because of what might result,
it was not only necessary to try and collect all the
three together, but to further prepare people's minds
to receive such a great event without taking any part
in it. M. le Prince had himself already prepared them,
when he had espoused the cause of the Cardinal
against the people. His troops also had admirably
seconded him in this by pillaging and ravaging the
country-side as they had done. Meanwhile, as, in
spite of the warning of the President de Maisons, this
prince as yet suspected nothing, instead of changing
his behaviour, which might have destroyed the
suspicions entertained as to his fidelity, he began to
plot in the province of Guyenne to get himself given
the governorship. He would much have liked to
exchange it for that of Burgundy which he held; for,
beside its being much more important both in revenue
and in a thousand other things unnecessary to specify
(since they are self-evident) it was besides a very convenient one for him. Indeed, he already had another
the other side of the Loire—that of Berri. But now,
although one must not be sure that he as yet entertained those great plans which he has since developed,
as it is a natural thing for everyone to wish to get on,
he made use of an opportunity which seemed to him a

favourable one to obtain both these governorships for himself.

The Duc d'Espernon, who had inherited from his father the characteristic of being very proud, ill-used the Bordelais, whose governor he was, a good deal. He had a perfect understanding with the Cardinal, who had an idea of marrying one of his nieces to the Duc de Candale, his only son; for this reason, the governor in question lent his aid as much as he could in the territory he governed, to help raise new taxes, with which his Eminence every day loaded the people more and more. Bordeaux, which is the capital of this province, and which took a great lead in it as capitals usually do with regard to everything, did not dare express all it thought. Château Trompette, which is as it were the citadel of that town, stopped this; but eventually, the natural disposition of the people to revolts being augmented by the sternness of their governor and the exactions of the tax-collectors, they all of a sudden rose against him. The Marquis de Sauveboeuf, a gentleman of the vicinity, who had a private cause for complaint against the Duc d'Espernon, as well as against the Court, by which he had been a good deal ill-used, placed himself at their head. They armed some vessels so as to become masters of the Garonne, and the revolt having every moment gathered strength from the hatred they bore their governor, they laid siege to Château Trompette.

At that time I was already a lieutenant in the Guards, a circumstance which entailed my mounting guard, which was a more important thing than it is to-day, the reason being that, thanks to God, everything is now, as it should be, in a state of submission to its

King, instead of which, at that time, his person was
not in great safety on account of the little respect left
in the minds of many people. Consequently, everything depended on the vigilance and fidelity of those
who were guarding him, and all the posts which had
anything to do with this were valued in the highest
degree possible, wherefore M. le Cardinal was very
friendly towards us, while we were thus employed, so
that, should anyone make any attempt to bribe us, we
might not fail to let him know. Meanwhile, as I
seemed to him to be even more wanted in that part of
the country than at Paris, he sent me post-haste to
Brouage to find the Comte d'Augnon, who was governor
there.   I gave him orders from the King to equip ships
for sea with the utmost diligence, and to succour the
Duc d'Espernon.   This concerned him more than
anyone else, because he was vice-admiral, a position
which was not then of the importance it is to-day, but
which has since become a very great one.   For
instance, when it was proposed to give it some time
after to the Comte d'Etrées (who now holds it), he
refused to accept it, from the fear that it might stop
him from one day becoming a Maréchal of France.
He was already a lieutenant-general, and he thought
that, being as far advanced as he was, it would turn
out an obstacle to his fortunes ; accordingly, M. Colbert
had to promise him, after the King had done so, that
this post should in no way prejudice his claims, and it
was only upon that condition that he accepted it.

The orders I had for the Comte d'Augnon were not
only by word of mouth, but set down in writing
besides.   However, M. le Prince, who was well pleased
to embarrass the Cardinal, had already been before-

hand with him, so as to oblige him to have recourse to himself to pacify the province and thus to get it placed in his hands. He had secretly sent one of his gentlemen to the comte, and they had agreed together that, instead of acting with the haste enjoined, he should do everything in such a slow way as to wreck the plans of the Court. This I clearly perceived, directly I arrived at the governor's. He discovered a thousand difficulties about whatever I might propose to him, and on my clearing all of them away, as far as good sense would allow me to do, although I understood nothing about naval affairs, which were under discussion in this interview, I soon saw that he was behaving with a remissness which could only be very suspicious, instead of with that earnestness which one would naturally have expected from a good servant of the King. But now, my mission being finished, and having nothing more to do with him, I had no sooner described what I believed myself to have discovered to his Eminence than I saw two deputies of Bordeaux arriving at his house. The Duc d'Espernon had, by order of the Court, granted them a passport to come and see him. Both these deputies were mortal enemies of the governor, which, had he been master of the situation, would have been the cause of his refusing it to them. The principal object of their deputation was to lodge complaints against him. Amongst other things, they accused him of having treated them like a tyrant and, although they did not dare to say that they would continue to be rebellious, unless M. le Prince was appointed governor in his stead, they caused it to be pretty well understood, by saying that their province would never willingly be obedient to authority until a prince of the blood should be at its head. They said also that, were M. d'Espernon not removed, some discontent would always linger in some place or other, which could only have bad results, so much so that the interest of the Court as well as their own lay in not refusing them this satisfaction. Meanwhile, M. le Prince was secretly doing all he could to be chosen for the post, while the Comte d'Augnon, according to his advice, took such a long time to put to sea, that Château Trompette found itself in extremities before he was in a condition to relieve it ; indeed, this fortress surrendered before he had confronted the enemy. The Bordelais demolished it without waiting a moment's time, although they were treating with the Court. They acted with such speed, because they thought that, this being done, it would be easier for them to prevent its reconstruction, than it would be to obtain its demolition, were it left standing. This was a daring stroke: but, as the weakness of the government allowed it, it did not prevent their obtaining the greater part of what they asked for. They got rid of their governor, and, M. le Prince being installed in his place, the Duc d'Espernon went sometime after to take up his own governorship in Burgundy. Folks were no more contented there than they had been in Guyenne. The inhabitants, who for a long time had been ruled by the first prince of the blood, only viewed the change with regret. M. de Tavannes, lieutenant-general of the province, who also deemed it an honour to take the orders of the Prince de Condé, was no more pleased than other people. M. le Prince again secretly fomented these feelings of discontent, so that, although he had no longer any right to give orders in this province, he yet reigned there just as absolutely as he had ever done.

That year he had not joined the army. The Comte d'Harcourt, who, as I have elsewhere said, had distinguished himself in a number of encounters, had taken his place in Flanders. He began by laying siege to Cambrai, but the enemy having relieved it before his lines were finished, he could no longer continue his undertaking. He marched in another direction, a circumstance which in some measure obscured the glory which he had gained by a number of great successes. M. le Prince, who had wanted to stay in the Cabinet, where he began to enjoy himself a good deal more than with the army, was delighted at what had happened, which seemed likely to further enhance his own reputation, although it was already at the highest point. The more the Comte d'Harcourt passed for a great captain, the more reason was there for praising him, for he had always laid his plans so well that such a thing had never occurred to him except once at Lerida. The Cardinal, who disliked his triumph, very nearly died of grief. In the meantime, as he was clever and crafty, he tried to make M. le Prince lose not only the reputation which all this had given him, but further, to make all the blame for it fall upon his shoulders. He secretly had the rumour spread that he had refused to take the command of the army, and that, had he been with it, nothing would have happened that year. Besides this, these rumours, added to the refusal which his Eminence had just given him of the governorship of Pont de l'Arche, threw M. le Prince into such a great passion against him, that he said a number of things to him which

did not appear seemly coming from the mouth of
a prince of his rank. For, as he was more fit to
strike a blow than anyone else, people would have
liked all his actions to correspond with his reputation,
and it seemed that, as he had had recourse like
a woman to biting words wherewith to show his
resentment, they had in no way done so. It was
thought that this kind of insult was a weapon much
more fit for women than for a hero like him. All the
army knew of these scandals, just as well as the whole
Court and the whole of Paris, and, although the Comte
d'Harcourt did everything he could to gain the friendship of the officers, there were none of them, at least
among the most important ones, who did not proceed
to inform M. le Prince that, should his differences with
the minister go any further, they would not hesitate to
embrace the Cardinal's interests against his own. The
Cardinal, who had this in common with his predecessor, that he tried to have spies everywhere, got news
of this through a man called Du Tot, who believed
that, to make one's fortune, one must attach oneself to
the minister in preference to everything else. An
attempt had been made to win him over, as he was
in the service and well enough liked by the soldiers.
Debas, a creature of M. le Prince, one who was from
my province, had been employed in this; but Du Tot
had told him in formal terms that he was the servant
of M. le Prince, but not to such a point as to declare
himself against him whom the Queen-mother had
selected to hold the reins of state. He would not, he
said, enter into a discussion as to whether he was
worthy to do so or not; it was not for him to judge
of this, but for the Queen, and, until the time when

she should have deposed him, he would remain faithful to him until his last breath. Indeed, continued he, he made no distinction between failing in fidelity to him or to the King, until such time as he should have been proscribed. The Cardinal was very pleased with this answer, which he only heard a long time after, that is to say, when Debas, who was then trying to corrupt others, let himself be corrupted. As Du Tot made a point of being an honest man, he preferred that he should hear of it from someone else than himself. He contented himself with doing his duty, without attempting to praise himself. For this reason, although I have just now given him the name of "spy," I do not think I had much reason for doing so. One may let a minister know of what is happening prejudicial to the service of the King without sullying one's honour; this is all he did, and therefore it is only fair to do him justice.

Be this as it may, his Eminence, perceiving that a great storm was brewing against himself, considered that there was no better expedient to divert it than to carry out his resolve. Meanwhile, so as not to be censured in the world, and in order on the contrary to find defenders when the friends and creatures of M. le Prince should rise against him, he granted him the governorship of Pont de l'Arche after having a long time refused to do so, and with much firmness too. He even had this refusal widely announced, so that everyone might think, as was true, that M. le Prince had rather extracted this favour from him than he himself had granted it. M. le Prince, who had not yet all the experience he has since gained, reckoning this as a great triumph, boasted of it in private to

those whom he thought his friends, but, as many of
those to whom one gives that name are far from
deserving to bear it, there was one who went so far as
to report it to his Eminence. This increased the
reasons for resentment which that minister entertained against him, and having made the Queen
share his displeasure, her Majesty thought it best to
take measures with the Parlement, so that it might
not espouse his cause. Not that that body had much
cause for doing this, for in addition to having declared
against it in the civil war, he had further had the
houses of all its members so plundered, that one
might have said that he had been intent upon such
a course of action. The Cardinal had obtained this
from her as a favour, not that he then dreamt of what
was to happen, but so that, sharing part of the public
hatred with himself, their interests might in the future
become but identical. In this, his policy was not bad:
on the contrary, it was that of a clever Italian, but, as
it frequently happens that the plans one has made turn
out quite differently from what one expects, instead of
so uniting their fortunes, he found means of making
everything which occurred contribute to his ruin. To
undertake this stroke, it was necessary to associate in
his fortunes the Duc d'Orléans, who was a meek prince
and allowed himself to be ruled. His rank as uncle
of the King gave him a great position in the State, and
in some measure made up for the small consideration
he was held in for any personal qualities. M. le Prince,
who knew him better than anyone else, had tried by
his tact to efface any resentment which he might
retain about the affair of the officer.[1] Meanwhile,
as a single word of the Abbé de la Rivière, to whom

1 See Volume 1, page 359.

the Court had recently given the bishopric of Langres, and who had absolute power over his mind, was more than enough to make his schemes fail, he took measures with him, so that, very far from opposing him, he might favour his plans to the best of his endeavours.

This bishop was a man from the dregs of the people, but who for all that was none the less greedy. When he came to monsieur, he would have thought himself too happy if he had been given a small benefice of five or six hundred "livres," but his good graces, into which he had quite immediately entered, having procured for him some abbeys and eventually a bishopric, he dreamt of equalling the Cardinal, whom the voice of slander reported to be of like birth to himself. Those who knew the real state of things did not believe this, although the hatred they bore him, just like the others, made them disposed towards everything which could do him harm. The Bishop of Langres might have discovered the truth just the same as these people did, but, as he was very desirous of not knowing it, in order that so much fault might not be found with him for trying to equal the Cardinal, he began to want to don the purple, not finding that the camail[1] and the mitre honoured him sufficiently. So it is that, as one advances, one always aspires to something one does not possess. Be this as it may, this bishop, finding no disposition at Court towards making his schemes succeed, turned in the direction of M. le Prince, who did not fail to proffer him all the advances possible, so that at the right time he might check his master in the event of someone cropping up to try and make mischief between them.

[1] An ornament worn by a bishop over his lawn sleeves.

2—2

The Bishop of Langres did not refuse his friendship and, as he knew that M. le Prince had for some time placed himself upon a footing to obtain, by fair means or foul, everything he might want for himself or his creatures, he thought that he would once more do for him what he had already done for so many others. Accordingly, their interests requiring that they should both unite against the Cardinal, M. le Prince deemed himself in such great safety on account of this, as to think himself at the top of the tree; so coming to an open quarrel at every moment with this minister, the latter became so bitter against him, as not to be at rest till he had had him arrested.

For this he had either to again win over the Bishop of Langres, with whom he had for some time trifled, promising him afresh that the King would ask of Rome the hat he so much coveted, it was necessary, I repeat, to find means either of deluding him again or at least to make him lose his master's confidence, so as to get the latter to sanction the resolve which had been taken against the Prince de Condé. Without him one dared not carry it out. The danger was too great, and it would have been the means of arousing the whole State against the government of the day. Finally, although the one course seemed no less difficult than the other, on account of the obstacles which appeared on all sides, his Excellency nevertheless decided that, from the disposition of the Duc d'Orléans' mind, he would succeed better with him than with the other. The bishop was too well trained in his work to let himself be caught a second time, whereas, if someone who had a little sense and tact was to be found, he might hope to make the duc do everything he wanted.

There were then three parties in the State : that of the Court, commonly called the Mazarin party : that of the Prince de Condé, and that of the Parlement, called by the name of Frondeurs. This name had been given to it because, during the height of the civil war, some members of that body had advised not only that very severe measures should be taken against the Cardinal, but further had maintained that, to ruin him entirely, a proceeding of this kind was necessary, in such a heated manner that they had come to abusing their own colleagues. Their rage arose from these latter not sharing their feelings as they desired, and being, on the contrary, inclined to smooth over matters. The first of these parties was composed of most of the courtiers, the second of a great number of military officers, some even of those most esteemed, the third, of the Duc de Beaufort, of the Coadjutor[1] of Paris who was a brother of the Duc de Retz and of the whole of the people of that great city. These citizens did not really know what they wanted : had they known, they would but have thought of keeping peace. They had already suffered so many evils from civil war that, although this one had lasted no longer than six weeks, more than six years were yet necessary to efface its effects. But the word " tax," which is hateful to the populace, (and the horror of which the Parlement was further clever enough to add to by reporting that the Cardinal had all the money it was producing sent into Italy) making them ready for all the ideas one wanted to impress upon them, their simplicity reached such a

1 The Cardinal de Retz, Jean François Paul de Gondi, born 1614, died at Paris, 1679.

pitch that they began to believe that taxes would be totally abolished, owing to the Parlement taking up the matter.

As it was a great thing to have these people, who are almost equal in number to the whole of the rest of the kingdom, on one's side, the Cardinal (who knew that he was not liked by the Parlement, and that, consequently, directly that body perceived the arrest of the Prince de Condé, it would make use of the opportunity to ruin him), tried not only to alienate the Duc de Beaufort and the Coadjutor from it, but also to embroil them with the Prince de Condé to such an extent as to make them keep that body in the path of duty through the delight they would feel at his fate. This was difficult enough for him to do in the case of the first-named nobleman. The resentment he still retained on account of his imprisonment, when he had been treated with much severity, was yet so active in his mind that he could not hear the Cardinal spoken of without disgust. For instance, although his Eminence was thinking of giving one of his nieces to his elder brother, which in his idea was to bring about a reconciliation, up to that time it had produced so small an effect that he wished him just as much evil as ever. As to the Coadjutor, his mind was no better disposed in his favour, as he not only aspired to the purple, but also to depose the minister so as to him-self take his place. He regarded the Cardinal with just as much envy as a lover does a rival who happens to be favoured. Besides, he was none too well pleased with the Queen, who had not received the offers of help, which he had gone to make her on the day of the barricades, in any too gracious a manner.

She had indeed scarcely looked at him, either because she knew him to be possessed of ambition enough to make her feel sure that he was capable of inciting these disturbances rather than calming them, or because she was in such a bad humour at what had just happened, that she was unable to think over things as thoroughly as was her custom on other occasions.

These difficulties, which were great enough to have discouraged anyone but the Cardinal, did not nevertheless discourage him. As, in matters of cunning and knavery, he would have been very sorry to give way to anybody, he thought of something which nobody perhaps but himself would have dreamt of. He posted men at night, who fired musket shots into the carriage of M. le Prince, while he was passing over the Pont Neuf. By good luck he was not in the carriage, but one of his lackeys (for thus he himself termed them, and I may well do the same thing after his example) having been wounded, he believed, as appeared to be the case, and as the Cardinal was well pleased he should suspect, that someone had wished to assassinate him. Nevertheless, he did not know who was at the bottom of it, unless it was the minister. He believed that, except him, he had never offended anyone, but his Eminence, to whose advantage it would not have been to have left him under this impression, having soon disabused him of it and made him believe that, far from an attempt of this kind being his work, the Coadjutor was much more the right person to be suspected, he strengthened this slander by some circumstances which were likely to thoroughly impress this idea upon the prince's mind beforehand. The circumstances in question were that, in a conversation which the prince had had with some persons of rank, he had slightly lampooned the Coadjutor. He had described him as being more amorous than pious, and, as truth offends more grievously than anything else, and as even that which has merely its appearance often produces the same effect as truth itself, the prince was all the more inclined to believe this was the case, knowing from a good source that his words had been repeated.

Appearances were sufficient to condemn him. He made a violent attack upon him. He openly blamed the Coadjutor, and, the matter being reported to that functionary, and the prince even declining to hear his defence, the fear which he was in of his violence (tales of which abounded on all sides) made him seek a protector in the person of the Cardinal. His Eminence got him cheap, because he saw that he had need of his help. They both joined together against the prince, and, as the Coadjutor was one of the friends of the Duc de Beaufort, he promised the minister, while making his pact, that he would get him to join them if he could. He also promised that, should he be unable to do so, he would at all events be answerable for his not siding with the prince against him. M. le Cardinal was satisfied with this promise, and, perceiving that he had nothing further to fear in this quarter, now only thought of striking the blow he had contemplated for such a long time. The thing was very cleverly carried out, just when the prince least expected it. The minister, having found means to get the three princes, against whom he had conspired, assembled together on the pretext of some business the

Comte de Matignon had with the Council, had the comte secretly informed that he must not only beg M. de Longueville to be there, but also make him see that his brothers-in-law were present. This they did without suspecting anything, and were in this manner arrested and taken to the Château of Vincennes, where the Cardinal confided them to the keeping of Debas, who was a shrewd Gascon. The latter had been my comrade whilst I was with his Eminence, and never did man better understand the secret of deceiving the public than he! Everyone thought him incapable of knavery, so much so that those who had not quite the same opinion of the Cardinal said, when speaking of him, that he was a living contradiction of the proverb which informs us, that servants are usually like their master. However, in the end, after having played his part so well for some time, he showed clearly that it was but too true that faith should be placed in this proverb. Indeed, he got hold of a hundred thousand crowns which the Comte de Seulemberg, Governor of Arras (who has since become Maréchal of France under the name of Mondejeu) had confided to him.

The worthy Guittaut, captain of the Queen's Guards, accompanied by his nephew De Comminges, was the individual who arrested the three princes, and, as there was a danger of their being rescued on the way, his Eminence promised the Comte de Miossens, lieutenant of the company of gendarmes of the guard of the King, that, provided he should safely conduct them to prison, he would procure the bâton of a Maréchal of France for him. It is he whom we have since seen calling himself the Maréchal d'Albret, a shrewd Gascon, and a man of inordinate ambition; this is shown by the fact that such an honour, which is usually bestowed only as a reward for great deeds, cost him but the trouble of going two leagues by the side of a carriage containing three prisoners.   However, this is nothing to be surprised at.   He was one of those people with whom everything succeeded, and one who, if I may use an expression which is usually employed to designate a lucky man, was born with a silver spoon in his mouth. It is true he could boast of a fine name—the name of D'Albret is one with which no others can compare ; so, if it had been his by right, it would have been more excusable for him than for the Maréchal de Turenne to be unwilling to be called maréchal.   Scions of the family of D'Albret, had there been any in existence, would indeed have considered themselves dishonoured by such a thing, but as there is a great difference between bastards and legitimate heirs, one must not be surprised if he whom I speak of showed himself less delicate than those from whose left side he sprang.

Be this as it may, I have not been far out, it seems to me, in declaring that he was born with a silver spoon in his mouth, since in his youth, being on the point of returning to his native province from lack of money, he had found a lady who paid him so well for certain services he had performed for her, that he obtained the wherewithal to buy a company in the Guards.   He had also obtained a good many other favours from this lady, in short, it was to her he owed his good fortune.   It is true that he was not the first ; a circumstance which well deserved that she should pay him better than if she had presented him with an entirely virgin heart.   As apparently she had a fancy for the tribe of bastards, a former lover of hers had

been a man who was a by-blow of her own family.
Besides this, she had had many other lovers, some
bastards, some of legitimate birth. Somebody one day
had been near telling this to her husband, who was a
hero of the first rank, but, as there was no need of his
being told for him to know it, and as he was of opinion
that in these sort of matters it was much better to
pretend to be blind than too clear-sighted, he replied
to the individuals who spoke to him, who from feelings
of delicacy talked as if of things far away and as
meaning someone else than himself, that for his part,
were his wife a flirt, he would be so annoyed to be
told about it by anyone as to believe that the only
reward he could give to such charitable folks would
be to run his sword through their bodies. His would-
be informants needed no more to make them shut
their mouths. They heartily agreed that he would
never escape from a state of cuckoldom, as men sometimes claim to do who kill their wife's lovers; but they
may say what they like, I do not see that they escape
any the more by so doing. On the contrary, I think
that, instead of extricating themselves from the mire,
they but sink the deeper into it. Indeed, it is but
publishing their misfortune, and from being like
Cornelius Tacitus, whom at first they resemble, they
become, as says a common proverb, with some wit at
least on the part of the individual who first originated
it, like Cornelius Publicus!

M. le Prince being thus in prison, his friends and
parasites, who were in despair, had the added grief of
seeing a display of fire-works given by the city. Nevertheless, the cry of "*Vive Mazarin*" was not heard as "*Vive
Broussel*" had formerly been. The inhabitants contented

themselves with only celebrating the memory of the justice, which they believed had been granted them in depriving of liberty a man who had not only robbed them of part of their property, but had also so thoroughly blocked the roads into the town, that it had not been his fault he had not made them die of hunger.

After they had committed a thousand follies about this, as was usually their way in matters which they thought concerned their interests, they calmed down their great ardour which made people, who had any brains, laugh. M. le Cardinal, to whom I paid my court much more assiduously now that I was no longer in his service, seeing me one day in his room, where there was scarcely anyone else, asked me what I thought of such an unexpected change. At first, I would say nothing in reply : not that I did not know what I ought to answer, but perhaps from fear of displeasing him by speaking freely to him. Nevertheless, my silence only increasing his vanity the more, "Have your say," said he, "and know that I do not approve of you alone being silent about a matter in which it seems to me I deserve at least some praise." "I am sure of it, Monseigneur," I replied, "since you have done everything you could to succeed : but to believe that things will turn out for you as you think, is something I will not agree to so early in the day." He would not let me say more, and having as it were snatched the right of speaking away from me,—"You are playing the clever man," he continued, "but, to show you that you are just as likely to be deceived as other people, I want you to come in my carriage with me this moment : I desire, I repeat, to show you by the extent of the public acclamations, that you are wrong not to believe that I am now as popular with the populace as in the past I was the contrary." I would say nothing more to him, from fear of paining him by continuing to try and disabuse his mind. Meanwhile, we got up into the carriage as he desired, his Eminence being in the back with M. de Navailles, and myself in front with Champfleuri, the captain of his guards. The carriage we were in was magnificent, the horses the same—all of them the best he had in his stable, for he wanted to attract everybody's attention ; but, instead of succeeding in his wishes through all this, just the opposite happened to him. The more his equipage was worthy of the admiration of the Parisians, the more they made it a subject for abusing him. This I clearly perceived from the way they were talking to one another, even had not their looks shown it me well enough. Not a man took off his hat to the Cardinal, who was regarded by the people as one only tricked out at their expense. We traversed the city from the Palais Royal to the Porte St. Antoine, without a soul presenting himself before us to acclaim his Eminence in any way. Navailles, who was already desirous of his returning to the Palais Royal, tried to divert him on the way with jokes, so as to spare him the pain of what he saw, but he had no desire for laughter, especially after having boasted so magnificently, as he had done, that he had only to show himself to disillusion me of my ideas, and so nothing could equal his confusion on his return. I began to talk as Navailles had done to dissipate his annoyance, but, as he knew that I was a long way from being as easy-going as he was, he did not take it in the same way.

Indeed, to tell the truth, this man was as clever a
courtier as the Court has ever seen. The fortune he
made there clearly shows this. From being a cadet
de Gascogne[1] as he was, to have amassed an income
of more than a hundred thousand livres is a good proof
that he knew more than others. True, that the daughter
of his eldest brother, whose property he had, complains
a little! Whether she is right or wrong, is a thing I will
not go into nor will I mix myself up with it. I have
enough to do with my own affairs without embarrassing
myself with other people's. If he has done well or ill,
let those whose business it is look to it—it does not
concern me.

In the meantime, the three prisoners were transferred
from the Château of Vincennes to that of Marcoussis
and from there to Havre de Grace. Information
arrived that the Vicomte de Turenne, who had
allowed himself to be won over to the side of the
Prince de Condé, was advancing towards Champagne,
which he reckoned he would march through without difficulty. His intention was to come and extricate him from the prison, which was incapable of
resisting his army, but his Eminence having provided
against this in the way I have just described, the
Vicomte de Turenne laid siege to Rhetel and captured
it. The archduke had given him some troops which
he had joined to some regiments of his own. All these
made up an army of from thirteen to fourteen thousand
men. Turenne alone was in command without the

---

1 The cadets de Gascogne were more celebrated for their
devilry and daring, than for their worldly possessions, which
were as a rule very trifling. Cyrano de Bergerac, it will be
remembered, served under the famous Carbon-Castel-Jaloux as
a "cadet de Gascogne."

archduke being there in person, as I perceive many historians declare was the case, but this is just where they must not be believed, since it is certain that the prince in question was at Brussels. I speak of this as an expert, I who soon after found myself among the troops who had to do with the Prince de Condé, and who totally defeated him.

I had not made a bad estimate as to the feelings of the Parisians towards his Eminence. The hatred they bore him made them soon forget the wrongs they deemed themselves to have received from the Prince de Condé, so, weeping for his misfortunes with the same eyes which one had seen flash with joy at the news of his imprisonment, they raised a great outcry that he and his brothers should be set at liberty, and that the Cardinal should be expelled from office. The Parlement, which secretly made them do this, and which, since the peace, had done a number of things which showed plainly enough that it would never obey the minister except by compulsion, soon joined with the malcontents to assist them in their revolt. There were in it the seeds of rebellion which the peace had never rooted up, so, suddenly regaining its former strength, it recommenced its sittings in defiance of their having been forbidden to do so by the Court. The Cardinal secretly opposed this before openly doing so. He complained to the Coadjutor, who had promised to keep this body (the Parlement) faithful to him, that he was keeping his word badly, and that, after having made him believe it would make no move, it was doing worse than it had ever done. He told him that it was his business to stop it, since he had undertaken to do so. The Coadjutor had not a word

to say to this. It was true that he had given his word
to the Cardinal to restrain the Parlement at any time
it should be inclined to make a disturbance, but, as
his Eminence for his part had promised to obtain a
Cardinal's hat for him and it did not arrive, this
functionary took no trouble to satisfy his remonstrances. Both of them were only trying to cheat
one another. The whole question at first lay in doing
so in such a cunning way that no one should discover
it, but as this was very difficult now that they knew
one another better than they had at first done,
suspicion followed the friendship they had mutually
promised, hatred then ensued, and at last a fixed
desire to ruin each other.

The Vicomte de Turenne, after having captured
Rhetel, also thought to get the whole frontier of
Champagne under his sway. This was not difficult
for him, while matters remained in their present state.
There was no one to defend it, and the conquests
which the minister had taken it into his head to make
in Italy for his private ends, kept troops there, which
would have been much better employed in Champagne
than in a country separated from us by a barrier which
could not be forced without apparently running against
the will of God. For indeed, when one looks closely
into things, it seems that there is truth in saying that
He has decreed that there should be limits to kingdoms,
and that they could not have been better defined than
by the chain of mountains which separates that country
from our own. The same thing applies to the Pyrenees,
which God also appears to have placed where they
are, only as a division of our crown from that of Spain.
But in short, as it is not a new thing for men to go

against the wishes of the Sovereign Lord of all things and even when they are laid down in Holy Writ, so, when all that can be said rests merely upon a presumption, there is no cause for surprise in their contravening them with even greater audacity. People soon smother all their better thoughts to further their ambition, and the desire they have to dominate the whole world makes them not only cross mountains but whole seas besides, if it is a question of getting what they want.

Be this as it may, the necessity of defending the province of Champagne obliging this minister to abandon these vain projects to do what was most needful, the Cardinal made some troops which were on the other side of the Alps return, and gave their command to the Maréchal du Plessis. He had served a long time and, wherever employed, had never been considered other than a good captain. It was a necessity for him that he should not only have this reputation, but also deserve it, to make any head against the Vicomte de Turenne, who was already in a way to make himself equally feared and esteemed. To these troops the Cardinal added the regiment of guards and, as we exceeded the enemy in infantry, the Maréchal du Plessis made no difficulties about marching straight on Rhetel which it was his design to recapture. The Vicomte de Turenne was too far away to relieve it in time, should it be a little pressed; so, as the success of this undertaking only depended upon making haste, the maréchal entered upon it with so much keenness, that the siege was finished before the Vicomte de Turenne could even have arrived on the heights of Sonpuis. He had abandoned all his schemes in other

quarters to come to the help of this fortress, and he
had hoped to succeed, because he had with him the best
cavalry of Europe. In the first place he had with him
sixteen hundred horse of his own, which were all as
well equipped as the King's guards are to-day. The
men were picked as well as the horses, and besides
that, there were the old troops who had formerly
fought under the great Gustave and under the famous
Duc de Weymar. As the Vicomte de Turenne had
not as yet had news that the fortress had surrendered,
he still continued his advance with the same haste he
had employed since he had set out: however, on
reaching Sonpuis, he learnt not only the fate of
the town, but further that the maréchal was coming
to meet him, to save the trouble of his going to find
him. The Cardinal, who had received a courier from
the maréchal, thought that it was of such great importance that he should be present at the battle for
which the former was making preparation, that he at
once took post-horses to join him. He had previously
provided himself with ten thousand louis d'or, which at
that time was a large sum for the Court. He wanted
to make presents to the soldiers so as to cause them to
fight more bravely. There is no doubt that he must
have been very anxious to gain the day, since he was
willing it should cost him so much. Thus, to overcome his natural bent of mind was a thing just as
remarkable as his good luck. Indeed, ten thousand
louis d'or were to him as much as ten millions to anyone else, and although they did not come out of his
purse, it is certain that this move must have cost him
a good deal to make before finally determining upon it.
Eventually, however, he reflected that it would per-

haps be the means of making the Parlement return
to its duty. He feared this body more than any army
and could not even hear it spoken of without trembling.
He was always calling to mind the day of the barricades, and as he had observed that, for having dared
to arrest two or three of its members, a hundred
thousand men had immediately rushed to arms, he
thought with much reason that he would never be in
safety till he had taken means either to win it over,
or to reduce it to such impotence that it should no
longer be in a position to hurt him.

No sooner did the Vicomte de Turenne become
aware of the arrival of the minister and his intention
in coming, than he thought he ought not to decline a
battle. He flattered himself that the valour of his
cavalry would make up for the faults of his other
battalions; for this reason, instead of drawing up his
troops in battle-array, as is usually done on such an
occasion, he was satisfied with putting some squads of
infantry amongst his squadrons. In this way he
marched towards the enemy whom he expected to
scatter at once, but the maréchal, who had posted
his foot-soldiers in advantageous places, and who had
commanded them not to fire without orders, having
made them fire their volleys in their faces so to speak,
notwithstanding all the bravery this cavalry possessed,
so many of them fell that the remainder were totally
scattered. The maréchal profited by this disorder.
He at once had them charged by his squadrons, who
had not worn themselves out much at the siege and
who were fresh and vigorous. This charge completed
the rout, and the cavalry having retreated at a gallop,
it was in vain that the Vicomte de Turenne tried to

rally them to a charge ; he could never do so, so much so that every man having taken his own line of flight, he himself was forced to do the same. The maréchal detailed some squadrons to pursue the fugitives, a great many were captured and the same fate would have overtaken the Vicomte de Turenne, had he not been well mounted and well acquainted with the roads. He retired to Stenai where he only arrived on the fourteenth day. This fortress, which belonged to M. le Prince, was holding out for him, and had received a Spanish garrison, so as to be in a better state to defend itself.

The Cardinal, having after this victory returned to Paris, thought that now he ought to take the Parlement in hand ; so, not thinking that it would still be in a condition to lay down the law to him, he spoke very haughtily to some of its members, whom the Queen had sent for to the Palais Royal to reprimand for their constant plots. The Parlement, indeed, had been quite taken aback by the late victory which had placed the Court above its enemies. At last, however, having taken into consideration the fact that, should it allow the Cardinal to completely crush M. le Prince, it would perhaps be impossible for itself to afterwards resist him, it arranged to have a petition presented to itself by Madame la Princesse, asking for the liberation of her husband. The mother of the prisoner had already presented one during the early days of his detention which was to the same effect. It had however been rejected on account of the Coadjutor, who was now arranging the new one, being at that time on good terms with the Cardinal. As this functionary then had hopes that the latter would have him given the cardinal's hat which he had promised him according to the terms of their agreement, he had taken good care not to allow any attentions to be paid to it, but eventually, his Eminence having tricked him just as cleverly as before he had tricked the Bishop of Langres, there was no longer anything to stop him openly declaring for M. le Prince, unless it might be fear lest desire of revenge for his attempted assassination might lurk in his mind.

The friends of M. le Prince, who had been constantly working for him since his arrest, perceiving that, in spite of the goodwill of the Parlement, he would find it hard to get out of his present quarters, unless the Coadjutor should interest himself in his case, held counsel together to determine how they should proceed in an affair of such delicacy. This prelate wanted to have assurances given him in view of the fears he entertained. This appeared to them but just, so much so, that they themselves offered to go bail, that not only would M. le Prince never think of the assassination again during his lifetime, but would further become his friend. This they told him, that he might be satisfied with their declaration that all the people in Paris as well as themselves were equally disabused of the idea that he had had anything to do with what had occurred on the Pont Neuf. Indeed, for some time now, everyone had begun to perceive that all this had only originated from the Cardinal, and people detested his knavery the more, whilst he secretly continued to congratulate himself upon his plot having turned out so successfully.

The Coadjutor was of opinion that something was to be said for the word of so many honest men,

especially in a matter which spoke for itself as did
this one.   In the meantime as, before thoroughly
declaring himself for M. le Prince, he wanted to make
some terms with him, he came to the conclusion that
he would never obtain a guarantee of this unless he
himself ratified it.   This ratification was, so to speak,
impossible in his present position.   Debas, who had
followed him to Havre, and who was quite devoted to
his Eminence, still continued to keep an eye on him ;
so carefully indeed did he do this, that he was near
being jealous of his shadow.   Clever and suspicious as
he was, he had nevertheless been several times tricked,
and even under his own eyes.   One of his guards, who
had been bribed, managed to convey letters to M. le
Prince in a crown - piece which had been specially
scooped out on one side and which had been so
cleverly put together again that, but for the fact that
it did not weigh as much as others, it was exactly similar
to them.   There would have been no need for so much
mystery, had this guard been able to communicate
with M. le Prince in secret, or cleverly give him a
letter without anyone noticing.   However, Debas
never let his prisoner out of his sight, or, if he did
leave him, his son, who was his second self, at once
took his place.   Accordingly, everything being dangerous with a vigilance such as theirs, it had been
necessary to have recourse to this artifice to convey
information to M. le Prince and obtain news of him.
This particular expedient had been adopted, because
he was in the habit of frequently playing at quoits,
sometimes with the Prince de Conti, sometimes with
the Duc de Longueville, and sometimes even with the
younger Debas ; for, as regards the father, far from

having anything to do with him, he hated him so bitterly on account of his rough manners, that he had all the difficulty in the world in putting up with him.

The guard had been the cause of the adoption of this stratagem, because, once won over, he had been questioned as to how the prince passed his time. The man had stated what I have just said, and further, that he was in the habit of paying him to pick up the quoits. Accordingly, he was instructed as to what he had to do, which was that, when he gave the scooped out coin to the Prince de Condé, he should either squeeze his hand or wink his eye in a way to make him understand the secret. This the guard did not fail to do, and the prince who was clever, having easily understood from the lightness of the crown-piece that it was destined for other purposes than to play quoits with, put it in his pocket and took another in its place. By these means it was hoped to give him news of what was going on; but, as the agreement which the Coadjutor wanted for his own safety, contained many paragraphs and could only be put in the crown-piece in several instalments, it would have been likely to have wasted a good deal of time had not the death of the Princesse de Condé (the Dowager) smoothed away the difficulty. Her death was utilised to ask permission of the Court to interview her son about the will she had made. This was so natural that the Cardinal had no suspicions about it. All the same, he would have refused, had he not been afraid that there would be an outcry against him. He knew his conduct was being watched, and that the least thing which gave cause for fault finding would not be likely to be forgiven. Perrault who, as I fancy I have said, had been arrested at the same time as his master, but since liberated, was therefore allowed to go and see him. Debas kept him under strict observation, so that he might speak of nothing to him but the object of his visit; but as, however strict one may be, it is very difficult in these kind of interviews to prevent oneself from being deceived, the president slipped into his master's hand a paper which contained everything he was wanted to know.

M. le Prince was so little unconvinced about the attempt at assassination, which he maintained the Coadjutor had tried to make upon him, that he felt quite an extraordinary repugnance at granting what was asked of him for that individual. Nevertheless, as he saw nothing worse than prison, and as this was to procure him his freedom, he eventually consented to it. One does not know, in spite of this, whether he did so in good faith and whether, even at that time, he did not entertain ideas of breaking his word.

Be this as it may, having not only signed this paper, but having further returned it to Perrault in the same way as it had been given him, the Coadjutor no sooner verified that it was drawn up in the manner he desired, than he turned his back on the Cardinal. Up to that time he had been careful with him. Although he was aware of his craftiness, he had not dared to declare himself without being sure of M. le Prince. Otherwise he was afraid of the Cardinal's becoming reconciled with him to his own ruin, and that he would be left without any support or prop between two enemies of such a formidable kind. Being at last guaranteed against this danger, he employed all his endeavours with the Parlement to try and obtain from it the exile of the one and the freedom of the other. His idea was to raise himself on the ruins of the Cardinal's fortunes and, as M. le Prince had bound himself by a clause of this agreement to grant him his protection to make him succeed in this undertaking, he reckoned that his success would be a certainty.

II

WHILE all this was going on, the Duc d'Orléans, whose place it was to play the chief part in the State, had allowed himself to be trifled with by the Cardinal to such an extent, that one might say that in the latter's hands he had completely divested himself of his authority. He let himself be ruled sometimes by all the world, and sometimes by his wife, who had not the sense to see that all the people whom she permitted to approach her only gave their advice with the intention of deceiving both herself and her husband. She was a sister of the Duc de Lorraine, and he had married her against the wishes of the late King, who had not only had his marriage declared void by a decree of the Parlement, but who further, as long as he lived, had never consented to relent in the matter. For this reason they had for several years been separated from one another, and it had only been since his Majesty's death that the present King had consented to their coming together. This princess had all her features excellently moulded, so that, if looked at in detail, she was a very beautiful woman,

but, taking her altogether, hers was at most a waning
beauty and one devoid of all the charms which vivacity
bestows; the only spark of it she showed in her life
was in being ambitious beyond anything one can
imagine. Accordingly, although she had not the
intelligence to be troublesome, she had not been
sorry to see disorders arising in the State, so that she
might keep up her position without being obliged to
draw all her claims to consideration from the Court.
She could not in particular bear the Queen-mother,
not that she found anything in that princess unworthy
of esteem, but because her station was above her own.
She was also none too fond of M. le Prince, especially
since the insult he had put upon the Exempt of Guards
of her husband. The Cardinal, who tried to make
everything serve his ends, and who would have been
well pleased to see jealousy prevailing between these
two families, had cleverly had it hinted to her that M.
le Prince was devoured by ambition, and that, in consequence, he wanted not only to raise himself above
the duc her husband, but also despised him so much
that he appeared to have forgotten the difference there
was between a son, a brother and uncle of the King,
and a first prince of the blood.

The little sense, which she possessed by nature, had
not enabled her to find in herself any of the qualities
to withstand this deceit, and she had blunderingly
fallen into the trap, the more so because, during the
time of the victories of M. le Prince, his Court was
usually so large as to have put her husband's to shame.
The Coadjutor, who had himself been a witness on a
thousand occasions of the ideas of this princess, and
who knew that, the better to succeed in his designs,

he ought to win the duc over, thought that, far from availing himself of her as a channel to success, he must hide everything from her with great care, if he wished to lead matters to a happy issue. Accordingly, he made the duc promise to tell her nothing about what he wanted to discuss with him, and then no longer abstained from opening his heart. The duc, like himself, had friends in the Parlement; the respect paid to his birth attracted some, and besides this, all the others were well pleased to have him at their head, because they flattered themselves that his shadow guarded them against the reproach which some people levelled at them " of undertaking things beyond their powers." Be this as it may, the Duc d'Orléans, who had had a share in the imprisonment of M. le Prince, was now disposed to obtain him his liberty, for he allowed himself to be swayed by every breeze. He joined with the Parlement and with the Coadjutor for the carrying out of this undertaking. Not only did the Parlement reply to the request of Madame la Princesse, but further, it decreed that representations should be made to the King and to the Queen with a view to obtaining the liberation of her husband. Her Majesty, who, although devoid of all that cleverness which is said to exist in some women, yet had a courage beyond her sex, thought that the Parlement was arrogating to itself an authority which was not its right. She sternly reproved it for meddling with a matter of this kind, and declared in formal terms that such a thing was beyond its powers, adding that a day would perhaps come when it might repent of its action. She also told its delegates that it was not the business of the Parlement to mix itself up in State secrets, and that, by acting in such a way, it wished apparently to follow the example of England which, after having driven its King from his capital, had further inhumanely murdered him. The Parlement was shocked at this comparison ; so, matters becoming more and more strained, his Eminence began to fear that he might soon be obliged to withdraw into Italy. Indeed, the Parlement of Paris had not been alone in declaring itself for the Prince de Condé, that of Bordeaux had done just the same, and although the Cardinal had appeared to have quelled this storm by taking the King there, it was a long way from being entirely calmed down. This province still supported the prince, and as it never loses an opportunity, as I have already said, of revolting, but welcomes it with all its heart, the minister was afraid of the two Parlements uniting. He foresaw that, should such a thing happen, there were yet others who might perhaps do the same thing, especially as there was hardly a single province which was not discontented with his ministry. Besides, the Comte de Grancé had retired to his government of Gravelines, apparently quite ready to form a party on the grounds that, after the battle of Rhetel, some Maréchaux de France had been created and he had been left out. He claimed to be as worthy of this honour as others, and wanted to obtain by force that which had not been given him with a good grace.

As these were times when those who knew how to make themselves feared got everything they liked, he was considered to be in the right. Be this as it may, this would not have much embarrassed the Cardinal, had this been the only affair on his hands ; he knew of a remedy, which was to grant the comte what he asked for ! But it was not the same thing with regard to other people, since it was his own place which they wanted, and he was in no mood to give it up. This caused him to take every kind of means to appease the Parlement, but as he must have owned the riches of a Croesus to satisfy all its members, not one of whom did not want to be bought at a very high price, the storm which had been brewing against him for so long began to threaten him in such a menacing way that he deemed himself forced to yield ; so, making a virtue of necessity, he left the Court and went to Havre de Grace, to comply with a decree of this corporation, which declared that the Prince de Condé and the two other prisoners should be set at liberty. Some other decrees had also been directed against him, and being anxious to avoid dealing with them as they did not suit him at all, he left the kingdom, after having protested to the prince that it was not he who had been the cause of his misfortunes. The Prince de Condé thought what he liked about this, and having seen him leave without regret, he returned to Paris, out of which city a great number of people came to meet him. He would have been surprised had he known with what joy they had received the news of his imprisonment, but as no one had as yet taken the trouble to enlighten him on the subject, he received the proofs of their goodwill with pleasure, for he flattered himself that this was a repetition of those which they had shown him when his great deeds and repeated victories had rendered him celebrated throughout the kingdom.

The Queen, who had studied enough under the Cardinal to know that one must dissimulate, if one wanted to make oneself worthy of the place she occupied, bestowed a thousand caresses upon the prince, although at heart in despair at his return and at the departure of the Cardinal. Besmaux followed him to Breüil, a pleasure-house of the Elector of Cologne, to which he retired, and his Eminence proceeded to Sedan. On his way there, Fabert lent him I do not know how much money which was not his own. His friends had given it him to keep, and as it was a considerable sum and the disposal of a deposit is never allowed, this loan, made as it was against all forms and even with much peril, injured his reputation a good deal. Who could affirm indeed that this Minister was ever to return to Court, he whom the Parlement had proscribed in a decree and who saw all the princes of the blood arrayed against him! Accordingly, people did not fail to say, when they heard how Fabert had treated him, and when it was evident from what afterwards occurred that he had no reason to regret what he had done, that he must have been a magician to have carried out such a stroke as this!

While the Cardinal was at Breüil, he was accurately informed of everything which was going on at Court by the Queen herself, who was dying of desire to make him return. She deemed that her pride was concerned, and that to yield in this sort of way to a body of rebels, was to make a breach in her authority. The Prince de Condé, who was yet young and a lover of pleasure, spent the first days of his return in debauchery and without thinking too much of what he had to do. He deemed his victory complete since his enemy had abandoned his position, and, without fore-

seeing what might happen, he began to despise everybody. He hardly looked at those who had taken up
arms against their sovereign to get him out of prison!
The Vicomte de Turenne was of this number and even
so to speak the chief one, he who had dared give
battle for his sake! Consequently, he was overcome
with sorrow at the ingratitude of the prince and inwardly swore never again to relapse into the same
mistake he had just committed on account of being
so badly rewarded by him. M. le Prince found a
good deal to regret inhis own be haviour when, some
time after, he threatened to take up arms against his
King.

It is not known, to speak the truth, what really
urged him to commit such a great fault against his
Sovereign, unless it was that he saw the King's coming of age drawing near, and was afraid that after
that time the Queen would make the Cardinal return.
As this minister was not more than a hundred leagues
from Paris, and it was notorious that her Majesty was
continually sending him couriers, he on that account
thought that his Eminence still had just as much
power over her as formerly. Besides, he observed that
in his absence the Queen only consulted Servient, De
Lionne and Le Tellier, three of his creatures, on all
matters of importance, a fact which greatly displeased
him. The Prince de Condé had returned from prison
with the idea of acting as regent in the Council, and
that nothing should happen except according to his
wishes. He found himself far from such a thing, and
being born with great ambition and more fit to
command than to obey, he sought for means of
satisfying himself. All the same, he did not at

first show any signs of what he was thinking about, and modelling himself upon the example of the Queen, who, the better to deceive him, looked kindly at him, he paid her his respects with all the marks of submission and obedience which she could desire from a subject. However, after both had been dissimulating for some time, the Queen, on the advice of the Cardinal, formed the idea of having the prince arrested again. This De Lionne and Le Tellier formally opposed, on the ground that it would reunite the party of the prince with that of the Coadjutor. Already they had begun to quarrel afresh, not that the prince was not totally disabused of the idea he had formerly held as to the Coadjutor having wanted to assassinate him, but because he had come to the conclusion that, should he carry out the agreement by virtue of which he had emerged from prison, far from obtaining the authority in the Council to which he aspired, he would but be changing masters. The idea of the Coadjutor was, as I have already said, to take Mazarin's place, and as he had secret and powerful bonds with the Duchesse de Chevreuse, the Prince de Condé, who was of a haughty spirit and who did not let himself be easily governed, was afraid that not only would he be obliged to bend to his will, but to hers as well. They had by their influence already made one Garde des Sceaux: this was the Marquis de Châteauneuf. They further expected to fill the most important posts with their creatures without letting him have much share: so, being anxious to deliver himself from this new slavery, which was in no way to his taste, he made use of the Prince de Conti to succeed in his designs. The latter, by a clause of

their agreement, was to marry Mademoiselle de Chevreuse, who was a well enough made young princess
and capable of rendering his life more pleasant than it
had up to that time been.   Consequently, he was
more in love with her than with his breviary, which he
had never caressed too much.   His great ardour had
displeased his brother who, on leaving prison, had
dreamt of breaking off this marriage, and the agreement he had made, at the same time.   He had told
him his idea without as yet telling him anything about
his plans.   He had pointed out that princes ought
to make love in a different way from common people,
and that, even were this not the case, he ought to
keep within bounds more than anyone else, since
he had always been one of the cloth, and consequently,
people could not see him suddenly pass from such a
high position to such great weakness without being quite
scandalized. The Prince de Conti, who wore underneath
his cassock the same passions which others wear under a
cuirass or a shoulder-belt, scoffed at his advice, or at
least, if not jeering openly, he did not fail to treat his
mistress just the same as usual.   The Prince de Condé
was quite indignant with him, and, as he wanted his
brother, like other people, to yield to his wishes, he
began to adopt a tone towards him different from the
one he had up to that time employed.   He began to
make a thousand jokes to him about his mistress, and,
finding nothing in her personal appearance to take
hold of, he taxed her with bad behaviour. As her
mother had private friends, of whose advice she availed
herself in the great plans which she was contemplating,
he accused the daughter of making use of them for

other purposes than her mother did. He gave him to understand that the Coadjutor, the Marquis de Laicques and Caumartin, on leaving the duchess's room, were wont to enter that of his mistress. She had, he said, a " large appetite," so much so that, if he wanted the leavings of these three persons, he had but to take her as his wife. The Prince de Conti, head over ears as he was in love, swallowed this slander as truth. Accordingly, without going into things further, he became so disgusted that he broke off with his betrothed. The Coadjutor had a shrewd suspicion that this blow came rather from the elder brother than from the younger one, but, as he was not yet quite sure of this, he thought it better not to break with him entirely. He wanted first of all to thoroughly clear up his suspicions, hoping that, if it was only jealousy which had made the Prince de Conti act in this way, it would not be difficult to cure him of it. Matters being in this state, the advice of M. de Lionne and Le Tellier, at the moment when the Queen and the Cardinal had conceived the idea of again laying hands on the person of the Prince de Condé, did not seem ill-timed either to her Majesty or her minister. Both accordingly resolved to delay its execution until such time as the Coadjutor should have no further grounds for suspecting the truth of the arrest. Meantime, they instructed both men to delay at least till he heard of it. They reckoned that, this once done, not only would there be no appearance of a reconciliation having taken place, but further, that it would be easy for them to gain the Coadjutor over to their interests. De Lionne and Le Tellier were two men of very different character;

one was all mystery, the other straightforward enough, although he occupied a position in which persons endowed from birth with sincerity soon lose it. The two men accordingly behaved very differently in the mission confided to them ; one made use of very round-about methods to gain his ends, the other went straight to the point without troubling to make such a fuss about it. He sent one of his clerks to tell the Coad-jutor that he would very much like to speak to him, and so, if he would appoint a meeting-place, would be there for certain. The prelate was quite willing, and, having informed M. de Lionne, went to the " Chartreux." They met at a certain monk's, whose name was Dom Julliot. Both came *incognito*, and, although M. de Lionne was ready enough to form a bad opinion of ladies' virtue (since he possessed one at home who gave him no cause for happiness) he began to laud the virtue of Mdlle. de Chevreuse to the skies, so as to increase the irritation felt by the Coadjutor at M. le Prince's having availed himself of this pretext to break with him. Further, having prepared his mind to listen to him the more readily, he declared that, if he were willing to effect a recon-ciliation with M. le Cardinal and lead the Parlement to no longer oppose his return, he should be given all the assurances he might reasonably desire of being invested with the purple the first time the Pope should make any cardinals. Such a proposition was attack-ing him in his weak quarter! He, the Coadjutor, wanted, at all hazards, to become a cardinal, and as he could no longer hope to be Prime Minister, now that he no more had the Princesse de Condé to help

him, he promised M. de Lionne to do everything in
the matter which the Queen wished. Nevertheless,
before binding himself to anything, he was anxious
that her Majesty herself should ratify the promise she
was now making. This interview lasted a good three
hours, since they could not see each other again afterwards without risking being recognised, and were
desirous of settling everything at one single sitting.
The Queen confirmed with her own lips to the Coadjutor what De Lionne had told him on her behalf,
and having agreed together to keep the matter secret,
the prelate was no sooner reassured in this quarter
than he broke with M. le Prince in the most open
manner possible. He loudly complained that he was
not a prince of his word, and that, even had he
performed greater deeds than he had done, this defect
totally wiped them out.

M. le Prince was too clever not to see that the
Coadjutor must be certain of powerful protection to
break with him so openly. He at once concluded
that it must be the Queen's, and as it was impossible
for him to hold out against both influences, if he did
not also lean upon some person who could balance
their action, he paid his court to the eldest daughter
of the Duc d'Orléans,[1] who was a princess more fit
to wear a soldier's tunic than a skirt. She had high
aspirations, although at heart possessing a violent
desire to be married. For some time past she had
been old enough for this, being on the point of passing
the age of twenty-four, but, though she was then a

[1] La Grande Mademoiselle, the Duchesse de Montpensier,
born in 1627, died 1693.

very beautiful princess and the richest in Europe, the minister (Mazarin) had not chosen to give her to the numerous foreign princes who would have much liked to take her. The Court did not wish her to carry them her fourteen or fifteen millions, and this sum (to which her property amounted) seemed sufficiently large to be reserved for its own use. M. le Prince, who knew her desire and the obstacles in its path, adroitly made use of this state of affairs to win her over to his interests. He was aware that she possessed great influence over the mind of her father, and that if she undertook to gain him over to his side, she would be more likely to succeed than anyone else. In order to make her serve him the more willingly, he proposed the Duc d'Anguien, his only son, as her future husband. Nevertheless this offer was not one to tempt her. A child of seven or eight years old, such as he, was not the thing for a beautiful princess in the full strength of her desires! However, as she foresaw that the same difficulty which had up to that time prevented her from being married would continue to exist, and that thus she would remain a spinster for ever, she preferred to hope that she might one day have this young duc for a husband to the prospect of having none at all. She knew that he would grow bigger as time went on, and calculated that, although she must then be of a very disproportionate age to him, her great riches would take the place of merit, even if the years which would have elapsed between then and now would have effaced from her counten-ance the flower of beauty which was there at present. Indeed, this princess took such a fancy to the marriage that she became the advocate of M. le Prince with her father.

It was impossible, with so many plots on foot, that the populace should not be carried away to commit some act of rebellion. It is an essential quality of setting a bad example, that it corrupts those who have the least leaning that way; so the Parisians, perceiving that they were ground down by taxes, and that the princes of the blood, who are usually the support of the State, were so at variance with the Queen as to give every appearance of seconding them, if they forgot their duty, proceeded to beat the clerks who raised these taxes. They even threw one or two into the river Seine, which threw them into such terror that most of them abandoned their offices.

The King only entered Blois after having made a treaty with that town, which detained him for at least two or three days. He had even more trouble in treating with the city of Orléans, which would not open its gates to him at all. While going through this part of the country I sought news of Rosnai,[1] whose evil behaviour yet lay heavy on my soul. Although several years had already elapsed since his insult to me, I had not yet forgotten it—on the contrary, I was resolved to be revenged the moment I could; however, what I discovered was not of a nature to please me. I found that he had shown himself there but from time to time, and like a man who had all the "Archers" of the province at his heels. This made me ask those who told it me, if he was involved in any trouble? They replied that they knew of none, saving that he had once had a misunderstanding with a passing stranger. The report was current that this was the cause of his absenting himself,

1 See Vol. I. p. 6.

because this stranger, who was then but a youth, was considered by him and all the country people as a fellow who sooner or later would do him a bad turn.

By this I understood that this stranger was no other than myself, and on my afterwards asking for news of Montigré, the people answered that he had gone to Toulouse, to conduct a lawsuit against Rosnai; that they had been engaged in litigation since I do not know how long, and that a certain decision of Messieurs les Maréchaux de France, which had intervened between them, had not been able to terminate their disputes. There was a fear of Montigré's getting the worst of this lawsuit, as he was an honest man, and were this to happen, he would be irretrievably ruined. The latter had helped me too kindly for me not to feel solicitous about his affairs. I at once wrote to him to offer him friends in that part of the country as well as money. At the same time, I enquired if Rosnai had put in an appearance to plead against him. I was resolved to travel post according to his answer, directly my duties would allow, but the news I received from him saved me that trouble. He sent me word, that he saw him no more than he did a "werewolf," nor could he tell me what part of the world he inhabited, but, for the sake of his own peace, he would have wished that I should have divested his enemy of the desire of pleading, as well as of that of showing himself amongst honest folk. I admired the strength of fear and what it was able to do. Meanwhile, as I always kept myself posted as to the doings of this "screech-owl" who, as it seemed, loved only darkness, I learnt some five or six months later, that not only had he won his suit, but that

Montigré, who had been cast in more than ten thousand crowns damages and costs, had immediately died of grief.

I lamented him, as was right, after what he had done for me, but, as there was no remedy for what had befallen him, I contented myself with praying to God for him and having some masses said for his soul.

The Cardinal still continued to desire to make one of his nephews captain-lieutenant of the King's Musketeers. He had only had that company broken up with this end in view, hoping that, when it should no longer exist, Treville would show himself more tractable than before. He had secretly had him informed about this, and had not concealed from him that, if he did not arrange matters with him, he must never expect to see it re-established. Treville, who was as proud in misfortune as in prosperity, had not been alarmed at these threats, and had replied to those who spoke for the Cardinal, that, as long as the King might please to dispense with his Musketeers, he would remain at Court without employment, but that, should a wish seize his Majesty to again set them on foot, he hoped he would do him the justice to give him back the company, which he did not think he had lost from ever having failed in his duty. This reply had disconcerted the Cardinal and as, when once he wanted anything, he did not soon yield, he caused a number of propositions to be made him, which appeared advantageous, so as to get him to abandon his claims. Treville, who was not a man like anyone else, would not listen to them. His Eminence became incensed against him, and as he had the tendency of which his country is accused, and had not yet lost it since he had been in France—that is to say, love of revenge, he did all he could to get him to take some false step. The moment was very opportune. Treville had a brother-in-law in the Parlement, and had he not been as attached as he was to the King's service, the rebels would have made him a good offer to secure a man of his worth. However, as his fidelity was above being shaken by all the ill-treatment which could be bestowed upon him, he remained firmly attached to his duty. This did not cause the Cardinal to give way, and being aware that men, no less faithful than he, were often passed off as traitors, especially when one possessed the cleverness to tinge one's suspicions with some show of truth, he tried to insinuate to the Queen that Treville was dabbling in the rebellion of the Parlement. He even told her that he knew for certain that he was about not only to join the rebels before long, but further to cause part of the regiment of guards to pass over to their side by means of his brother-in-law. He added, that there was no other way of stopping this than by seizing their persons, nor must a minute be lost; for, should one of them hear the least rumour that they were suspected, they might not only secure themselves against the punishment they deserved, but further take measures which might be prejudicial to the State.

The Queen did not always do all the Cardinal wished—a long way from it. Accordingly, far from resembling the late King, who had exiled him some days before Cardinal Richelieu's death, to content that minister, and who had not, so to speak, dared to make

him return before his eyes were closed, she took quite
another course. She answered that she knew Treville
too well ever to suspect him of treachery, that he was
proud, sometimes even more so than was right (since
one should learn, when once at Court, to bend to the
powers that be); however, although she perceived this
defect in him, she would never do him the injustice of
believing him guilty of what the Cardinal was now
trying to persuade her. His Eminence, who perceived
himself, as it were, thus accused of slander, wanted to
justify himself, and, not being able to do so except by
continuing to insist that he was guilty, and that his
information came from such a good source that it was
impossible to suspect it, the Queen could not refrain
from replying that he himself did not believe what he
was saying, but was well pleased that others should
believe it, to satisfy his spite. She said that she had
now for some time observed that he had inherited this
from Cardinal Richelieu; that he disliked Treville,
and she had not a very good idea of what the reason
might be; however, this dislike seemed to her so ill-
founded that, whatever he might do, she did not think
that he could ever make her swallow it.

These words were such strong ones that, whatever
was the Cardinal's respect for her Majesty, he could
not remain silent. He tried to exculpate himself and
did so in terms which so gravely displeased this
princess, that she was forced to tell him more unpleasant things than before. He withdrew quite
confused and quite mortified, and, the serious business
he then had at Court obliging him to go away for
some days, he left Besmaux with her Majesty to effect
a reconciliation. He ordered him to tell her that her

bad treatment would oblige him to leave the kingdom
more than all the decrees of the Parlement; that not
only the whole of France, but further, all Europe was
convinced she had confidence in him, but all the same
it must be very slight, since it could not prevail against
the shrewdness of a native of Bearn; that for many
reasons he would like the Parlement and all other
enemies to know what was going on, for, as they took
as sole pretext for their fractiousness the kindnesses
which they supposed her Majesty to bestow upon him,
nothing could better disabuse them than the little
confidence she reposed in his words. Further, since
there could be nothing more painful for a man who
found himself attacked by the whole of a great kingdom
(and especially for one like himself, who knew that all
the hatred borne him but arose from his embracing
the interests of her Majesty with a little too much
warmth) he was resolved to withdraw into Italy, since
he found himself deprived of the reward he expected
for his services. He had always done everything to
please her, and to prove that nothing equalled her own
interests in his mind. However, from present appearances, he seemed to have thoroughly wasted his time
and was in despair in consequence, but nevertheless,
could do nothing else, for, when one did everything
possible, one was not obliged to do more. The
Cardinal further instructed Besmaux to continue to
insist upon the imprisonment of these two men, and,
if unable to succeed, to at least request the Queen to
have them banished to some town far away from the
Court.

Besmaux was delighted to find himself thus employed by the Cardinal. He had already been

concerned in some other little matters, but, as it had
never been in connection with the Queen, nor even
with anyone who was within a hundred paces of her
rank, he became so jubilant that it was not difficult
for me to see by his manner that he had some great
reason for rejoicing. And indeed, this showed itself
to me so clearly that, although I was well aware that
one never ought to ask people secrets, I could not help
telling him that he was wrong to conceal his good
luck from his friends, as it deprived them of the means
of rejoicing with him. He made pretence of not
understanding what I meant, and, having asked me
for an explanation, I innocently told him what I
thought. He would not own the matter to me, in
which he was not far wrong, since, besides being
obliged to keep the secret, I should not have awarded
him much praise for showing so much delight, when
it would seem to me rather that he should display
nothing but sadness. Indeed, this business was not
too creditable to his master, and, however he might
acquit himself, his own honour would be concerned,
to my way of thinking. Be this as it may, not having
been able to extract any answer, but that I was puzzling
to try and find out, and was a sorry guesser, he betook
himself to carrying out his Eminence's commands,
and succeeded none too well. The Queen continued
to do Treville justice, and her good opinion of him
saving his brother-in-law, towards whom her feelings
were not altogether so favourable, it only remained for
the Cardinal to carry out his threats. He had had
this princess informed that he would return to Italy;
but he took care not to do a thing so agreeable to
France, one which would have saved it many men

and many millions.   Indeed, the civil war now raging
in the realm was only on his account, or at least, if
the ambition of certain people had something to do
with it (such as the Prince de Condé and certain
members of the Parlement), he might easily have
removed the cause, had he been content to restrain his
temper.   However, he took care not to thus abandon
the post of Prime Minister, a post in which he had
already amassed a quantity of money which he had
sent to Italy, and in which he contemplated amassing
a good deal more to satisfy his avarice.   Accordingly,
very far from altering his conduct to please the populace who loudly complained of it, he still continued to
sell such offices as might chance to be vacant, no
matter of what kind they might be.   He went so far
even as to sell those which had never before been sold,
such as the post of " Surintendant des Finances," for
which the Marquis de la Vieuville had given him four
hundred thousand francs.   This marquis had imagined
that, in consideration of this sum, he would let him
do as he pleased, and that afterwards he would not
take long to recoup himself; however, he had clipped
his wings so well that, had it not been that the
Cardinal could not see everything, he would hardly
have had "water to drink at home."   Indeed, his family
is no longer rich, and it would have been better for it
that he should have kept his money, and not had such
a good appetite.

His Emirence, who, after his threats to the Queen,
still wished that she should be grateful to him for
remaining, had her told by his " creature " that, if he
was not following the dictates of his just resentment,
it was because he took pity on the sad state in which

he found the kingdom. His desire was, to repair the
ravages made in it before he left ; this done, he hoped
she would not refuse to allow him to depart. His
Eminence showed good sense in speaking thus, and
even conscientiousness, since, as it was he who had
made the ravages, it was but right he should repair
them ; however, instead of succeeding as he expected,
he very nearly made a more serious one than all those
which had been made before.

No sooner was the Prince de Condé with his army,
than he made a sudden attack upon the Maréchal
d'Hocquincourt. He fell on his soldiers, who were
separated from those of Turenne, whilst they deemed
themselves in perfect safety. The whole Court fell
into terrible consternation, and was even in great
straits. It no longer drew any money from Paris, nor
from many provinces; and, as kings have this in
common with other men, "that they are only esteemed
according to the wealth which they are seen to possess,"
a number of courtiers were quite ready to change sides,
because they saw his Majesty's affairs in great disorder.
M. le Prince could not fail to see their state of mind,
for he had many allies amongst them, from whom he
perpetually received news, but, as he also had fair
friends, and ones who were much nearer his heart
than anything else, he left his army to the Duc de
Nemours, and went to see them at Paris.

His Eminence, who could have had no greater
piece of good fortune than to see this prince depart,
for he feared him personally more than the whole of
his army, was enchanted to know that he was in the
arms of his mistresses. He thought, as indeed seemed
very likely, that this would give him time, especially

as he was leaving the command of his troops to a prince who was no less amorous than himself. Both indeed were in love with the same lady, but with this difference that, although the two of them had given their hearts to the Duchesse de Châtillon, one was a far more faithful lover than the other. The Prince de Condé was but a flighty swain, who amused himself with flitting from flower to flower, whilst the duc took his passion seriously. All the same his mistress was not worth such a thing. She had, so to speak, "as many lovers as there are days in a year," and if one were to place reliance on scandalous reports, she was much of the same disposition as the Prince de Condé. Although she had a greater fancy for the Duc de Nemours than for anyone else, this did not prevent her from turning a willing ear to all who wished to make love to her. She and the duc had often exchanged rough words on this subject—to the extent even of wanting to leave one another. However, this prince's affection for her was so great that, in spite of his being as it were certain of his misfortunes, she made him believe quite the contrary, whenever she cared to take the trouble.

Lucky would it have been for M. le Prince, had the duchess been the only woman who deceived him! At least, he would have been able to have returned to take the command of his army, and give the Cardinal fresh trouble. However, his other mistresses having treated him worse than she had done, by merely granting him their favours, he found himself in consequence so incommoded that he was obliged to place himself in the hands of the surgeons. He concealed this misfortune under the guise of the necessity, which he made people believe called him to Paris. The Parlement was sitting there as usual, and the return of the Cardinal had put that body into such a bad temper with him, that, as I have already said, they were fulminating some terrible decrees against his person. One of them laid down the price of his head at fifty thousand crowns. Another ordered the sale of his library, so that that sum might always be ready for the man who should commit this murder. No minister could have been more severely handled, and as he had often heard speak of the Maréchal d'Ancre,[1] this last blow really made him wish to return to Italy. The fear of meeting with his fate made him speak to the Queen, whose courage was of quite a different sort from his own, since the least thing made him tremble, and her Majesty (who, on the contrary, only became more resolute as she perceived a danger growing greater) told him to take courage. She made use of the most expressive terms possible to persuade him, even to the extent of saying that his business was her own, but, as people are much more easily preserved from danger than fear, he continued to be in such a plight that he would willingly have hidden himself had he dared. The Queen was obliged (seeing he was not reassured by her words) to make the Vicomte de Turenne give him an assurance that the Parlement was not in a state to do him the harm he was afraid of. His Eminence might perhaps have thought something of this, had the vicomte been always at hand with his army; but, as this general had business elsewhere, he had scarcely gone away when the Cardinal resolved to ask the Queen for leave to depart.

[1] The Maréchal d'Ancre was assassinated in the reign of Louis XIII. with the connivance of that monarch.

Meanwhile, his Eminence conceived the idea of offering one of his nieces to the Vicomte de Turenne, to induce him to utilise all his military knowledge to extricate him from his wretched plight. He trembled lest he should once more declare himself against his sovereign, the more so as his eldest brother was at present in arms against him in the Province of Bordeaux. Naturally suspicious, he was not sure whether the two brothers had not some understanding, and if he ought not to be afraid of his turning his back, when his help might be most necessary. He communicated his ideas to Navailles, who at once encouraged him in them, thinking this would be a good thing for the Vicomte de Turenne, who as yet had neither office nor governorship, such as he soon afterwards obtained. He even undertook to mention the subject to him, hoping that, as he himself followed the career of arms, this general (who ought to be grateful to him for arranging this marriage) would prove his gratitude when they should meet. The Cardinal accepted his offers, so that the proposal was duly made. At that time the Vicomte de Turenne was a good Huguenot,[1] and thinking that he ought not to marry a woman of a different faith from his own, although this was common enough at the time, he replied to Navailles that he was much obliged to the Cardinal for the honour he wanted to confer upon him, but the sensitiveness of his conscience prevented his being able to profit by it. This answer, which was not that of a courtier (whose custom is to have no religion at all whenever his prosperity is concerned), alarmed the Cardinal

---

1 Turenne became a Catholic in the year 1668.

more than ever. He at once thought that the vicomte was only rejecting this alliance with him because he had a more delicate conscience than Cardinal de Richelieu, who had made no difficulties about making the Duc de Puilaurens perish by causing him to marry his relative. He thought, I repeat, that he did not want to be accused, like him, of having made this marriage, the better to catch a man he wanted to ruin. Accordingly, growing more and more imbued with this idea, he began to look so askance at the general, that the latter thought himself obliged to speak to the Queen about it. Meantime, as he believed that all this originated only from what had passed between Navailles and himself, he was obliged to tell her, so that she might the better appreciate his reasons. The Queen, who was very devout and who resembled the vicomte in believing that it was a very good thing for two people of different religions not to marry, bade him calm his mind and she would bring his Eminence to reason. She did, indeed, speak to him about it, and as this minister liked to get some good out of everything, he replied that, if he entertained any irritation against the general, it was only by reason of his interests. When, said he, he had caused a marriage with one of his nieces to be proposed to him, it was not because of his great wealth or of the splendid establishment he could give her. He knew what the fortune of a cadet of the house of Bouillon was; but, as in the present state of affairs, when everybody was glorying in being false to their word, he deemed that it would be advantageous to her Majesty to make sure of him, he had tried in this way to so thoroughly secure him, that, no matter

what others might propose to him, he would not be
ready to accept it.

Charles II., King of England, had been unable,
since his father's sad death, to find any means of re-
mounting the throne.   Not that he had gone to sleep.
He had been trying to arm all his subjects in order to
revenge the terrible parricide which had taken place,
but this had only served to increase his misfortunes.
As there were but few faithful to him, he had been
either so feebly seconded, or so ill served, that, after
having risked a great battle, he had had a good deal
of trouble to save himself from the hands of the rebels.
Eventually, after unheard-of sufferings and running a
risk, the mere recollection of which makes one tremble,
he had passed over into France, as to a place where
he might hope to find safer asylum than anywhere
else.   As he was the son of a daughter of France, this
alone seemed to him enough to banish all fears.
Moreover, he knew that the French prided themselves
on succouring the unfortunate and oppressed like
himself.   Nor had he been deceived in these hopes.
He had found not only the King and Queen, but also
the whole people just as much touched by his misfortunes as they could have been by their own.
Consequently, he had thought himself bound to be
grateful to everyone, and as, in the troublous state in
which the country was, we needed, just as he himself
did, people to alleviate our miseries, he had employed
himself in this so usefully at the time when the Duc
de Lorraine held the Vicomte de Turenne as it were
in his hands, that it was he to whom a debt of gratitude
was due for having extricated that general from the
predicament in which he was.   Yet Charles II. was

but twenty-one—an age when most people are unfitted for carrying on negotiations! However, as he had been brought up in adversity, he had learnt more in a year than anyone else would have done in several years; so, still continuing to be desirous of proving his gratitude towards a crown to which he deemed he was under an obligation, he entered the army, where he served in person, just as the humblest soldier might have done.

The civil war having ended, the Queen thought of nothing else but making the Cardinal return. He was bored to death at Sedan, indeed, boredom was his most serious malady. Accordingly, no sooner did he know that the Parlement had concluded peace, than of a sudden he found himself resuscitated. He no longer spoke at all of still being unwell, and, on the contrary, looking into affairs on the frontier where he was, the Queen exaggerated this activity of his to everybody, declaring that without him the Prince de Condé would certainly have gained other victories besides those he had just done. This opened the eyes of all those who had wished to blind themselves. The Cardinal de Retz was wild with fury and rage to find himself so grossly tricked! However, as his mistake was now not to be remedied, and as there was no one who was in a mood to espouse his interests to such an extent as to recommence the war for his sake, he was obliged to angrily "champ his bit." The Queen discovered that he was attempting various manœuvres and various plots, with a view to replunging the State into the troubles out of which it had but just emerged. This obliged her to think more than ever of having him arrested, and perhaps she would at once have done so

in spite of the Cardinal's advice, had he not added to
what he had already told her, "that the pear was not
yet ripe," and that, before culling it, she ought to
alienate from the Cardinal de Retz his principal friends
in the Parlement.   Did she not make sure of things in
this quarter, there was danger of the Court of Rome
wanting to interfere ; for, more often than not, it was
wont to meddle where it had no business.   His
Eminence (Mazarin) had concluded by saying that,
although her Majesty was only responsible for her
conduct to God and to the King, her son, the Court
in question aspired to looking into everything which
had any reference to the persons of the Cardinals.
One ought to deliver oneself from enemies at home
before drawing strangers upon oneself; for, when
attacked at home and abroad, it was but by a kind of
miracle that any resistance could be made.

The Queen placed faith in his advice, and tried to
win the Parlement over, before carrying out the resolve
she had formed as to his Eminence (De Retz).   She
won over some members of that body by fair words,
and having softened by presents those who appeared
to desire something more substantial than words, so
as to thoroughly assure their fidelity, she was soon in
a position to execute her plans.   This was highly
necessary to re-establish tranquillity in the realm, and
to repulse the Spaniards, who had just retaken Gravelines and Dunkirk once more.   Besides, it was quite
obvious that the Cardinal in question, with a mind as
uneasy and turbulent as his, was not able to keep
himself quiet.   His ambition was entirely alien to his
character, and all who knew him declared that no one
was more unfitted to govern a kingdom than he.   For,

very far from possessing that coolness which is
absolutely essential for such an important undertaking,
he had such an extraordinary temper that he would
lose control of himself, if he entertained the least idea
that he had grounds for being angry. But what
further made it more apparent that there was a
stronger reason than this for making sure of his
person was, that it seemed as it were impossible for
him not to create disturbances as long as he was at
liberty. Further, he was ruined, because he had
already spent so much to succeed in his plans as to
have no other means of repairing the ravages he had
made in his fortune, but by occupying the position
he had so long coveted. He owed nearly three
millions, and it was thus that a man, the duties of
whose office obliged him to point out to others that
it was wrong to be ambitious or to harm one's
neighbour, had strayed away from a morality so holy
and so true! He had let himself drift into this state,
because, from his disposition, he saw nothing which
could make him happy but the government of the
kingdom. Be this as it may, the Queen, having
exactly followed the advice of Cardinal Mazarin,
contrived by her prudence to conduct matters to such
a state of maturity, that, before two months were over,
she found herself in a position not only to have the
Cardinal de Retz arrested, but also to make her
minister return. Mazarin was desirous that the one
should precede the other, that is to say, that the
person of his rival should be secured before his own
return was discussed. He thought that there were
two reasons which rendered this absolutely necessary.
The one was that, if by chance her Majesty should

chance to fail in her stroke, and the Parlement
should view her attempt with disfavour, he would be
obliged to leave the kingdom for a third time, were
he to have come back.   The other reason was, that
people would not attack him about it so much if he
was not on the spot (although there might perhaps
be a suspicion as to his being the author of the
business) as if he were at the moment head of her
Majesty's Council.   The first of these reasons was
fairly good, and one might even add that, should the
populace rise in consequence of the arrest, he need
have no fear of its laying hands on him, since he was
out of its powers where he now was.   But as to the
other, it was so weak that it did not deserve to make
the least impression on his mind.   Although he was
away from the Court, it was not necessary to know
very much about what was happening not to feel sure
that all the blame would fall upon him.   Accordingly,
present or absent, he might feel certain that all the
good and all the harm would be laid to his charge.
His precautions in this direction were then very useless, and even so out of place that, had he made his
delicacy known, all who might hear about it would
have been more likely to laugh at it rather than give
their approval.

The Queen, who concerned herself much less in
looking into everything than in following her inclinations, did as he told her, and having caused the
Cardinal de Retz to be arrested, no one made any
disturbance because, though people clearly saw that
the deprivation of his liberty announced the speedy
return of Cardinal Mazarin, they were so pleased
at having a taste of peace, that they did not want,

by undertaking fresh things, to lose a benefit of which they had been deprived too long for their own comfort. Besides, as the prisoner had never played any other part than one exactly opposite to that which he should have done, the love borne him was so slight that no one worried about what had happened to him. He was conducted to Vincennes and placed in the same room which the Duc de Beaufort had escaped from some time back. However, such stringent orders were issued for care to be taken that he did not do the same thing, that he soon saw that, while these orders were carried out with as much exactitude as they then were, any attempt of his would be useless.

Some days later, the Marquis de Vieuville chanced to die, and as it was the first day of the year 1653, between four and five o'clock in the morning, his Suisse (porter) was so saddened at the thought of not getting any New Year's presents, that he would have hung himself had he not been prevented. He was discovered to have already gone in search of a rope, but someone having noticed his despair, people tried to calm his mind. This was very difficult with a Suisse who recognised no other God but money! However, a person cleverer than other people having promised to get him into the service of whoever might succeed to the post of Surintendant, the porter eventually consoled himself for his loss with the hope of a greater profit. The post was divided between Servient and M. Fouquet, Procureur-Général of the Parlement of Paris. It was given to the latter as a reward for the services which he had rendered to his Eminence in his company during the civil war.

As to the other, he obtained it because the Cardinal reckoned that he would make him do everything he wanted, and to speak frankly, he would only be his clerk. Accordingly, he gave him all the best of the post of Surintendant, whilst he left the other all the unpleasant portion. He gave the power of "lier et délier,"[1] to Servient, that is to say, of delivering bills[1], or, to speak more plainly, having them paid whenever he chose, for we were then at a time, when his Majesty's wanting to do good to someone availed nothing, if the Surintendant des Finances did not approve of it. Whatever bill one might have, it was but a song, unless it was passed by the minister in question. I am well aware that this procedure still prevails to-day, but there is this difference between then and now, that at present, once a bill is issued, everything works automatically without one's being obliged to pass through the hands of a number of blood-suckers, which in those days was quite inevitable. Cardinal Mazarin was himself one of these blood-suckers, and even one of the most cruel, so much so that, when he had caused one of these bills not to be met, a thing which often happened, he would send out emissaries to arrange the price he would let it pass at. He knew very well how to get paid afterwards, and it is by means of this charming profession that he acquired a portion of the immense riches he left to his heirs at his death.

Nothing of importance occurred between the imprisonment of Cardinal de Retz and the return of Mazarin, except the death I have just spoken of. The

[1] "Lier et délier," really an ecclesiastical term, meaning "to give or refuse absolution," though here used in the sense of 'holding control over the finances."

King went to meet this minister, to whom he deemed
himself under an obligation, because he was given to
understand that everything he did was but in his
interests. As he was not yet of an age to know how
to discern between his good servants and his bad ones,
he of necessity had to rely on those who should have
known them better than himself. Everybody hastened
to pay his court to the minister, well divining that he
was about to become more powerful than ever. I did
the same thing as the others, because, after having
been his servant as I had been, I did not see how I
could reasonably get out of doing so. However, I
avoided those transports which savoured more of the
slave than of a grateful man, so much so that I let
those who were in the greatest hurry go before I
myself went. The Cardinal reproached me for this,
upon which, not being much astonished, I answered
him that all those in whom he observed so much
eagerness would have done just the same thing for
his enemies, had they found means to overcome him.
As for myself, who did things in quite a single-minded
way, and without humbug, there were a thousand more
reasons for relying upon my fidelity than on all their
simperings. Upon this he at once said to me :

"Artagnan, I did not know the French before I
governed them, but the Spaniards have great reason
for calling them rogues. There is nothing one cannot
make them do for money, and even by the mere hope
of making a fortune. Formerly, I imagined that it
was the nation of the world most worthy of being
esteemed; what further gave me this opinion was,
that I saw people resisting Cardinal Richelieu with all
their strength. However, if I am to judge those times

by these, they were certainly his enemies, only because
he would not buy them. A few pistoles, more or less,
would have attained his object ; and this is the idea I
shall always hold until such time as I shall have
discovered someone who is either clever or honourable
man enough to disillusion me."

I did not like his entertaining such a bad opinion of
a kingdom where there are so many brave and honest
people. It seemed to me unjust, as well as full of
ingratitude, coming from him who had entered France
as much a beggar as any painter, and who had already
married one of his nieces to a grandson of Henri the
Great ! For eventually, notwithstanding the obstacle
which the Prince de Condé had wanted to put in the
way of the marriage of the Duc de Mercoeur with a
Mancini, the duc had taken this step, although all his
enemies had secretly told him that he was about to
contract a marriage which would bring him no honour.
To dissuade him, they had even tried to insinuate that
the position of the Cardinal was as yet so ill established
that it wanted a mere nothing to upset it.   However,
either because he was in love with his niece, or because
he thought everything he heard about this originated
merely from jealousy, he carried out the match in
spite of everything they could say. It even seemed as
if his father would refuse to give his consent—a circumstance which made him adopt the course of
marrying her secretly. Nevertheless, whatever face
the Duc de Vendôme pulled, he was one of those
people of whom the Cardinal had spoken. He made
himself the slave of money, and therefore he was not
so particular about the matter as he wished people to
think. Consequently, no one could dissuade those

who flattered themselves on knowing things from a good source, that all his son did was not done in concert with himself. Nevertheless, he did not wish this idea to prevail when the Cardinal returned to the Court. He withdrew, as if displeased at his coming into favour, but this was only to play his game the better with him, so much so, that his anger entirely cooled down, when he saw himself offered the post of Admiral which for a long time he had wished for. His Eminence made no further difficulty about disposing of it, now that the Prince de Condé had gone away. He was well aware that, after what he had done, he would not care to return so quickly to heap reproaches on his head.

III

AS I disapproved (as I have just said) of the liberty his Eminence was taking in insulting our nation, I asked him if he did not exclude Treville from the bad opinion he held about it. It seemed to me that the latter had never by his conduct given any cause for being numbered amongst the people he had just mentioned. At least, one could not say that he had made himself the slave either of Cardinal Richelieu or any other man, since he had never been willing to give way to anyone else than his king. I told the Cardinal that he, more than others, was able to judge of this, for Treville had made a stand against him just as much as against Richelieu, and had preferred having his career wrecked to showing himself complaisant towards him.

The Cardinal, in reply, answered that there I was quoting an instance of a fool who only deserved to be excluded from human society. Indeed, just as there was a meanness in paying homage indiscriminately to everybody, so was there a madness in refusing it to him whose due it was. Consequently, when Treville had dared to resist both Richelieu and himself, he had shown himself more fit for the mad-house than for the praise which I was trying to bestow upon him. Whenever a man was of real worth (as I had declared the individual we were discussing to be), he based the whole of his conduct upon prudence, and, as prudence demanded that one should bend to whoever was in power, Treville had been wrong every time he had not done so. The Cardinal added, that perhaps he was not entirely without some feelings of repentance for this behaviour, and that, were I to speak the truth, I would own that he had spoken on the subject to me. Even were this not the case, he knew very well that he had spoken thus to someone else. He was very glad to casually mention this, so as to teach me that he had been right to accuse him of being a lunatic. Of this I could not doubt after what he had just told me, since Treville had himself admitted that he was a regular madman, when he accused himself, as he had done, of being the sole cause of his own disgrace.

I did not like to contradict him, although, from my knowledge of the character of Treville, I entertained strong doubts as to his being capable of doing what was imputed to him. I was afraid of upsetting the Cardinal, were I to freely speak my mind; so, preferring to talk about someone else, I asked him if Marigny, who had grievously offended him, though he had never given him cause, must also be counted amongst the slaves to whom he had referred. I added that I did not think that this at all events was the case, for here was a man who (instead of paying

homage to him, as he declared all Frenchmen vied
with one another to do) had showered a quantity of
insults upon him. As a matter of fact, neither I myself
nor any respectable person approved of such behaviour;
so I would not take this particular instance to concoct
a hero, on whose model I would advise no one to
mould himself. Much rather did I consider him a
slanderer and a regular lunatic; but anyhow, whatever
he was, he was always consistent and not what the
Cardinal had said. Marigny had no turn for flattery,
having a much greater one for satire.

This Marigny was a man who, from joyousness
of heart, and without ever having had anything to do
with the Cardinal, had taken pleasure in writing
scandalous verses against his ministry and person.
As one pleases people more by satire than any other
form of writing whatsoever, this had been the only
thing necessary to gain him not only friends but a
reputation for cleverness besides. These friends,
nevertheless, were not like a captain of the régiment
de la marine, whom his Eminence some time later
caused to be thrown into the Bastille, for having
criticised his conduct, but in a serious way, as is
usual amongst respectable people. This captain, being
in prison, told those who thought to please him by
abusing the minister, that, were it not that he feared
being called a flatterer, he would tell them that they
were not speaking the truth. Truth should be en-
closed in certain limits, and whoever overstepped
these was a slanderer, rather than a truthful man.

But to return to my subject. The Cardinal, perceiving that I went on to cite Marigny as an example,
capable of confuting what he had told me, replied that

in that case, I was speaking of a man whom we should wipe out from the human race by reason of his evil tongue. He would willingly ask him what he had done to cause him to tear him to pieces in his satires as he did. He saw nothing strange in a person's being in a rage with an individual who had given him cause for displeasure. Nature always had a leaning towards vengeance, and when one was unable to give one's enemy a sword-thrust, one was often delighted to give him a "lash of the tongue." Marigny, however, whom he had never done good nor harm to, could only be regarded as a monster thirsting for blood, against whom everyone ought to declare himself. In consequence, I had cited another bad instance in the same way as I had Treville, because a monster and a fool, as both were, must not be reckoned amongst men.

This was all I could get out of the Cardinal, and as I knew very well that it would not be sensible to dispute with a greater man than oneself, I agreed to all he wished. Nevertheless, I could not let his first contention pass, deeming that he had wrongly insulted our nation. I know not if my yielding, or my character, which was different from the one he had just attributed to other people (but which he could not attribute to me), gained me his favour, but eventually he told me that, although he had admitted no exception to his indictment, he was yet obliged to own that I was not like the people he had just spoken of. I had, he continued, never paid him court except as an honourable man should, and, although there were many people who, in his place, would like others to grovel before them, he well

knew how to distinguish between what arose from
a free and right submission, and what was done
through baseness. He bade me take care to continue
to live as I had begun, and he would remember me
at the right time and place. I should have been
delighted at these promises, had I not known that too
much trust must not be placed in them. Besides,
I perceived him so eager for riches, as not to be able
to flatter myself that he would bestow them on anyone
else, especially as all was fish that came to his
net. In the meantime, as he was in a position
to assist people when he wanted to, I sought for
something which would cost him nothing, and which
might make my fortune. Some days later, I was
told that a Portuguese, Dom Lopes by name, who
dealt in precious stones, had just died suddenly
without ever having been naturalised. I asked him
for the " confiscation "[1] of his fortune, which certainly
amounted to one hundred thousand crowns. This
Dom Lopes was well enough known at Court for all
its frequenters to be aware that he possessed a good
deal of property. The Cardinal, to whom he had often
sold precious stones, knew this just as well as myself,
and perhaps better than others, for it was a peculiar
characteristic of his, that, directly he was told that
anyone was well off, he wanted to know all the ins
and outs, so that he might become his heir, whenever
occasion should present itself. Accordingly, having
too good an appetite himself to bestow such a choice

---

1 "Confiscation." The fortune of a non-naturalised foreigner
at this time went to the King. This and other laws relating to
the disposition of the property left by foreigners were only
suppressed by a decree of August 6th, 1790.

morsel on another, he without hesitation replied, that he was sorry that I had not been the first to come and ask him this favour. He would, he said, have been charmed to procure it for me, but, having let myself be anticipated by someone else, the thing was already done. Dom Lopes lodged at the house of one of my private friends, who had given me the news. He had died on his return from town, and, as his host wanted to oblige me and himself as well, because I had promised him that, if he was able to discover anything which I could ask for, we would divide it together, he had hastened to me without losing a moment. I therefore knew that nobody could be aware of what I had just announced to the Cardinal, which making me divine his evil intention, "Monseigneur," said I, "you accused the French some days ago of being great cowards; allow me to tell you, no matter what interest you may take in the nation which I now have to indict before your Eminence, that the Italians are great rascals. Dom Lopes' landlord, who is a countryman of yours, has this moment told me that his tenant has just fallen dead in his rooms, and that he had at once set off to come and let me know, after having ordered his wife not to divulge a word of this news to anyone, before I should have spoken to you about it. Nevertheless, your Eminence clearly perceives how impudently he has lied to me, since you are not only already informed as to this death, but further, the favour he urged me to go and beg of you is also granted to someone."

The Cardinal, when he had heard me accuse his nation of rascality, had blushed, either from anger or shame. He had believed, as many others in his place

6—2

would have done, and as indeed was the truth, that
my words only referred to himself, but, being delighted
at the ending I had just given to them, he replied that
he was not surprised that the Abbé Undedei, who was
the man who had asked him for this "confiscation,"
should have had news of it sooner than myself. My
Italian, added he, had done for another Italian what
he did not think he ought to do for a Frenchman.
This was natural enough, but even had it not been the
case, he would not venture to maintain that there were
not rascals of his nation just as well as of others. In
all countries there were good and bad people. All the
same, he was sorry that this had happened exactly to
my prejudice, but another occasion would be found to
oblige me when I least expected it, and a better one
perhaps than this was.

The abbé he meant was a man who, to depict him
as he really was, served him as trustee in many things.
He already had several benefices in his name, and
whenever there was some windfall like this, which he
did not wish to appear to enrich himself with, he
immediately gave it to him. He knew very well that
he would return it, and that, thus escaping the public
hatred, he would none the less have what he wanted.
This abbé, who was in the secret, was always quite
ready to declare that he had asked the Cardinal for
anything, although often he had not heard a word
about it. I therefore calculated that it would be
useless for me to question him on the subject, the
more so as, even were he in a mood (which he was
not) to confess the whole thing, I should not have got
much good by so doing. What was said was said,
and the Cardinal was not the man to retract the words

he had spoken, since his interests were concerned. In the meantime, his Eminence, being afraid that I should not stop there, and that I should ask him the truth, thought he ought to warn him. He instructed him as to what had happened with reference to myself, and that, were I by chance to speak of it, he must not fail to put me on the wrong scent, as he himself had done. He told him further, that I was in a great rage with the landlord of Dom Lopes, and that I believed that he had deceived me; consequently, he was to confirm me in this idea, because, in spite of its being an unimportant matter that he should justify himself to me, or let me believe all I liked, yet, as it was always a good thing to possess the esteem of everybody and especially when it cost but a few words, he thought proper to use his best endeavours. The abbé had been to see Dom Lopes several times at the house where he died, and knowing that his landlord was not an Italian, as I had declared to the Cardinal, (but as I had been pleased to tell him, to give some outlet to my resentment), he replied that my daring, in having presumed to speak as I had done, had been unequalled. What I had said about his nation, I had meant to tell him about himself. For a young fellow like myself, this was the height of insolence, and, if he would listen to him, he would banish me far away from the Court. This would teach me my duty another time, and respect towards those whose due it was. The Cardinal did not trouble so much about any affronts which might be put upon him as about his private interests. I had spoken to him, some days before, about a post which he had to sell, and for which I had found a bargainer who wanted to give him ten thousand

francs more than other people offered ; thinking, therefore, that he might very well miss this stroke of business,
if he let loose his anger as he was advised to do, he
made reply to the abbé, that there were certain things
which a minister ought to pretend to ignore, and others
which he could not pass over in silence without im-
perilling his authority.   Those which he might pretend
to ignore were principally when admission of a knowledge of them was a proof of one's bad faith.   He could
not, said he, have me exiled without everyone's knowing
the reason.   I myself would be the first to tell everybody, and, the matter being in no way to his advantage,
it was better to pretend ignorance than to purchase
satisfaction by the loss of one's reputation.   The abbé
(who was a man of the very character which the
Cardinal had painted our nation to me as possessing),
hearing him speak like this, thought it best not to
reply.   He agreed to everything he wished, and, the
better to pay him court, told him that by this he was
showing himself worthy of the position he occupied,
and that, even in the smallest things, he shone beyond
anything he could express.   Finally, he declared his
reasoning to be so clever and subtle, that he had not the
least word to urge against all that he had propounded.
It had not been the fault of the abbé, as we have just
seen, that I had not been hopelessly ruined ; for, when
one is once banished from Court, and especially
through such a thing as this, it is very rare that a
person can ever return.   My own good luck, or rather
the avarice of his Eminence had saved me ; but, as
there are people who, when they, so to speak, stab
you, want you to be grateful to them, this abbé told
me two days later at Court, where I found myself

alone with him, that he advised me to thank him, for,
had he been less my friend than he was, he might
have done me a terribly bad turn with the Cardinal.
I was quite unable, at first, to understand what his
meaning might be. I did not suspect that his
Eminence had told him of what I had said; so,
begging him to let me know in what way he had
served me, so that my gratitude might be proportionate to the good he had done me, he replied that it
was all very well for me to pretend not to know, but
I was not so ignorant as I wished to appear. I must
remember that I had passed off the landlord of Dom
Lopes as an Italian. There was no need to say any
more, for my natural quickness, which he well knew,
would not now make it a difficult thing for me to
divine everything else! I certainly did now guess
what had happened, at least a portion of it—but not
all of it as it had occurred; for, had I done so, I
should not have failed to thank the abbé for the trick
he had tried to play me. This he richly deserved;
for, after having wanted to ruin me as he had
attempted to do, he wished in addition, that I should
thank him for not having done so! I will let the
world judge after this, if I was wrong in accusing his
nation of rascality; and, even had it not already been
suspected of it (as it was), his conduct alone was
enough to give it such a reputation. Be this as it may,
being not only unaware to what extent he deserved to
be despised and scorned, but even believing, as he
wished me to do, that I owed him a debt of gratitude,
I praised him as he was very far from deserving.
Nevertheless, as I knew his devotion to the person of
the Cardinal, I took good care not to show my irrita-

tion before him, as I might perhaps have done before anyone else. On the contrary, I told him that the words of which his Eminence had had reason to complain had escaped me thoughtlessly, and that I had not been long in feeling sorry I had uttered them, since they had no sooner left my lips, than I would have wished for many reasons to have recalled them.

I deemed it best to speak thus in a moderate way before him, although I really still thought what I had told the minister. I continued to see the Cardinal as usual, well knowing that I must not give way to my angry feelings to such an extent as to do myself harm by discontinuing to pay him court. He spoke afresh to me of the bargain I had tried to make for him, in which rather an obstacle had arisen. The individual who wanted the post, which he wished to sell, was a young man of great expectations, whose mother was still alive. She was the widow of a conseiller of the Parlement, and as she would have much preferred him to embrace his father's profession than become a hanger-on of the Court, she had had her son informed that she would disinherit him and would even marry again herself, should he not do her bidding. I told the Cardinal of what was going on, and as his own interests were concerned, he became very alert. " All of you," said he to me, " are always looking for people to give you advice, which most frequently kills your soul and body by making you pursue shadows. Not one out of a hundred of these pieces of advice succeeds, but what will you give me if I bestow a piece on you which will make your fortune ? " I could not divine what he meant by this, and finding that it bore no reference to the conversation we were having,

it appeared queer to me that a man who, in such a
position as his, should be an example of wisdom and
prudence, should diverge from his subject to such an
extent as to make those discussing it with him lose
sight of it. Accordingly, not being able to conceal my
astonishment, but doing so in respectful terms, and
ones which could not draw upon me the treatment the
Abbé Undedei had recommended, he replied that I
was no Gascon; I must have been changed at nurse,
for the Gascons had a keener penetration than I, who
had not only not even dreamt of what he now wanted
to tell me, but who yet did not understand it, though
it ought to appear as clear as daylight to me.

No sooner did I hear the Cardinal reproach me thus,
than I began to carefully ponder over what he could
mean by all this. But, being obliged to admit my
ignorance in spite of all my thinking, " Poor man,"
rejoined he, " go and hide yourself, since you do not
understand that what I want to tell you is, that what
you ought to do is to marry that widow and profit by
this present chance of making your fortune. Go and
see her from me, and tell her that I beseech her to
agree to her son's treating with me about the post I
want to sell him; further, that he will be sent back to
school, if ever he presents himself for a councillorship;
that he himself has owned to you that, instead of
going to study law, his only care has been to go and
play tennis and haunt the taverns. Tell her that this
is a bad disposition out of which to make a good
judge, and that, consequently, she must not mind
seeing him adopt a career in which he will succeed
better than in the one she wishes him to embrace.
You may add that I am ready to grant her my pro-

tection and also be useful to her when occasion may arise." The Cardinal went on to say that I must put on my smartest clothes to pay this visit. As the widow was already inclined to remarry, if her son took this post (or most probably this was but a pretext she was making use of to avoid unfavourable criticism), I should soon make an impression upon her. People should help themselves, if they wanted to make their fortunes, for good luck did not always come to look for those in need of it! He jokingly added that he asked for no fee for his advice, except the arranging of his bargain.

I considered that he was not now reasoning too badly, and having promised that I would follow his advice, I dressed myself as smartly as possible and went to see the widow. She listened to the speech I made her on behalf of his Eminence in accordance with his instructions, and at once answered me that, although she would much like to please him, she could, nevertheless, not do so now. She could not sanction her son's abandoning the profession of his father; if even he did so, I might tell him she would at once marry again. These words were not lost on me. I rejoined that, as it was more right to side with fathers and mothers against their children than with children against fathers and mothers, I presented myself to her to carry out her revenge; her son was most certainly resolved to go his own way in this affair, no matter what obstacles she might place in his path; so, if she wanted to make him quickly repent of his foolish behaviour, she could not find any man who would embrace her interests so ardently as myself. At the same time, I told her a lot of things about her beauty which, as a matter of fact, was not great. In former years, indeed, she might have been beautiful, for it is a common saying that "the Devil was handsome as a young man." Nevertheless, I do not approve of this comparison; but, if it has been made, it is only to impress upon us that what one may find ugly at a certain time need not always have been so. Indeed, as this lady had a son of from twenty-five to twenty-six years old, and as the mother of such a son can no longer lay claim to be a beauty, at least with any chance of being believed, she might well have told me to go and pour out my stories somewhere else, had she chanced to be in a mood to do herself justice. Nevertheless, whether the Cardinal had hit the right nail on the head, when he had told me that she only wanted some pretext to marry, or that I seemed to her none too badly made and so aroused her desires, she did not remonstrate against my offers so severely as to give me grounds for despair. On the contrary, she softened like a woman who would have much liked me to be speaking the truth. She did not of course tell me this, but, as there are things which one understands by silence just as well as if they were formally explained, I made no fuss about asking permission to pay her a second visit. This she consented to, without my being obliged to be too pressing—a further circumstance which made me perceive that my affair was going on none too badly.

In the meantime, she wanted to know who I was. I satisfied her curiosity, and noticed that she was enchanted when I had told her my name, and that I was a lieutenant in the Guards. Apparently she had been afraid that I was some adventurer, a kind of person who abounded around his Eminence. This made our conversation last some time, and, seeing that she was taking an interest in it, I told her everything I could, to give her a good opinion of my rank and myself. Not that it is ever seemly for a man to praise himself, it had much better come from someone else than oneself; however, I deemed, if ever such a thing was pardonable, that it was so on the present occasion. Indeed, I acted thus much less from vanity than to disabuse her of any idea which might be harmful to me. I was afraid of her confusing me with the mass of rogues, who entirely filled the house of his Eminence, and, if once I allowed her to get this idea into her head, it would afterwards have been difficult for me to change her opinion. She received what I said in my own praise very well, and, taking it in the same spirit in which I spoke, that is to say, as simply a proof that I was a gentleman, and not an innkeeper, like the man I have before spoken of, she asked me that very day if I would not buy a company in the Guards, directly I got the money to do so. To be asked a thing like this at a first interview was getting on well! Mayhap, she would have done better to have shown more reserve. For, although this does not mean much, and she might even have said it from indifference, as there are certain things in which a lady ought to be extremely circumspect, she should weigh even her lightest words, since it is not the only thing for her to be virtuous, if she does not further keep herself quite free from suspicion.

Having parted as I have described, I told her son, whom I had informed that I was to see him on behalf

of the Cardinal, what answer she had given me about
his affairs. At the same time, I enquired of him if he
was resolved to displease her and so expose himself
to what she threatened. He rejoined that, provided
M. le Cardinal would grant him the honour of his
protection, he would not pay any attention to such a
trifling matter. His mother would get over her rage
when she saw that matters were settled, and even did
she go so far as to marry again, he would console
himself as other children did when the same thing
happened. I considered this a very youthful reply.
His mother had at least eighteen or twenty thousand
livres as income and, although I have never been
accused of being too fond of money, I yet deemed that
he would have been doing much better to be a plain
conseiller in the last " Présidial " of the kingdom than
lose such a fine establishment. However, his desire
was so great that he proceeded to say, that not only
was he determined to do what he told me, but further
to give his Eminence a thousand pistoles more than
he had offered, so as to secure his protection when
there should be need of it. This was attacking the
Cardinal in his weak spot, and being delighted to
pay him my court by letting him know this news,
which would please him as much as if he had great
need of the money, he entreated me with clasped
hands, so to speak, not to let this opportunity slip.
At the same time he told me, the more to encourage
me, that I did not know what I owed to him. I at
once thought that he must have asked the Queen for
something for me, and as one is naturally curious in
such a pass, I pressed him so much to let me know
what he meant, that at last he could not prevent

himself from telling me that, had he been willing to listen to the Abbé Undedei, he would have banished me far from his side. This speech was one to give me an even worse opinion of the Italians than before. I remembered that the abbé had taken care to imply to me that he had not desired my ruin, and that on the contrary he had tried to save me. Meanwhile, I learned that, far from matters having happened as he had described, he had done his best to get me exiled, from which circumstance I concluded that I had not been far wrong when I formed the opinion that dissimulation and treachery were the appanage of people of his nation.

I made the best excuses I could to the Cardinal, and the thousand pistoles which I gave him hopes of beyond his expectations having rendered me white as snow in his estimation, I do not know that I might not even have got the abbé banished, had I cared to ask for such a thing. Eventually we separated mutually pleased with one another, I because he promised me never again to think of the words which I had let slip, he because I had impressed upon him that he might count upon the thousand pistoles not escaping him.   I now set to work to see that the matter was carried through.   In the meantime, as, whilst serving others, it was not right that I should forget myself, I went again to see the widow, by whom I was even better received than on my first visit. She now spoke plain French to me, and I, on my part, having spoken afresh of the plan I had of participating in the revenge she wanted to take on her son, she asked me straight if she might rely upon my word. I answered that she was wronging me and herself as well, if she entertained any doubts about this. I was glad to let her know that I had never deceived anyone, not even my enemies. This was my character. Besides, she ought to know herself well enough to be aware that not only was she capable of arousing desires but also of setting them in a blaze. Consequently, I was already consumed by ardour to see my fortunes united to her own by bonds which could never be broken. This might be settled whenever she pleased, and I hoped that it would be to-day rather than to-morrow.

This speech did not fail to touch her, at least I had reason to think so from the answer she gave me. She told me that, if things were as I said, I might rely on soon being a captain in the Guards; she had the money quite ready to buy me a company and to procure for me an even greater position, if I was not satisfied with a captaincy. I was delighted to hear her speak so. For a long time now I had ardently wished for a post of this kind. Several times already I had spoken to his Eminence on the subject, and he, not being any more backward at promising than had always been his wont, had at once replied that it should be done directly he saw an opportunity. This opportunity had presented itself some time afterwards, a company having chanced to be vacant, but, as he had found there was some money to be got, he had remembered me no more than if I had been nonexistent or if he had never made me any promise. I had thought fit to remind him of my interest in the matter, but the only answer he had given me was, that "what was delayed was not lost." These six words had made me patient, but since

then he had again dealt with two or three of these
companies under my very nose, just as if what he
had told me was but a regular dream. So, as I no
longer relied upon him, my joy at seeing myself in
such a fair way to dispense with his protection was
great in the extreme, since such small confidence could
be placed in his statements. I hoped, as indeed I
had reason to do, that this pleasure would not fail
to be mine, now that I was about to have some
money. I had, if I may say so, done my duty with
some distinction. This had given me a reason for
pressing him more than I should have done, had I
felt that I had been lacking in it. Be this as it
may, thinking now only of settling my marriage, so
as soon to see myself happy in getting what I had
so long desired, I went to see the widow every day
with much assiduity, and was every moment received
more agreeably than I had been at the commencement
of our intimacy.

Meanwhile, her son's affairs were settled, and, either
because he had up to that time imagined that my visits
to his mother were only on his own account, or because
his anxiety to obtain the post he was seeking made him
incapable of thinking of anything except that which
could facilitate his schemes, he had as yet taken no
offence whatever, or if he had done so, had been unwilling to show any signs of it. Now, however, having
nothing further to desire in that quarter, he began to
consider that, property being an excellent thing and
what one could not do without, it would be a very bad
move to let his mother's slip out of his hands. For this
reason, closely observing the attentions which I began
to pay her, he became so uneasy that he no longer

slept day nor night. He might have said something to me about it and taken a high hand with me, in the way one usually does in these sort of cases. For, although duels still continued to be forbidden with much stringency, people did not fail to occasionally evade the prohibition and to fight as much as ever. Regularly appointed meetings were passed off as chance encounters. However, either because he was such a good servant of the King as not to like to contravene his orders, or because he deemed me more inclined to do mischief than himself, far from proceeding to such extremities, he, on the contrary, told me that he was not sorry that I was about to become his stepfather, for he clearly perceived that his mother was bent on committing the folly of marrying again, and, as this was the case and it was not in his power to prevent it, he was ready to bestow his benediction upon both of us.

He made this speech to me in such an airy manner, that I thought there was no deception in what he said. I consequently did not scruple not only to embrace him, but to declare besides, that, as he was behaving like this, I should always live on such good terms with him and such friendly ones, that he would have no reason to regret his kindly view of our courtship. I was well aware that both his mother and myself were quite free to do as we liked, but being of a disposition which preferred to be at peace with the whole world, I was highly delighted at the course which his reason and natural good sense had caused him to adopt at the present juncture. Everybody was not always ready to do themselves justice like this, and he would do much better than if he had behaved in another way. I would ask him only for a little time in which to prove this truth to him, and the only judge of it I should seek would be himself.

His mother was informed by me of what he had said. She was just as pleased as I myself, so much so that, at once forgiving him for his disobedience in consideration of his recent gracious behaviour, we both fixed the next Monday as the day for our marriage. We ordered our clothes in view of this event, and having published the banns on the Sunday, we were ready for our betrothal the same day, so as to complete our marriage on the morrow, when the curé of St. Eustache, in whose parish she lived, came to tell us that an objection had been made. This news surprised both of us, but not each of us to the same extent. As I was not thoroughly posted as to this lady's mode of life, and had taken more care to make enquiries about her property than about anything else, my first idea was that she had had an intrigue with someone who was just as anxious to win her as I was. This cooled me down considerably, and at once perceiving it, no sooner had the curé taken his leave, than she glanced at me without daring to say a word. This news had as it were prostrated her, so much so (especially when she saw my face) that she had not even asked the divine who it was that was raising this opposition. The curé for his part had thought it most discreet to tell her nothing, believing her to know enough about it not to need enlightenment. He was afraid of causing her to blush, and that she would be obliged to cast down her eyes in my presence. He knew these things were usually the sequel of some love affair, and therefore he was anxious to

spare her the confusion which she must especially feel
before me, because, to be reasonable, such a thing
could not be agreeable to me.

The lady in her distress would never have broken
her silence, had I not forced her to do so by asking
what the meaning of all this was. She said, in reply,
that she knew nothing about it at all, but that
all she could tell me was, that it was very painful for
herself, since my expression showed clearly enough
that I suspected her of some intrigue. In spite of
this, she had never had any especial love affair with
anyone, either before or after her husband's death.
Consequently, she had no reason whatever for expecting
what was now taking place. She had always been
virtuous, so much so that not only had she never
given any man grounds for opposing her banns, but
even for daring to say that she had ever uttered a word
to him which could be construed as an engagement.
For eight years now she had been a widow, and if I
liked to make enquiries, I should discover that since
then she had lived in such great retirement that it
was an impossibility to accuse her of having seen
any man who did not belong to her family. The
frank way in which she spoke at once convinced me
that she was not as guilty as I had imagined. I had
at first got some curious fancies into my head, which
had obscured my understanding; so, immediately
ridding myself of these ideas, I decided that I ought
not, on account of a false alarm, to abandon the hopes
I had formed of possessing her twenty thousand livres
of income. I therefore asked her pardon for my
suspicions, telling her (to make her the more appreciate
my return to her allegiance) that she ought to be

7—2

delighted at this occurrence, since it must demonstrate that not only I did not want to lose her, but must further convince her of the confidence I should always place in what she told me.   She must certainly now perceive that, after being thoroughly alarmed, I immediately recovered at a single word of hers.   She admitted that this was true, but added that, all the same, she did not know whether she had any great cause to rejoice at it, for a woman who fell into the hands of such a suspicious husband had every likelihood of passing some evil hours with him.   Jealousy was a strange thing, and although people said it was only the result of love, as it could nevertheless be but the outcome of a diseased kind of love, my moods were not less to be feared than death itself.

I was not in any way jealous.   To be so, I should have had to have been in love, which was very far from my case!   I was no older than this lady's son, and to be fond of a woman who might have been my mother was not the sort of thing very much in my line, but I coveted wealth and a good position, and the news which the curé of St. Eustache had brought us having seemed to me to announce the loss of both these things was what had produced the particular state of mind which the lady had observed me to be in.   Nevertheless, as little by little I began to be reassured, I tried to make my peace with her, which I succeeded in doing only with a good deal of difficulty. This done, I enquired of her from whom these objections arose, and being no wiser than myself (having been so much affected as to have forgotten to ask) she replied that, whoever the man was, he must be an impostor.   Her surprise at the news, and above all

at my reception of it had prevented her from finding
out from the curé, but as I began to admit my mistake,
and she herself was also beginning to regain her senses,
horses must be put in the carriage, and both of us go
together to find out who was at the bottom of all this.

We did as she wished, and, not finding the curé at
home, we spoke to one of his curates. He told us that
the objection arose from a gentleman named Le Bègue
de Villaines, who was from the province of Berri. This
gentleman had taken up his residence at the house of
an attorney called Harouard, and the latter would
probably give us all the information we desired. His
advice to us was to set out and find him, for, if we
wanted to know more than he had just told us, we
should have to enquire of others than the curé and
himself. We thought fit to believe him, and from his
house betook ourselves to the attorney's, who lived
quite close to Notre-Dame, just in front of a little
parish church there is there. The widow had already
vowed to me, on leaving the curate's house, that she
did not know this M. de Villaines, and that she had
never even heard him spoken of. On the way, she
reiterated the same statement once more, which highly
delighted me, because I felt glad that a lady whom I
desired to make my wife should not only be known as
virtuous, but, in addition, as being above all suspicion.
On account of this, I formed the opinion that it was
but a joke someone had tried to play us, and was
unable to say if she or I was its intended victim. All
the same, I could not conceive that it could possibly
concern me; I was unaware of having any enemy, the
more so as the whole of my behaviour had always
been so circumspect towards everybody, that it was

easily seen that I tried rather to please everyone than
to displease one single soul.

Harouard was honest enough for a man of his
profession (in which honest men are very scarce) : consequently, we had no sooner told him what had brought
us, than he replied that he did not know this M. de
Villaines. It was however true, that a handsome
enough man, whom also he did not know, had that
morning come to his house to beg him to take charge
of the legal notices which might be given to him
touching this affair. To secure him, he had said that
this business could not fail to be carried to the Parlement, and that M. de Villaines, on the strength of his
reputation, had already cast his eyes upon him to
defend his interests.

As all this appeared to us a regular plan to play us
a joke, we asked this attorney what sort of man was
he who had come to see him. Our idea was to try
and recognise the perpetrator of this hoax from the
portrait he should give us, so as to thus find out whom
we had to deal with. But, in spite of his frankly telling
us all he knew, the result was just the same as if he
had told us nothing at all. Neither the widow nor
myself knew anyone who at all resembled the man he
described. The lady appealed to the Officialty, where
she was summoned. First of all, she requested that
her opponent should appear in person, taking an oath,
as she had already done before me, that she had never
known this M. de Villaines nor anyone connected with
him. There was a lawyer at this court who held a
brief for the other side, and who asked for a month's
delay for his client to appear in. His pretext was,
that not only was his house more than sixty leagues

from Paris, but that he was also unwell. The judge reduced this by half, and only gave him a fortnight. This period of time, which still seemed to me a very long one (not on account of my love, which was very moderate, but on account of my impatience to know who had played us such a trick), was hanging very heavily on my hands, once the first day was past, when at the end of the week I thought I descried the man whose picture the attorney of the Parlement had painted. He had described him as having a red doublet embroidered with silver, a black wig and a beaver-hat of the same colour with a white feather. He had besides told us that he had a tuft of blue ribbon on the brim of his hat, as was then the fashion. Passing over the Pont-Neuf in a sedan chair, I perceived, in the carriage of my future step-son, a man exactly answering this description. This made me rather suspect that it could not but be he who had been to Harouard's house, and further, that it was the step-son alone who had set him to work. This I told his mother, whom I went to see after dinner. She agreed with my views, and we mutually arranged to have her son watched, so as to discover who this "red doublet" might be. By these means we found out that he was an adventurer without birth or reputation, whose only profession was frequenting gaming-houses. This increased our suspicions : for, as exactly a man of that stamp was needed to sustain an imposture of this kind, this individual would be more suitable than anyone else who might have his own or his family's reputation to look to. The lady wanted me to go and find him and threaten that, did he not withdraw from his lawsuit, I would have him cudgelled to death, but,

being of opinion that she was going a little too fast to
follow her advice (for, far from the matter being
cleared up as she declared it was, I saw many difficulties ahead), I begged her to restrain her impatience
until such time as our suspicions should be verified.
What puzzled me was that the man did not call
himself M. de Villaines. He went by the name of
the Chevalier de la Carlière—a title which apparently
had not cost him much—at all events his chevalier-
ship had not been expensive, since they would not even
have taken him at Malta as a "Chevalier servant."[1] He
was only the son of a mason, though, to see him, one
would have said he was that of a Maréchal of France.

We also placed a spy at Harouard's door, and at
that of the lawyer of the courts, to see whether the
man did not go to one or the other's house, but this
spy, having done nothing but waste his time and
trouble, I bethought myself of sending Athos to lodge
in the same hostelry as the chevalier. First of all I
made him disguise himself. I hired for him at an old
clothes' shop a black suit and a mantle of the same
colour, and having begged him to call himself a lawyer
whilst at the hostelry, he made a number of litigants
who lodged there believe that he had come specially
from Pau on account of a lawsuit with which a com-
munity of that part of the country had entrusted him.
This was thoroughly believed because, though he had
not the appearance of a lawyer, they did not make
too careful enquiry. Besides, people do not always
look what they are: witness a certain referendary
whom I sometimes see at Court, who has as much
beard as a guardsman, and who would look much

---

1 A "Chevalier servant" was one who entered the order,
without being able to give proofs of being of noble birth.

better at the head of a regiment of cavalry than on the
"fleurs de lis."[1] For everybody ought not only to work
at his profession, but also to have the appearance of
doing so. A beard does not suit a magistrate unless
it is "à la Moignon, or à la Novion." A beard "à la
Vedeau" is more the beard of a sentry than of a councillor
of the Parlement, so all those people who equip themselves out of their rôles take leave of good sense at the
same time. They only get themselves laughed at, but
enough of beards : I had much better return to my
subject.

Athos having thus declared himself from Pau, La
Carlière, who had no great judgment, at once asked
him if he knew me. Probably he was aware that I
came from there, and, although he merely knew me
by reputation (and I should not have been too pleased
to be well known to a man like him), his eagerness to
speak was the cause of his making this enquiry.
Athos, who had as much judgment as the other had
little, no sooner heard him speak of me than he
thought his trouble would not be for nothing. He
believed, I repeat, that I was both right in my
suspicions and that he himself would not be long in
clearing up the matter. He accordingly replied, the
better to cause him to fall into the trap, that, although
Bearn was not too big a district, it was impossible to
know everyone there ; that he had, it was true, heard
talk of my family and myself, but he could not say
that he knew me as an acquaintance without telling
a lie. He had heard, he added, only two days before
he had set out, that I had made a large fortune in
Paris, and that I had married a rich widow, which
should suit me well, since I had no riches of my

1 On the bench.

own. La Carlière rejoined that he did not know who had told him this news, but it was totally false. The fortune I had up to now made was nothing in particular. It was true I was a lieutenant in the Guards, but as for my having married the widow I spoke of, he must scratch that out of his books. He added that he quite agreed I had thought of marrying her, but it had never come off, unless he was very much mistaken.

If this chevalier of a new sort had been imprudent in merely asking Athos if he knew me, it was being much more so to speak to him so plainly! Had he had the least sense, he ought not to have opened his mouth about this matter, but, as he had none, he continued on his way, without taking precautions against it leading him over a precipice. Athos, without giving any sign of anything, answered that he could not go bail for all the rumours which were current in the provinces. He had really believed in that rumour, because he had heard it at the house of the lieutenant de roi at Bayonne, but, since he declared it was not true, he was ready to trust him rather than the man who had said so, for, being on the spot as he was, he would know more of the matter than one who was so far away. His civility pleased the chevalier, and, from the manner he spoke, thinking nothing less than that he was on my side, he begged him to let him know confidentially if I were of the family of D'Artagnan as I claimed to be. I had agreed with Athos and the lady that, should the chevalier by chance put a question like this to him, he was to tell him all the scandalous things possible. My idea was, that it was the chevalier who had been to Harouard and that my future son-in-law had made him go, so all this would soon come back to his mother with the object of disgusting her with me. I had consequently given Athos his lesson in writing, so that it might be reported to her word for word. It could make no impression, for I had warned her beforehand and she had highly approved of this stratagem, which indeed succeeded admirably. Athos, after pretending a little shyness, as if he feared being put down as a scandalmonger, told La Carlière that, since he was curious to discover my origin, no one could speak more positively about it than himself. Eighteen or twenty years ago a lawsuit had taken place at Pau about my genealogy. At that time he was the clerk of a lawyer to whose house all the papers had been brought which had to do with the matter. His curiosity had led him to carefully examine these papers, and either he was a fool or I was no more a gentleman than his valet. He now remembered that I was the grandson of a tinker who had gone to the wars and, having made something of a fortune there, had taken the name and arms of the family of D'Artagnan.

La Carlière, who was the man who had been to Harouard, was delighted at this discovery. He had been sent there by the lady's son, as we had suspected ; so, believing that no sooner should she hear me spoken of like this than she would not receive me again, he went to tell his friend the news. I heard from Athos, whom I secretly saw in a house which I had appointed as a meeting-place, everything which had passed at the hostelry. I formed the same opinion as he had done, and at once thinking that I should not have long to wait to hear something about it, my forecast soon came off. The son no sooner learned what I have just recounted, than he had a letter written to his mother by his confederate. It was dated from Paris, and contained the whole story of my origin without one syllable being omitted. What was besides a curious thing about this was, that the next night the strangest concert one ever heard speak of took place in front of this lady's windows. All the whistles (as I believe) of the tinkers of Paris and the suburbs had been borrowed, and, as the sounds extracted from them were mingled with those of a quantity of pans and kettles, the most horrible music ever up to that time heard was produced. It is true that this is what usually happens, or at least a part of it, at the weddings of old people who remarry young ones, but, as we were not yet come to that, and as, besides, the lady was not of so decrepit an age that she was to be thus coarsely insulted, it was easy for us to perceive that this new sort of rough[1] music was directed not so much against her as against me. Indeed, if some of these instruments were usually to be observed in ordinary "rough music," the addition of the whistle meant something mysterious, and could only have to do with me.

No more was necessary to make me resolve to revenge myself on a man who made war on me more like a fox than a lion, I mean my future son-in-law, who, under the pretence of friendship, had, fooled me so finely, that I had been the first to praise his good qualities to his mother. This was why she had so easily forgiven him. However, things having changed a good deal

---

1 "Rough music," known in the north of England as "riding the stang," has not yet entirely disappeared from English village life, and is still occasionally resorted to in cases of unpopularity or bad behaviour.

since then, she was so eager to see him punished for
his perfidy, that she would herself have incited me to
vengeance, had she not been afraid of outraging good
taste and natural feeling by so doing. I had, nevertheless, no need of anyone to excite me against him.
I was by nature an enemy to deceit, even if it had
only someone else as its object, and as his treachery
directly affected me, I sent to find him, to let him
know that I wanted to cut his throat. I did not discover him all that day, either because he feared something, or because he was making preparations for a
terrible thing which he was contemplating. Nor did
I find him all the next day, without being able to think
of any other reason for it than the one I have given.
Seeing my trouble wasted, sorrow overcame me to such
an extent, that, letting my resentment fall upon his
crony La Carlière, I regaled him, as he was leaving
Morel's, with a shower of blows from a cudgel. I
pretended, by way of excuse, that he had trodden on
my toes coming out of that establishment, where the
game of dice was played and where one always found
a mixed company, that is to say, people of quality and
scoundrels. He could not muster up courage to draw
his sword to defend himself, which made me so sorry
for him that I regretted having treated him as I had
done. It even seemed to me that my honour was
tarnished by insulting a wretch such as he. So, ceas-
ing all of a sudden to thrash him, I told him that he
must not believe all this was for having trodden on my
toes. "Ah," said I, "I recognise you, my friend, as
being M. le Bègue de Villaines and not the Chevalier
de la Carlière. The Chevalier de la Carlière has too
glib a tongue to let himself be thrashed without at
least abusing his aggressor, but a "bègue" (a stammerer)

can no more speak than a rascal do anything else than
turn his back to be beaten, as you have done."

He was very surprised to hear this speech of mine,
and as he was already confused enough with the blows
with which I had regaled him, he tried to bolt to the
corner of the street, so as to escape in the direction of
the Hôtel Salé. He had no long way to go to do this:
Morel's house was in the " Marais," in the Rue de la
Perle, fifty paces at most from the hotel in question. I
do not know if he concealed himself there, or if he
went on, for I did not give myself the trouble of
following him. Be this as it may, having immediately gone to describe to the lady what I had just done,
I told her that her son had acted wisely to avoid me,
for, had I found him when searching for him, it had
been my intention to see if he was as courageous as he
was crafty and evil-speaking. The widow told me I
had done well to regale my chevalier as I had, which
would teach him to be wiser another time, but as such
a thing might bring trouble upon me, were I to draw
sword upon her son, she would beg me to do nothing
of the sort. It was to be hoped that the warning I had
given his friend would act as a reprimand to himself,
and if the worst came to the worst, and should he not
amend his behaviour of his own accord, she would no
longer refrain from advising me to have no greater
consideration for him than I had had for the chevalier.

I thought that this was too much for a mother and
a lady of good family to say. A lady like this should
not wish her son to be treated as one treats the riff-
raff. But she was so enraged at the " rough music,"
thinking that only old women were treated in such a
way, that she had lost possession of herself. Indeed,

it is attacking a woman in her most sensitive quarter
to tell her such truths, so much so, that she would
pardon her own death as easily as a joke of this kind.

Of all the ways of offending women there is none
which upsets them more than anything which deals
with their age. The more truth there may be in what
one says, the greater offence they take, and, as this
lady was past forty, every word which might convey
the impression that she was more than thirty was a
dagger-thrust to her. For this reason, some three
weeks or a month before, she had wanted to scratch
her son's eyes out, because he used often to come and
hum about her ears a song which at that time was a
new one, and which had been composed for a person
of about her own age. The words of it were these—

> "*Once that she's come to forty year,*
> *A dame must bid farewell*
> *To love and laughter. Fickle swains*
> *No longer fear her spell.*

> "*Careless of ancient loves, they fly*
> *To seek some winsome lass*
> *Still in her spring-tide, bright of eye,—*
> *Ah love, like time, must pass!*

She had, nevertheless, taken good care not to let him
know that her anger arose from any idea that she
herself was attacked by this ditty. She had pretended
that he sang badly, and that his voice was no less
jarring upon her ears than the most disagreeable thing
in the world.

Our chevalier having thus been so excellently regaled, we were both awaiting the end of the drama,
which he and his friend had been kind enough to

arrange for us, with more patience than before, when her son played us another trick which we had been far from expecting. As he had money and property, he found a clerk of a Secretary of State, who, for five hundred pistoles, promised to obtain for him a "lettre de cachet" to have his mother shut up. The steps they took to obtain this were these. They invented letters and answers written by her to a brother of hers in a foreign country. He had gone there on account of a duel which had caused much stir at Court. Owing to it, he had forfeited all the property of his family, which would have come to him after the death of his eldest brother, who had been referendary and had died childless. These letters, by reason of the way they were interpreted, contained some reference to State affairs, so, as more is not necessary to ruin anybody, the "lettre de cachet" was issued and very cleverly made use of. A jubilee[1] occurring about this time, the lady (who was very pious), having left her house with only a companion to go and visit the churches, was arrested whilst leaving the Hôtel-Dieu. As is usual on these kind of occasions, she was thrown into a carriage, and the guards, who were too well instructed as to their duty to overlook anything, having made the companion enter it, at the same time the blinds of the carriage were pulled down and both ladies con-ducted to the house of the man who had arrested them. The leader of the escort believed the lady to be a real criminal, so, all she could say to announce her innocence to the minister, or to have letters conveyed to her relatives being of no avail, he made her the next morning get into a carriage drawn by six

1 A general indulgence granted by the Pope.

horses, which was to take her to the prison which had been appointed.

Her household was very surprised when the dinner-hour arrived and they did not see her return. However, they waited till two o'clock without being otherwise alarmed. They believed that piety had caused her to visit several churches, and that this was the reason of the delay. But at last, three o'clock having struck, and no news having yet come to hand, the servants went to make search at her friends', to discover whether she had not stayed to dinner with some of them. Two hours more having elapsed without their being able to find out what had become of her, and the lackeys having returned home just as wise as when they set out, the lady's servants began to be plunged into real trouble; so, thinking they ought to inform her son, the latter would not come to the house without a good escort. Probably he was afraid that, should he go alone, he might by chance meet me, and that I should treat him as I had treated his crony. This fear, besides, was the stronger because he knew that he had added a fresh crime to his previous one; so, as, after what I had said and done to La Carlière, he was not ignorant that I already knew one of the conspirators, he had a good idea that I might very well guess the other, and therefore did not think it convenient to risk himself rashly.

The escort he desired consisted of four or five of his relatives—lawyers and men of distinction, to whom he went to announce the disappearance of his mother. They were very surprised, as one could not have failed to be at such a thing. They questioned him as to what he thought had become of her, and taking care not to confide in them, since he would have been denouncing himself, he insinuated that I might very well have abducted her. The better to make them believe this, he told them that, though on first acquaintance she had passionately wanted to marry me, she had become so disgusted since the serenade I have just spoken of, that he knew from a good source that she had dismissed me. I had, however, said he, not consented to accept this dismissal. Far from it, I had returned as usual to see her, but had apparently met with such small success as to have resorted to the violence of which he suspected me to be guilty. At the same time he explained to them the mystery of the serenade, but, as there was one of these magistrates who had formerly been Intendant at Pau and who knew my family, he told him to take good care not to spread this "dream" abroad, for he would make himself a laughing-stock. There was no one who did not know who I was, and when people were so well known, all the slander one might heap upon an individual must recoil on the head of its originator. Consequently, if his mother should have become disgusted with me, such disgust must have arisen from some other quarter than from my birth, which was more likely to arouse rather than to extinguish her desires. Nevertheless, as all these gentlemen were very far from having any idea of his malice and thought him an honourable man, they resolved on lodging an ordinary legal complaint about the abduction of their relative and to make careful enquiries in all the convents, if by chance she had not retired to one of them before taking any further steps. However, all their enquiries having proved abortive, they became so carried away by passion, that they presented a petition to the lieutenant criminel for permission to arrest me.

The magistrate in question was a very extraordinary man, which all Paris knew him to be. He never refused a petition when presented to him accompanied by money. Should, however, this assistance be lacking, he would examine petitions from one end to the other and made no exception in favour of anyone, whatever protection they might have on their side. I have forgotten to say that this petition had been preceded by an information which had been lodged against me. My presumptive son-in-law had caused all the servants of his mother to be heard, but their declaration having rather exculpated than incriminated me, the lieutenant criminel had told the relatives that, if they wanted to bring this matter to a successful termination, they must bring other witnesses than those who had been produced. Indeed, these had said nothing but that I had been every day at their mistress's house, that we had eaten and drunk together very frequently, and that she had, some days before, ordered them to treat me with the same respect as if I was already their master. I let people imagine the effect of such evidence, and if my accusers must not have been mad to try and bring a suit against me on such grounds! The lady's son, when he perceived this, had recourse to the expedient usually employed by those who wanted to gain this judge over to their side. He caused money to be offered him, but as the magistrate had, unluckily for him, learnt that I had been to M. le Cardinal and that he was according me his protection, instead of consenting to receive it, he sent me word that he would much like to speak

to me.   I was totally at a loss to divine what he
wanted of me.   I did not know him at all, but having
pondered well over the matter, I concluded that a
soldier, who had been arrested for theft and who was
of my guard, was the cause.   I imagined that he had
remembered me, and that this magistrate, who was not
wont to forget himself when his profit was concerned,
wanted to feel my pulse, to save this wretch's life.
This thought inspired me with such contempt for
him, that, instead of answering his request, I did not
even trouble to let him hear from me.

When he perceived this, he spoke of it to a gentleman
who was a relation of his, named Seguier de la Verrière,
in the suite of "Mademoiselle."   This gentleman, whom
he had before asked if he knew me, was a friend of
mine.   He it was who had told him of my having
been to M. le Cardinal, and of his having been kind
to me; so, having complained that I had not done
him the honour of giving him news of myself, though
he might well expect such a thing, after what he had
done for me, the magistrate once again begged him
to let me know that he had something of importance
to communicate.   He even added that it concerned me
more closely than I thought, in order that I might
not be so negligent on this occasion as I had been
on the other.   La Verrière very much surprised me,
when he told me this.   I replied, with that cordiality
which prevails between good friends and honourable
men, that he knew his relation just as well as myself.
He had a bad reputation, and it was this which had
prevented my replying to his civil message.   My idea
had been that he wanted to ask me for money to
save a wretch from the gallows.   Perhaps, indeed,

this fresh attempt was made only with the same end
in view, and I would beg him to let me know his
opinion, for, if it coincided with my own, I should
stop where I was, without consenting to go and see
him. At the same time, I enquired if he knew at
all what was wanted of me, knowing that, without
any reference to his relationship, he would make no
mystery about the matter. La Verrière, who was an
honourable man whom one could trust, told me that he
had sounded his relative on the subject, but that he would
never tell him anything about it; he was therefore
of opinion that it was not about what I thought
that he wished to speak to me. His reason for
thinking so was that, were it for such a small matter,
he would have made no mystery about mentioning
it; he would even have told him to drop me a word,
the more so as it would have been easy for him to
turn this off in a creditable way, without as yet allowing
his own self-interest to appear. In short, La Verrière
concluded that he must have something of importance
to tell me, and even of such great importance as
not to confide it to anyone but myself.

I allowed myself to believe him, so much so that,
having gone to see this magistrate, he much surprised me
when I learned what had happened. I had already been
as astonished as anyone could be by the disappearance
of the lady, but perceiving besides that I was accused of
abducting her, I found myself so carried away by rage
and grief that I do not know what this judge could
have said about me. I must have seemed much more
brutal than polite, for, instead of thanking him as I
should have done, I railed against the lady's son, whom
I did not fail to accuse of being the author of what

had occurred. The trick he had already played upon
his mother and myself was a sure proof to me that I
was not deceived. I told the lieutenant criminel
this, and he replied that there was indeed some presumption that it was true, but the proof was not clear
enough to base certain confidence upon it. Besides,
he was not the man to have had his mother killed,
which also would have been, as it were, impossible for
him to have done, without some news of it reaching his
ears. He was furnished with accurate information
regarding all the murders which were perpetrated in
Paris. None had occurred for nearly three weeks past,
so, if the young man were guilty of that which I
accused him of, it was at most only of having had his
mother abducted. Nevertheless, people could not be
shut up like this without someone getting to know of it.
He would, for my sake, enquire of all the prévôts if any
suspicious carriage had been observed to pass by. The
prévôts had spies out from the break of day to well on
in the night, so, unless very particular measures had
been taken, this affair would not long remain secret,
always supposing that my suspicions turned out to be
true.

These promises were of no use to me, because,
although the carriage in which the lady was had been
seen to pass, this functionary did not dare to tell me
anything about it, as the matter concerned the King.
Besides, as he did not think the lady was in it, he
believed that, even should he speak about it, it would
be of no use to me whatever. He could not guess that
she had done anything which concerned the King, nor
that a son had been wicked enough to reduce a mother
to such a deplorable condition by means of a false

accusation. Be this as it may, not being able, after making a thousand useless enquiries as to her fate, to get rid of the suspicion which I entertained against this young man, I resolved to despatch him to another world. Nevertheless, I did not dream of carrying this out by evil means. My resolve was to fight with him, and oblige him to tell me what he had done with his mother, that is, if the fortune of war should place me in a position to ask him such a thing. However, no sooner did he perceive that I was trying to cross swords with him, than he secretly sold his post. At the same time, he crossed into foreign countries, under the pretext of travelling. I would have followed him, had I, like himself, been of a mood to throw up everything, but coming to the conclusion that my prosperity was concerned, I was as patient as was possible for me to be, from fear of having reasons for regret if I were to do things without mature deliberation.

IV

THREE months passed away without my hearing any talk of the matter. Notwithstanding this, I still continued to prosecute my enquiries, but I had got just as far with them as on the first day, when I received an unsigned letter, and one, the writing of which was unknown to me. It set forth that the writer had undertaken to give me a great bit of news, which must closely affect me. It could not be confided to paper for very important reasons, but before six weeks, or two months at the latest, I should hear it out loud. More information could not be given, for indispensable reasons. I was to live in hope till then, for my troubles would certainly not last longer.

My first thought, on receiving this letter, was that my enemy had had it written to further make game of me. Nevertheless, I had to be patient, without even knowing whence the letter came. For, as it was undated, and I had not been at home when it had been brought, I could not enquire from the postman.[1] I went the next day to him to find this out, and, having

1 Cardinal Richelieu had, in 1630, established a regular postal system, with twenty postal zones.

shown him the letter, he replied that he could not with certainty say from what place it had come. He carried letters from so many places, that he was afraid of taking one for the other, but, all the same, he thought it was from Bordeaux, and would even assure me that this was the case. The postage he had made me pay coincided with this well enough, but, in short, whether it came from there or somewhere else, all this was useless enough, since I did not know to whom to address myself to extricate me from my uneasiness. Two months and a half elapsed without my discovering the outcome of this letter, which made me more than ever believe that this was a new joke someone had played me. Finally, as I no longer expected anything, since the period of time named had already passed away fifteen days ago, I received a fresh letter, in which my pardon was asked for the writer not having kept his word. Excuses were made in it, couched in the most honourable terms imaginable, and these phrases ended with a formal assurance that, before three weeks were over, I should have every reason for being content.

This second letter gave me more pleasure than the first, since it seemed to me that, if there had been nothing to be hoped for me, the writer would not have taken so much trouble. I consequently again waited patiently during the time asked, and scarcely two days after it had expired, one of my servants came to say that a gentleman was asking for me. As every moment I awaited news of the person who had written to me, I asked him if he knew who it was, for, had he done so, I should have clearly seen that it was not the man I awaited with such impatience. He answered no, which so much raised my hopes, that I was very near running to meet him, the sooner to make sure of my business. Reflecting, however, that, even were I to fly instead of run, the man could tell me nothing on the steps, I waited for him in my room with a stout heart. A moment later, I saw enter a tall well-built man, who, after having civilly saluted me, said that he had not the honour of being known to me, but that it was he who had twice written to me. I was delighted to perceive that it was the individual whom I had so long been waiting for, and, having had a chair placed for him near the fire, I made my servants leave the room, so that he might speak to me more at his ease. He proceeded to say that he was a gentleman of Gascony, who had had the misfortune to be shut up for ten years in the château of Pierre-Encise, that he had got out but two days before writing me his first letter, and had not been able to let me know its intent, for fear of its being seized in the post and bringing some fresh trouble upon himself. A mere nothing was needed to get a man thrown into these kind of prisons, especially when one was observed, on leaving them, to attempt to send news to the relatives or friends of other prisoners! What he at that time had to tell me, and that which he was now going to do, was to inform me that a lady, who had been imprisoned in this château five or six months before, had great confidence in me to get her innocence established. She had been unable to write to me for lack of ink and paper, but now sent word that this affair had apparently been brought upon her by the same man who had opposed our marriage. I was not to lose a moment in succouring her, for, were I to delay a little

time, sorrow would soon send her to the tomb. She
did nothing but weep day and night, and he was even
very much afraid that the long time he had taken to
give me news of her might have thrown her into
despair.   Nevertheless, he could not have done any
more, for, at the end of such a long imprisonment, he
had been obliged to go to his estate to see his wife
and children.   At first, he had reckoned not to be so
long, but, not being born rich, and as in this world
one did not do all one wished, all this time had been
necessary for him to procure the money requisite for
his journey to Paris.

The reader may judge of my surprise at hearing
such news! I could not doubt that this was the lady
whom I had so long sorrowed for, and even had I
still doubted, I should not have remained in that
state long, since he mentioned her by name to me.
He added that she had been incarcerated in a room
above his own, that he had pierced the fireplace, which
had the same chimney as that in which he lighted
his fire, and had spoken to her by that opening, and
had by these means finally learnt her sad fate.   He
left me a moment after, saying that time must be so
precious to me after what he had just said, that everyone
who should make me lose it could not be otherwise
than insupportable.   He would, however, come from
time to time to see me, to know what I had done.
Meanwhile, did I need him, he lodged in the Rue
d'Orléans at the "Golden Scissors."   I had only to
write him the shortest note to bid him come, and
he would at once betake himself to my house.   I had
but to address it to M. de las Garigues, which, as a
matter of fact, was not his real name, but the one

which he had assumed in the hostelry for certain reasons of his own.

I thanked him, as was right, for the trouble he had taken, and having gone to the house of M. le Tellier, Secretary of State, to whom I had the honour to be privately known, I related as succinctly as I could the affair of the lady, so that he might assist me. This he promised to do, telling me that, as it was not he who had issued the "lettre de cachet," he would discover from the other Secretaries of State who it was who had given it, so I must furnish him with not only the name and position of the lady in writing, but further make three memoranda all exactly alike, in order that he might send them to the three Secretaries of State, which there were without counting himself. I was enchanted at his promises, and having gone from him to the house of one of his chief clerks, named Boistel, a friend of mine, I begged him to give me three sheets of paper with a pen and ink. This was soon done, and my three memoranda being completed on the spot, I at once took them to M. le Tellier, whom I found no longer at home. M. le Cardinal had just sent for him on some business, and betaking myself to his house (not to speak to him there, but to watch when he went out, so as to return to his lodging with him), I remained two hours without his making his appearance. Eventually he descried me in the ante-chamber while leaving the minister, and having signalled to me to come to him, he very obligingly asked me if my memoranda were finished. I replied yes, and having bidden me give them to him, so as to return me an answer as quickly as possible, I would not do so, on the pretext that I should be acting much more politely by bearing them to his house than by thus casually giving them to him. The truth, however, is, that I was afraid that, if I gave them to him, he would put them in his pocket and the moment after, remember them no more. The great matters, by which he was already overwhelmed and by which he has been even much more burdened since, gave me ground for fearing this forgetfulness. He told me however, that all these formalities were out of place between us, that I must give him the papers without fuss, for he would at once send them to his colleagues.

Seeing him so obliging, I obeyed without any repugnance. He did, indeed, give the packet to one of his lackeys, with orders to carry it to the valets de chambre of the three other Secretaries of State. He also bade him tell the man to whom he delivered it that, not only was it from him that these memoranda came, but, further, that he must impress upon his superiors that he would be grateful to them, if they completed this business as quickly as possible.

The lackey at once went where his master had told him to go, and having punctually executed his commission, I discovered the next day that all three memoranda had been returned to M. le Tellier with exactly the same answers. They set forth that the lady mentioned was not at Pierre-Encise, and that all the registers of the state-prisoners for a year past had been searched, and, from the examination made, it had been discovered that she was not there. No sooner had M. le Tellier shown me this answer than, without wasting my time writing a note to M. de las Guarigues as he had told me, I went myself to find

him. Fortunately he was at home, and, having reported
the answer I had just received, he replied, that there
was a misunderstanding in all this: that he had spoken
only the truth, when he had described the imprisonment of my friend to me, and that, as he could not
make out what this meant, the only and best advice
he could give, as I had friends, was to find out from
them the name of a lady, who had been incarcerated at
Pierre-Encise within the time he had mentioned to
me.   She was undoubtedly the one about whom I was
in trouble, and I ought to be the more sure of it from
his not telling me things picked up from hearsay, but
from his own personal knowledge.

I deemed that he was not in the wrong: so, having
returned to the house of M. le Tellier, I told him confidentially how I knew that the lady, whose name was
on my memoranda, was at Pierre-Encise, so that he
might not take ill my returning to the charge after the
trouble he had already taken.   Nevertheless, I made
this avowal to him only with all the precautions
possible, so as not to harm the man from whom I
had obtained this information.   I told him that it was
not only a natural thing for unfortunate people to try
and assist one another, but further, that anyone in
trouble would deserve to be punished by God, were he
not to earnestly attempt such a thing.   The interests
of the King were not concerned in this kind of affair,
especially when undertaken by just and reasonable
means, such as making manifest the innocence of an
accused person.   M. le Tellier, with his usual high-
mindedness, replied that it was unnecessary for me
to take so much trouble to exculpate the man who
had given me this information.   My interest in the

matter was enough to cause him to do his duty, and I should have a reply to my request at once in the same way, and as quickly as I had had to my memoranda. This his colleagues would not refuse him, especially when they learned that he took just as much interest in the matter as if it concerned himself. I thanked him as I ought for such lofty sentiments, and having again been but twenty-four hours in giving me an answer, I finally learned that the lady I sought had been arrested under her family name, and not under that which her husband bore. This was a scheme of her son's, to further put me off the scent and stop me finding out her fate.

The first thing I did after this discovery, was to make myself acquainted with the cause of her detention. It was M. le Comte de Brienne, Secretary of State for Foreign Affairs, who had had her arrested, but this gentleman, who was touchy and eccentric enough, having chanced at that moment to have had a dispute with M. le Tellier about something to do with their office, in which both thought themselves interested, M. le Tellier begged me to find someone else than himself to do me the service of which I now stood in need. I found two or three people who thought themselves sufficiently friendly with him to be obliged not to refuse my request. They did indeed speak to the comte in great confidence, but as the clerk, who had received the five hundred pistoles to expedite the issue of the "lettre de cachet," no longer had M. le Tellier above him to oblige him to bend under his orders, he turned the mind of his master so successfully, that, after several delays which he caused, they told me that they could not be more discontented

with him than they were. After having promised
them everything, he now sought for means to excuse
himself. They would not try and imitate him in
playing with me any longer. I must betake myself
elsewhere, since they preferred at once to own their
small influence with him, to giving me grounds for
blaming their great credulity.

The matter being thus finished, as far as they were
concerned, I had recourse direct to the Cardinal. As
it was he who had first advised me to make love to
the lady, I had taken care to keep him posted as to
all the progress I had made with her. He also knew
of my grief on seeing my plan collapse through the
misfortune which she had met with. He had even
told me that I must be very unfortunate to again
experience this misfortune, since it was not the first
time he had perceived me on the eve of an advantageous
marriage, and witnessed the downfall of my hopes.
Nevertheless, all this had failed at the most unexpected
moment, so that, if there was any consolation for me,
it should be that it was in no way my own fault. Be
this as it may, this minister not being able to be
annoyed at my speaking to him of a person with whom
he had himself started me, I described to him where
she was, and the need I had of his help to extricate
her. His Eminence was so eager to render services to
everyone when it cost him nothing, that he received
my petition favourably. He bade me give him a
memorandum on the matter, and he would send it to
the Comte de Brienne. I completed one a quarter of
an hour later, and, having gone with it to him, instead
of taking it, he told me to go and present it myself to
that under-minister. I went, and, either because he

did not think that I came from such a good quarter, or
that he was in his disobliging mood, as happened to
him often enough, he made reply that his ears had
already been tired out with this business, but that it
seemed such a bad one, that he was surprised at
honourable people being willing to meddle further
with it.

He was speaking to me thus only with the voice
of his clerk, who deemed himself obliged to support
his handiwork, fearing lest it should be discovered
that it was but the five hundred pistoles he had received
which had made him commit the piece of rascality
he had. But, as I was ignorant of all this, fear
seized me at hearing him talk thus, so much so that,
had my own interests only been concerned, I do not
know that I should not have abandoned everything
on the spot rather than risk making a false step.
Knowing the comte to be proud and vindictive enough,
I told myself that it might be possible that the lady
had plotted against the minister. The reason I had
for suspecting her was that she had an uncle, whom
his Eminence still kept in exile, and whose misfortunes
I had sometimes heard her deplore.

She had great need at this moment of having made
me fall in love with her, so as to surmount this
obstacle; indeed, as there is nothing which love does
not conquer, my fears would soon have disappeared
before it. Meanwhile, either because I was more
interested than I thought, or because my compassion
for her plight produced the same effect as love might
have done, I did not fail to return two days later to
the house of the Comte de Brienne, to ascertain from
him if he had no more favourable reply to give me

than the one he had already made. He received me even worse than the first time. I complained of this to the Cardinal, and knowing I must inform him, unless I expected to lose my suit, I casually said, without feeling sure if I lied or not, that there was a clerk of this Secretary of State who opposed me with his master. I had been told that he had let himself be corrupted with money, and that, as the son of my prisoner had a good deal, he had every likelihood of perpetually retaining him in his interests by new presents. So, as there was nothing more capable of smothering innocence than such a course of action, I saw great risk of seeing myself "fleeced," unless his Eminence were to accord me formally his protection. I only asked for justice, and if the lady were guilty, as was maintained, far from desiring to justify her, I should be the first to demand her condemnation.

His Eminence listened to my reasons, and as I had seized the opportunity of speaking to him when leaving the gambling-room, where he had just won fifteen hundred pistoles, he chanced to be in such a good humour that he bade me follow him into his study. He sent for one of his secretaries, and immediately bade him write off a note to the Comte de Brienne to at once bring him the register of the prisoners who were at Pierre-Encise. The comte did not dare resist an order like this, and being obliged to obey, he brought this register, in which I saw that the lady had been arrested for the reasons I have just detailed. I was enchanted to perceive that matters were not as I had suspected; so, nothing now preventing me from entirely devoting myself to her

interests, I begged M. le Cardinal to have the letters
mentioned in it brought to him, so that he might see
if they were as incriminating as was reported. He
was good enough to accede to my entreaty. M. de
Brienne sent the clerk, who had brought the register
with him, to get the letters. He was not long in
returning, and, having spread them out on the table
of his Eminence, I had no sooner cast my eyes over
them than I understood their import. I at once told
the minister this, and that the calumny was such a
clumsy one, that no trouble had even been taken to
forge the lady's writing. The writing was totally
different from hers, and even so different that no
experts would be needed to prove it. If his Eminence
would be pleased to keep the letters, I would in a
moment bring him some which I had from the accused
woman's own hand. Charity and justice itself demanded
that she should suffer no more, since she was innocent.
She was shut up like a miscreant, which was a very
sad thing, and at the same time very hard for a person
of some birth and one who had never given occasion
for anything of the sort.

The Cardinal, who was kind when he liked (which
was never), chancing by good luck to be in a good
mood just then, told me to go and fetch my letters
immediately. The matter should at once be settled
on the desk, without there being need of delaying it to
another time. Never did order seem more pleasant to
me than this one. I set out that very minute without
having to be told twice, and, having brought him these
letters, he at once perceived the deceit just as I had
been able to do. The Comte de Brienne himself could
not deny it, thoroughly prepared as he was; so, as all

9—2

now merely depended upon whether sufficient trust would be placed in me to believe that the letters I had shown were the lady's and that the others were not, his Eminence, who wanted to oblige me cheaply, bade me sign my declaration and attest that it contained the truth. I did so without hesitation, and even made myself security, "body for body," for what I advanced in favour of the lady. M. le Cardinal hoped that matters were as I said: then, having ordered M. de Brienne to grant me an order to extricate her from prison, this comte tried to put me off to the next day, and, perhaps, even to four or five days ahead. Upon this I begged his Eminence to grant a complete pardon, since he had already so manifestly obliged me. I declared that the clerk who had brought these letters might write the order and the Comte de Brienne sign it, and that there would be only the King's seal to be affixed, and, as this was but the matter of a moment, I should be able to take post that very day to deliver the lady from captivity. Half a day's journey in such a situation was a great alleviation to an unfortunate person: how much more so a time of longer duration, as was the one I was asking for! M. le Cardinal thought I was right and, things being done as I wished, everything would have turned out in the best way in the world for me, had I been able to have the seal affixed a quarter of an hour later, as I thoroughly expected to have done. However, the clerks, who were accustomed to do everything for one another, not being behindhand on this occasion (the man whose duty this was being apparently eager to enrage me, because he knew it would please his colleague who had received the five hundred pistoles), kept me going for two days without consenting to satisfy me. I even think that he would have kept me going much longer, if it had not been that I returned to M. le Cardinal to let him know the annoyance inflicted upon me. Eventually, his Eminence having taken the trouble to send again and even to threaten that, if people were audacious enough to make me wait any longer, he would send at least a dozen clerks to prison, my order was delivered to me, but not without difficulty. As a last piece of trickery, the clerk wanted to insist on its being sent by the courier. Perceiving, however, that I was determined to return afresh to his Eminence, and make complaint of this, the fear of harm befalling him caused the man to at last desist from persecuting me.

I set out the same day, pleased beyond measure at the succour I was about to give this poor woman. I considered myself as the cause of her misfortunes, since, without her kindness to me, her son would never have dreamt of being so unjust to her. As I was young and vigorous, I went a long way in a short time; I reached Lion very early, and having gone to take up my abode at the house of the brother of the Maréchal de Villeroy, who was archbishop, I proceeded thence to where my business lay. I delivered my order to him who commanded in this castle (Pierre-Encise), and this officer, having seen its contents, told me that he was deeply sorry for the trouble I had taken. He was very much afraid I had come too late. The lady to whom I had brought liberty had not the appearance of enjoying it very long. She was at the last point of illness, and as her disease but arose from grief, all he could now hope was that the news which I was bringing might perhaps resuscitate her from death to life. She had already received all the sacraments, in short, one only awaited her death.

I leave to the imagination my grief at a speech like this. I begged this commandant to show me to her, and, having at once conducted me to her room, I found her in an even worse plight than he had described. She did not recognise me, but this not being the case with her companion, who had been imprisoned in the same room, the latter ran to her bed to announce my arrival. "Madame," cried she, "here is M. d'Artagnan come to deliver you from prison. Did I not assure you that he had not abandoned you as you thought, and that a little patience was necessary?" I perceived from these words, that the length of time the gentleman I have mentioned had taken to let me know her condition had thrown her into despair. It was but too true: she had imagined that I thought no more about her, and this, added to the shock she had already sustained from her misfortunes, had caused her to fall into a slow fever, which had eventually reduced her to the plight she was now in. She well understood what her companion was saying, and casting her eyes to the right and to the left, to see where I was (for her sight was so dim, that she could hardly see three paces in front of her), she eventually perceived me, because I had approached her bed. "You come too late," said she; "whose fault it is I am unaware: you much better than I can tell. It will cost me my life, and I well know I am about to lose it." I tried to cheer her, and as I had no reason to fear doing harm to the man who had let me know where she was, since I had told M. le Cardinal how I had got the information, and he had not been displeased, I did not think I should be acting unwisely by informing her that, if my succour had been so long in coming, she ought not to blame me. However, this was giving explanations to a person not in a state to understand them; she had not two hours to live, and, indeed, expired at the beginning of the night.

I need hardly say, it appears to me, that I was very much grieved. This is easily to be believed without my being obliged to swear to it: consequently, though I had promised the Archbishop of Lion to go to supper with him, I was so little in a condition to keep my word that I despatched a note begging him to excuse me. My valet, who was there, did not conceal from him what prevented me, and, as the prelate in question was a very gentlemanly man, he sent one of his suite to testify his sympathy with me in my affliction. Assuredly it was a great one. I had lost a fortune which was not to be recovered every day—a woman, who had an income of twenty thousand solid livres, and who, besides all this, had loved me so much as to have reproached me more on seeing me for my inconstancy than bewailed her own misfortunes. Had I been really guilty, as she had maintained, it would have been enough to have made me die of grief and confusion; but, having nothing to reproach myself with on that score, I had but to overcome my sorrow for the loss of my time and my hopes. I did not think it opportune to again take the post, which I should have done in another frame of mind. I should then have returned pretty quickly to overcome the opposition which had been raised against our banns, and which had been left in the same state since the lady's imprisonment. Not that her presence would have been

necessary, unless people should have made attempts to
worry us any more, which, nevertheless, I did not
believe, after the way I had regaled my chevalier,
since he would certainly have been afraid of a fresh
thrashing, had he continued to trouble us further.
Besides, as it would not have been seemly for me to
return with her, I should have had to have returned
alone, so as to avoid the slander which would not have
failed to have been let loose, had we been seen travelling
together before being married. However, her death
exempting me from both these things, in spite of
myself I returned by Roüanne, resolved to take the
river there. I considered that this was a place for me in
which to muse quite peacefully. I reckoned on going
thence on a journey to St. Dié, to see whether poor
Montigré's death had not emboldened Rosnai to return.
He might think, as indeed was true, that I no longer
had anyone there to let me know of his stay. I was
eager to surprise him, and though it was playing a
" devilish Italian " to cherish my resentment so long, I
had every desire to be one on this occasion, although
on all others I did not scruple to declare myself
opposed to that nation.

I took hired horses from Lion as far as Roüanne,
and proceeded quietly to the latter place, so as to
abandon myself on the way to everything which my
sad thoughts might suggest. I made a thousand reso-
lutions which I never kept. I promised myself never
to become attached to any woman, and, having
embarked still in the same frame of mind, so resolute
did I appear, that there was no one there who would
not have said that I was about to give up the fair sex
for all the rest of my life. Indeed, so strong was this

determination in me, that, had we yet been in the time
of those knight-errants who have provided material for
so many volumes, I should not have failed to sport
some "device" to show all the ladies that they had
nothing to hope for from me.   However, as we were a
long way from those days, I contented myself with
making this resolution secretly, determined to keep it
better than I had done in the past.   In this way I
embarked on the Loire, after having taken for myself
alone what is in that country called a "cabane." I went
down this river to Orléans, where, enquiring if Mr.
Rosnai was at his house, I learned that he had some
days since appeared there.   As I did not lack for
money, I bought a fine horse in that town and another
for my valet.   These horses were absolutely essential
to me for my plan, as, before my purchase, I was neither
in a condition to undertake anything nor yet to escape,
did occasion need.   Rosnai (I do not know how) was
warned that an individual had enquired about him at
Orléans.   Notwithstanding the years which had elapsed
since our quarrel, my image was so firmly impressed
upon his imagination, that, had he been a woman and
about to conceive, he would not have failed to produce
a child resembling me.   He at once mounted horse and
fled far away.   Thus I missed my chance, and being
besides enraged at the loss I had sustained, I resolved
to make my vengeance fall upon someone else.   I
perceived, in addition, that it would be useless to
think of catching him, since he had concealed his
route so cleverly, that no one could tell where he had
gone.   The Chevalier de la Carlière was the object
which I made take his place in my mind.   I even
wondered why I had not given him the preference,

since it was more natural for me to think of him than
the other man, after the loss I had just sustained.
Indeed, as, after his friend, he was the chief cause of
my misfortune, it was quite right for me to punish him.
Be this as it may, considering, after having missed
Rosnai, that there was nothing which could satisfy me
but putting some fresh affront upon the chevalier, I
left the place I was in with the fixed idea of not spar-
ing him. I even reached Paris without this keenness
having slackened.   Meanwhile, as I was a little way
the other side of the Pont-Neuf, I was obliged to stop.
I found a terrible obstruction of carriages and carts
by reason of an execution which was about to take
place at the Croix du Tiroir[1]. This block threw me
into such a rage with the Parisians, that I could not
prevent myself a thousand times inwardly calling them
by the name of "loafers," which is their usual nickname.
For truly they are accustomed to be such fools as to
occupy themselves with certain things, which other
people would blush with shame at.   Nevertheless, if
there is one thing they should be blamed for, it is more
for running to all the executions which take place in
this city, than for anything else they may do.   In spite
of no week passing by without an execution taking
place in Paris, there are people who regard themselves
as lost if they miss one of them.   They rush there as
to a wedding, and, to see their eagerness and anxiety,
one would call them the most barbarous people in the
world, since there is a kind of cruelty in seeing one's
fellow-creature suffer. I did what I could to pass,
before seeing those about to be executed. I was not like

1 The Croix du Tiroir or du Trahoir was at the corner of
the Rue de l'Arbre Sec and the Rue St. Honoré.

all those I saw around me : already I would have desired to be a thousand leagues away. Far from enjoying these kind of scenes, there was nothing I would not have done to avoid them. For this reason, after having tried to force my way through, and seeing I could not succeed because of the crowd, I attempted to retrace my steps. I was already well in the middle of the Rue de l'Arbre Sec and so far on in it, that I was not a long way from the gibbets which had been prepared for those wretched people. Meanwhile, as the crush was just as great in front as behind, as the unfortunates came that way, I was compelled to stand aside like other people, to allow the archers who were escorting them to pass. The leading ones were already in sight, and from all appearance the criminals were not far behind. These archers had just taken them from Fort l'Evêque, a prison where coiners are usually confined. The condemned men were accused of coining or rather of having clipped some pistoles, at least, so the murmurs I heard around me declared. I also heard say that there was a woman of their gang, who was very pretty, a thing which inspired me with the curiosity to turn my head in her direction, when the cart, in which she was, approached me, but whilst making endeavours to look at her, I descried my Chevalier de la Carlière, who was quite close to her. He was about to be despatched, together with another man just as well-built as himself. Never was man so astonished as I at this sight and quite dumfounded. I became a good deal more so a moment later. The tumbril having stopped right in front of me, no sooner did my chevalier recognise my face, than he called out, "Ah! M. d'Artagnan, this is a nice ending for a man

like myself, who has moved in fine society. True it
is that I have well deserved my fate. However, nothing pains me so much as that which I did by evil
advice. I caused letters to be written by the person
you see here at my side, in order to ruin Madame
. . . . . She is in prison at Pierre-Encise. Strive
to liberate her : it will not be difficult, since I have confessed everything before M. le Lieutenant Criminel.
I ask her pardon and yours too, for I know your
interest in her."

These words, addressed to me before a crowd by a
man who was about to be hung in a minute, pained me
nearly as much as if I had been as guilty as himself.
Meanwhile, as he again entreated me to consent to
forgive him, so that he might die like a good Christian,
I found myself forced to speak, in spite of the confusion
I was in. Our conversation was, nevertheless, not a
lengthy one, as may be imagined. I contented myself
with the answer that I freely forgave him, and, the
tumbril passing on at that moment, the chevalier went
to the doom he deserved. Immediately all those who
had heard him address me began not only to eye me, but
also to warn their neighbours that one of the malefactors
had recognised an accomplice. In consequence, I soon
had a number of observers, who expected every minute
that I should be arrested, so that, before at most twice
twenty-four hours were over, I might be made to suffer
the same ignominy which the chevalier had just under-
gone. Only the people near me could not believe what
the others so easily concluded. For, as they had heard
word for word what the criminal had said to me, they
were well aware that I was not guilty, unless they
wished to deceive themselves. I became more con-

fused than ever, when I saw so many people with their eyes fixed upon me. I strongly suspected what most of them thought, for, as one is always far more apt to believe evil than good, it was enough that the criminal should have said a word to me for it to be interpreted to my prejudice. This made me make a fresh attempt to extricate myself from the crowd I was in. The onlookers were quite scandalised, because they imagined that I only did this to escape. They accordingly set up a hue and cry after me, no more nor less than if I had been a mad dog.

As these criminals were much like bullies, and as the archers might well think that all this disturbance arose only because some people had appeared to rescue them, they began to turn their heads in my direction and place themselves on the defensive. This caused some diversion in my favour. Their horses, which were restless, having jostled the people who pressed most closely upon them, they in turn pressed back upon others, and these did the same thing to those behind them, so much so that never had been seen such disorder and confusion as then prevailed amidst all this noble assemblage. This stopped me more than ever from extricating myself, and as the archers continued to urge the condemned towards the gallows, they began to make the woman, who was to dance this gloomy measure, mount the scaffold. Upon this, each of the onlookers began to avert their eyes from me, to cast them upon this wretched creature. Accordingly, I no longer had any more cause to show confusion, and this woman having at last suffered the penalty her crime deserved, and likewise the two others after her, the execution was no sooner over than the whole crowd dispersed, some in one direction, some in another. In this way did I find myself delivered, not only from the predicament I had been in for the last hour, but also from the encounter which I had previously foreseen.

Meanwhile, the time arrived when I was to pay the penalty of the mistake, which I had made in losing the bill I had formerly drawn to Montigré.[1] It had fallen into the hands of goodness knows who, but, in short, as it must have been into those of some wretch who tried to make money out of everything, he made such search to discover who this Montigré might be, that he at last discovered. As he was dead, he could not approach him with a view to obtaining some present in return for giving it back to him, but, as things were thus, he went to find his lawyer, whom he asked for the name of his heirs. The lawyer replied that there were none. He had died insolvent, and owed one man alone more than ten thousand crowns for costs and for other things of that kind, in which he had been cast. The man enquired who this man might be, to learn apparently, if he would be likely to make some arrangement about his bill. As I was the debtor, he concluded that, if my enemy got it into his hands, he might exercise his rights against me. The lawyer told him Rosnai's name, and the name of his agent in Paris. The individual at once went to find this man of business, and, having enquired of him where he could get news of his master, and seeing him equivocate (for he did not know his object in coming to ask for it), he told him frankly the reason of his visit. Rosnai was at Paris, concealed in a vile hole. His pettifogger went

1 See Vol. I., p. 52.

to find him, and reported to him (as he knew that he was only hiding on my account) that he had found an affair to cause me some unpleasantness. Rosnai enquired of him what this was, and, having been told, replied that he must take good care that this was not some feint to catch him. I could not get hold of him, I was perhaps by these means trying to lure him into some snare. He was not so mad as to trust in this, but, if the man who had come to see the lawyer was trustworthy, it would soon appear by his not scrupling to give up the bill without his being himself obliged to appear. The pettifogger thought he was right, and, as he had told the man to return, and he would then give him his answer, he awaited him with confidence. The man did not fail to make his reappearance; he was too sharp-set to let such an opportunity slip. He got a few crowns for his bill, and, no sooner was it in Rosnai's hands, than, by the advice of his pettifogger or from his own idea (for he was malicious enough to want no teaching), he had me given a writ secretly, setting forth my sentence to pay him this sum instead of Montigré. This writ, which was preceded by an execution which he had carried out in my house, seemed drawn up in due form. He further did all the other mean tricks usual on such occasions, when people try to carry through anything illegal. He even got me condemned by default. I took care not to oppose it, because all his procedure was of the same nature as the beginning of it, that is to say, entirely unknown to me.

All these proceedings were taken against me, and this master-rogue, who knew how to plead a good deal better than how to fight, having afterwards let the matter slumber for some time, I of a sudden found myself the victim of an affront, which a cleverer man than myself could never have avoided. Rosnai had had me condemned to pay the sum of money, or go to prison by default; so, being one day at the Palais[1] with ladies who wanted to make some purchases there, I found myself seized, when I least suspected it, by a dozen archers, who threw me into the "conciergerie," before I had time to draw my sword to stop them doing such a thing. Had I been alone, I should a thousand times more easily have consoled myself than at its happening to me in such good company. At the moment, I found myself utterly crestfallen, especially when I perceived that I had been placed between two barriers, so that the turnkeys might observe whether I was looking well, for this is the procedure with regard to those who are put in prison. These kind of people must have time, and a place to make their observations, so as to know their game, otherwise it might escape every day, and this is a precaution which they consider too necessary to make any omissions in.

One of the ladies with whom I had been was the wife of a conseiller des requêtes at the Palais. She had presence of mind enough to tell her husband, who was one of my friends, the accident which had just happened. In spite of his being in his chambers, where a matter of importance was proceeding, it did not appear so pressing to him as to go and see how he could help me, and he set out that morning and came to the "conciergerie." It was no laughing matter for me.

---

1 Lace stuffs and perfumes were sold in the great gallery and Salle des Pas Perdus of the Palais de Justice. Shops existed there up to 1842.

I had been stuck on a seat like a monkey, without even being allowed to cover my face with my hands. No enquiries were made as to whether I had a head-ache, and, did I try to put up my hands, a man would at once come forward to say, "Lower your hand, this is no place for concealment." My conseiller might, perhaps, not have been able to stop laughing at seeing the figure I cut, had it not been that he was afraid of paining me the more, should he yield to his inclination. He therefore took a serious tone, though he was in no mood for it, and on his asking me what might be the cause of the affront put upon me, I innocently answered that I had no idea, as, indeed, was true. I must, said I, have been taken for someone else, as I had nothing against me, either criminal or civil. He retorted that I had no curiosity not to have found out on my arrival. I ought to have enquired of the gaoler, who would have given me a copy of the entry of my committal, had I asked for it. In reply I said that, to follow his advice, I should first have had to have known of it. I hardly knew even now, when he was speaking to me, what an entry of committal meant. I had never heard anything of all this, and, having left my home at an age when one knows nothing about a prison, I, who had always exclusively concerned myself with a career of arms, was now no wiser than then. The only prison I had any knowledge of was that of our soldiers; but, as he was better informed about these things, I would beg him to do everything necessary.

The conseiller, without answering, ordered the gaoler to tell him why I had been arrested. The man at once obeyed, and, no sooner did I learn that it was Rosnai who had played me this trick, than I very nearly fell to the ground. I told him that I had paid,[1] and that the merchant to whom I had confided my money would prove it at the right time and place. I also told how he had returned me my bill, and how I had lost it. The conseiller replied that this was so much the worse for me, and that I should have difficulty in getting out of this trouble without paying a second time. The procedure, in virtue of which I had been arrested, was quite legal, but, luckily for me, the fortunate thing was that I should not die of paying twice over. Though it was not pleasant to do so, he would, nevertheless, advise me to console myself. Fretting was of no use, and, as the thing was done, and neither I nor anyone else could help it, the shortest way was to deposit the sum I was asked for—I could afterwards defend myself as I might deem best—always supposing that I would not take his opinion, but, meanwhile, I must, at all events, obtain my liberation. If, added he, I had not the money upon me (as happened every day to the greatest people), he would send home for it. He even believed that I should not have to wait for its arrival to regain my liberty, because, when he should have given his word to the gaoler to himself pay out the sum, he was certain that he would make no difficulty about opening the prison gates for me.

There was no need for him to take this trouble. I had fifty louis d'or with me, which was much more than was wanted to get out of this business. But, as I thought it very hard to pay what I did not owe, I do not know if I could ever have reconciled myself to follow his advice, had he not declared that, as long as

1 Vol. I., p. 52.

I did not take it, I should never leave prison, and that, as this affair would take a long time to be argued before being cleared up, I should have full time to be thoroughly bored. He was not sure even that I ought not to rather consent to the yielding up of the coins which I had to deposit, than to oppose it. No doubts were in his mind as to my having paid the sum as I had described, but, as I had no receipt, and form and even law appeared to be against me, I must learn to kiss the rod and leave to God the avenging of the injustice put upon me. As he had once before said, by good luck it was not much which was demanded of me, and he would now repeat it, so that I might not persist in prosecuting a suit, which would give me more sorrow than satisfaction, even were I to chance to gain it.

I was, for my sins, a little obstinate, though I had always heard say, that it was best to prefer the opinion of one's friend to one's own. Indeed, without reflecting upon his advice (so excellent and so sensible!), I was so self-opinionated, that I would only believe a portion of what he told me. As a matter of fact, I made the deposit as he had advised, but having, in spite of him, tried to oppose the paying over of this money, I began to play a part in which there is never any honour or profit. I tried to prove how I had paid the money. This would not have been hard, had one witness only been necessary, or had Montigré been still alive. He would not have refused me his evidence, and this would have confirmed that which the man whom I had paid could not have helped giving, directly he should be cited to do so. However, as in these kind of affairs there are written laws, which the judges are obliged to follow, they might be well aware that justice was with me, yet that did not stop them from condemning me as the loser. Nevertheless, this was only after a number of lawsuits—as many on one side as the other. I fell, by bad luck, into the hands of a lawyer who knew more than others about pettifogging. Knowing nothing, I let him act, and, besides, every day he would promise to get me my costs paid. In this way he got I do not know how much money out of me. But what hurt me more than anything else, though this was already enough, as I had not money at will, was, that I myself was cast in damages to Rosnai to the extent of two thousand five hundred livres. As the King had not yet abolished personal imprisonment for debt, as he has since done, this made me tremble. I had even been thrown into gaol for a lesser sum, so had good reason to fear I should be made to return there, since this debt was much more important than the other. Besides, had the King already forbidden the arrest for debt of people, it would not have affected me, since he had excepted those whose costs exceeded two hundred livres. I did not possess the money either in cash or in stock, without selling my post: so, not knowing what to do to pay it, I thoroughly hated myself for not having believed my friend.

The sentence of four months was, meanwhile, announced to me, and these had hardly expired, when I received an unsigned note from an unknown hand. I found it at home on my return from the Comedy, to which I had gone. I was asked for a pleasant enough rendezvous, and was told that I should the next day, between two and three after dinner, find a hired carriage drawn up at three paces from below the Porte

St. Antoine. I was to get into it and would find a
woman, who was dying for love of me. As (so the
note ran) I came from a province, where riches did
not abound, she would bring me three hundred pistoles
as a proof of her goodwill. Nevertheless, she did not
want me to recognise her, which was the reason she
would see me only with a mask on her face. My want
of money would have even made me allow her to have
a sack over her head, had she wished it! I betook myself to the rendezvous an hour before the appointed
time, so afraid was I of missing it. The lady had not
yet arrived there, but only a short time elapsing before
I descried a carriage approaching, I thought it was
hers : anyone else would have thought the same in my
place, as it at once stopped at the very spot she had
sent me word of. Accordingly, not doubting in any
way that it was she whom I had come to meet, I myself let down the shutter of the carriage, for there were
not as yet any fitted with glass as there are to-day.
It was M. le Prince, who, on his return from being
with the enemy, introduced this fashion into France,
which was previously unknown there, and which has
crept in since. Be this as it may, having got into this
carriage, beneath the curtain which was drawn I
beheld one of the most beautiful women in France and
one unknown to me. This lady had no mask on her
face, so that, not knowing whether she who had
penned the missive had not announced she would
wear such a thing, the more agreeably to surprise me,
or whether I was mistaking one carriage for another,
" Madame," said I, without further introduction, " is it
I for whom you are waiting here, or am I playing an
indiscreet part by presenting myself before you with-

out being sent for? It is true I have a rendezvous,
but the lady, who ordered me to come and find her,
also informed me at the same time that she would wear
a mask on her face, so I know not how to interpret
what I see. I came here with the idea of doing her
good service without being acquainted with her, but
what would I not do if 'tis you—you who are one of the
most beautiful women in the world?" My compliments, which promised much, might perhaps have
made her pay some attention to my person, had not
another had possession of her heart, so, after having
blushed at my words and at seeing herself alone with
me, a man whom she did not know, she replied, that it
was not I she expected, and she would advise me
without formality to get out of the carriage, ·for fear
of missing my rendezvous. The coachman, who had
seen me lower the shutter, had at the same time got
off his box to close it upon me. He had then re-
mounted it, and awaited the order of one of us as to
where he was to go, before touching it again. Accordingly, wishing myself to lower the shutter, so as not
to disoblige the lady, just as if it had not been painful
to me to see such a dainty morsel fall into the hands of
another, I found myself faced by three or four men
who bade me not take so much trouble, since there was
no need for it.

These men all had the look of archers, and this they
indeed were: so, in spite of my knowing that the period
of four months had not yet expired, I feared that
Rosnai had once again played me one of his tricks,
and turned pale as death. The lady did the same no
less than myself: she was married, and being aware
that she had no easy-going husband, immediately

suspected that it was he who was having her
arrested. At the same time, four archers placed
themselves at both the shutters, two on one side, two
on the other, and thus conveyed us to the Grand
Châtelet. We were both separated, and the lieutenant criminel having been ordered to interrogate me
on behalf of the court, where the husband was held in
much esteem, I did not trifle with this magistrate. I
frankly declared to him that I did not know this lady,
and that, another fair one having given me a rendezvous
at the same place where I had found her, I had got
into her carriage; that she had at once told me to
leave it, because she was not the woman I took her for.
I had tried to do her bidding, but had been at once
arrested. For her part, the lady said just the same
thing. Nevertheless, on being asked what she had
come to do there, and being heckled about it, she had
presence of mind enough to say that she had come to
watch for her husband, who was perpetually flirting.
He was pretty well known for this, because indeed he
was always doing what he wanted to prevent others
from embarking upon; so, having given more colour of
truth to her defence than she could have hoped for,
her husband was advised to leave the whole matter
alone, since, whatever success he might have, it would
but recoil upon his own head. His friends even told
him that he ought to be well pleased that his wife had
cleared herself as she had done; that, as there was
neither profit nor honour in going deeper into the
affair, this was the best advice they could give him.
He would not believe them, knowing that there was a
certain courtier who pressed his wife hard, and so took
as much pains to have himself declared a cuckold as

anyone else would have done to have proved her chaste.

As it was not I upon whom his suspicion fell, he abandoned the proceedings he had taken against me, sooner than those he had begun against her. I let them dispute as long as they liked, and, having left prison without trying to sue him for expenses, damages and interest, in spite of my lawyer promising to obtain me a judgment for them, I felt not at all pleased with this adventure, which had made me miss my rendezvous. Above all, I regretted the three hundred pistoles, which were to have been brought me, and of which I stood in such great need. For now the appointed four months were about to expire, and I do not think there were eight days left. Nevertheless, the lady who had written to me had been at the rendezvous, and had even arrived there a minute after I had been arrested. She had, in consequence, found a whole crowd of people, as occurs on these sort of occasions. She had been curious to know what this meant, and had made her coachman find out the reason. As there is always to be found someone who is better informed than other people, she had been given a fair account of its cause. Apparently, some archer had not been able to hold his tongue, and the news had spread in the neighbourhood. Such an accident should have made this woman chaste at the expense of the other lady. Like her, she had a husband, but either because he was less jealous than the other man, or that the lady's example did not affect her, she waited for me for two good hours without moving from where she was. All the same, this did not fail to weary her; she was far from thinking that I it was who had been captured with the lady, so she still continued to think that I should arrive from one moment to the other. Nevertheless, this was very useless, since for some time already I had been imprisoned. At last, having passed there the time I have mentioned, and not wanting to waste any more, she went away very puzzled as to what she ought to think of me. Indeed, if, on the one hand, she could imagine that I had missed the rendezvous from lack of esteem for herself, or perhaps, even because I had felt disgusted at the idea of the mask which she had told me she would wear, on the other, she felt sure that the three hundred pistoles she had spoken of would be a sufficiently attractive feature to make me overlook everything else.

Accordingly, whilst she did not know what to think of my behaviour, she learned from current talk that I had been arrested with the lady. This at first inspired her with an inexpressible jealousy. She at once concluded that she need search for no other reason for my missing her rendezvous, but, the matter having been cleared up by my examination and that of her supposed rival, she calmed the uneasiness of her mind. She was of opinion that she had been wrong to accuse me, and that she was the more obliged to wish me well, since this catastrophe had happened through love of herself; so, no sooner had she left the Palais, than she wrote me a second note. It was just in the same style as the first, except that, instead of the Porte St. Antoine, she chose the Porte St. Honoré for her rendezvous. There was also this difference, that, instead of the three hundred pistoles she had the first time told me of, she now promised me four hundred as a recompense, as she said, for my having been imprisoned on her account. I thought this note written in the finest manner in the world, though anyone else, who was not to get so much good out of it, might, perhaps, have deemed it more shameless than well written. I did not fail to appear at the spot she appointed at the right hour, and no jealous person was there to raise any obstacle at this rendezvous as on the other occasion.

We did not enter any house during the whole of the time we passed together after dinner. We only took a turn in the Bois de Boulogne, and, as I was eager to see her face uncovered, I besought her so persistently, that I did not believe she could refuse me this. She had, however, such control over her mind that whatever entreaty I might make proved useless. Her reply was, that she did not wish to forfeit my esteem, a thing which must infallibly happen, were she foolish enough to grant what I asked. As long as I did not see her face, she was sure of my not quitting her for anyone else, or, at least, did I do so, I should, perhaps, gain nothing by changing. Indeed, she was aware that if nature had illtreated her in one way, it had recompensed her in another. She must stop there, and not lose by her own fault in one minute what might with a little discretion be preserved as long as our intimacy lasted. By this she wanted me to understand that she was ill-favoured, and would lose by showing herself. Nevertheless, I would not believe a word of it, and was none too wrong. We returned in this way to Paris, and, having asked me for another rendezvous, I told her she might choose it wherever she liked, for she would always find me ready to be at her service. This next time we went towards Vincennes, and,

observing that I entreated her to enter some house
without always remaining in the carriage, as we had
done on the other occasion, she asked me if I knew of
any from personal knowledge, and I made reply, that
I knew of none: dissipation was not my way, but
I thought that, everywhere we might go, we should be
as well received as if we were skilled in such matters.
In the outskirts of Paris everyone made a trade and
profession of pleasing his neighbour, so we had only
to stop at the first door to get it opened on both sides.
She burst out laughing at my answer and, telling me to
take her where I liked, for she abandoned herself to my
guidance, we betook ourselves to Montreuil to a house
where there was a very fine garden. I asked her the
same favour as I had done on our first interview—that
is to say, to complete my happiness by showing herself
to me. She replied that I would then always be
incorrigible. She had already warned me that, had
I the slightest esteem for her, such a thing would
make me instantly lose it. Her answer did not satisfy
me, so much so that I pressed her more than ever.
Upon this she said that, as I was so obstinate in my
idea that there were no means of dissuading me, she
was ready to meet my wishes at the risk of everything
which might happen. At the same time, she took off
her mask and, indeed, did make me colder than marble.
Nevertheless, it was not on account of what she had
seemed to threaten me with—far from that, she was as
beautiful as a fine day—but because I at once recognised her as the wife of one of my best friends.
Indeed, this is why I had sometimes already told
myself, while observing her, that she had much of her
appearance. Nevertheless, what had banished the

thought of its being the same lady was, that I did not in any way consider her in a condition to make me the present she had done. Her husband was not rich, and she must have won this money at some game I did not know of, to find herself in a state to bestow such generous gifts.

She at once thoroughly understood that my position as an intimate friend caused me a tremendous struggle. "So," she said, continuing, "I was right in telling you that, no sooner should you see me, than you would at once cease to love me. I am, nevertheless, no less lovable, and I ought to appear to you much more so than any other woman, if you will thoroughly reflect on everything. Think what I am doing here for your sake, and, since my love for you is the sole cause, be convinced that you can never be grateful enough. Be sure, I repeat, that you can never pass in the mind of honourable people except as an ungrateful man, if you ever forget that the power of my love has made me not only override the honour I owed my husband, but also everything which I owe to myself. It also seems to me," she went on, "that, without in any way reproaching you, you should take into account the present I have made you. You are aware that we do not "shovel up money," if I may use the phrase, to show you that my husband and myself are not well off, but I learned in short, that you needed this help, and, although it costs me nothing, as I won it at basset, this does not disprove the fact that any other woman who had less consideration for you would have been eager to keep it."

I know not if it was these words which of a sudden changed my mind, or if her beauty alone produced that effect, but at last, forcing myself to quite forget her husband and giving myself entirely to her, I did what I could to demonstrate that she would never have reason to complain of me. Nevertheless, I felt scruples at having taken her money, and wanting to return her what still was left me of it (for I had already spent a good part to extricate myself from the affair with Rosnai), she would never consent to receive it back. She told me that, when a woman went so far as to give her heart, everything else should cost her nothing. This was the only reason she would give me and, as all her ways were just as fascinating as her appearance, I began to love her so madly that I would not live a moment without her. We had, however, in spite of our mutual affection (for she loved me no less than I loved her) to soon separate. The war at Bordeaux still continued, and, as it was a rising which might produce civil war all over again in the heart of the State, M. le Cardinal thought it best to send me to that province. For this reason, I was not pleased when his Eminence told me to grease my boots to set out for Bordeaux; but, as at Court one must not say all one thinks, and also still less show that one gauges a Minister's thoughts, I looked just as delighted as if I had been satisfied. He fixed my departure for the 15th of February, and made me come into his closet the evening before; he told me to set out for Poitou, and I should find orders there as to what I was to do. He had previously sent there the Abbé de Beaumont, Bishop of Rhodes, though he was the King's tutor, and this post does not allow the holder to leave the Court. He was an old courtier who had served his apprenticeship in a good school. He had been one of Cardinal Richelieu's men, and it is he whom we have since seen

Archbishop of Paris under the name of Péréfixe.[1] This abbé had taken as pretext for the voyage his wanting his native air to recover from a languishing sickness. Nevertheless, he was about as ill as I was, but a certain quack then at Court had given him some drug, which made the complexion yellow at will, and he had made use of it to cause people to believe that he was really unwell. The Abbé de Beaumont was not one of the greatest geniuses in the world; his good luck and his friends had conducted him more than personal worth to the position he occupied. Besides, the Cardinal who, very far from wanting to have the King brought up as befitted a great prince, would have been delighted to have made a sham king of him, so as to always keep the power in his own hands, had taken more care to choose a tutor devoted to his own interests than a clever man. Nevertheless, as it is the smallest minds which make the most fuss, so that one may think them everything they are not—no sooner had I gone to see the Abbé de Beaumont, than he took it into his head to look at me, just as he might have done at one of his schoolboys. He adopted the tone of a schoolmaster towards me, and told me that, M. le Cardinal honouring me as he was doing by his friendship, I ought not only to be very grateful, but further try to render myself worthy of his esteem. The very best thing I could do to succeed in this was, not only to be very discreet, but also not to exceed by a syllable the orders given me by him or by those he relied on. Having thus read me this lesson in a few words, he added, to show me, I think, that he had not wasted his time

1 Hardouin de Beaumont de Péréfixe, 1605-1671, author of the life of Henri IV.

under his former master, that not only must I proceed
to Bordeaux incognito, but also disguised as a hermit;
for this reason, I had done well to let my beard grow,
since it was necessary that my whole get-up should
correspond with my dress.

I had indeed allowed it to grow by order of his
Eminence. It may be that the abbé and himself had
simultaneously resolved on my wearing the dress in
question, or that the minister had decided upon this
merely by advice of the former. It had often made
my mistress, who did not like a long beard, grumble.
I had not known what excuse to make to her, so much
so, that we had very nearly quarrelled about it. She
had accused me of being very ill-natured in such an
earnest manner, that I had often had it on the tip of
my tongue to tell her that, if I disobeyed her, it was
only in spite of myself; that I had had superior orders
to do what I had done, and that she had only the
minister to blame if I did not obey her. Meanwhile,
as I already knew that secrecy must be maintained,
though the abbé had not as yet given me my lesson,
I contented myself with telling her to reconcile my
love and my duty, that there was a mystery in all this,
and that I would some day tell her the reason. This
woman, who resembled most of her sex, that is to say,
was extremely curious, would not grant me the time I
asked. She worried me to tell her my secret at once,
and, taking care not to do so, I was obliged to look out
for what is known as a " bouncing lie," to put her off
the scent. Accordingly, instead of telling her the real
reason for my letting my beard grow, I made her
believe that M. le Cardinal had bet me a company in
the Guards that I could never remain a year without

having it shaved off, that I had not wanted to tell her before, for, as this wager had been made only between us two, he might perhaps not be pleased, were he to discover that I had spoken to anyone about it. For this reason, I would beg her not to speak to no matter who on the subject, since she would most likely be sorry that I should lose such a chance through a slip of the tongue. She sincerely promised to say nothing, but, being a woman, and as, the more they are entreated to do anything, the less they do it, I had no sooner gone away than, the secret lying heavy on her soul, she tried to disembarrass herself of it. One of her friends having, whilst chatting, told her that I must have become hypochondriacal, by reason of my trying to distinguish myself from other people by a great beard as I was doing, she made reply that, were all mad people like me, lunatic asylums would no longer have any use. A company in the Guards was well worth the trouble of wearing a beard, and there was no one in France who would not be well pleased, just as I was, to obtain such a good post so cheaply. The person whom she told would have understood nothing of all this, had she not explained this mystery, but eventually, as, after saying so much, all the rest cost her nothing, she soon informed him of everything I had let her know.

The man to whom she told this news chanced to be just as credulous as she had been: so, the rumour going from him to someone else, and from the latter to a number of people, it eventually got round all the Court, that the beard I had set out with was a certain token of my advancement. This was the more easily believed, as his Eminence would often make wagers, which gave much more reason for talk than this one. True is it that this was when he knew what he was about and was sure to be the winner. For instance, whenever there was anyone competing for some benefice, and he had money to pay for it, he would ask him if he would wager that he would not soon obtain a bishopric or an abbey. The wager was proportionate to what it might be worth, for, at the same time, he would stipulate that it should be a bishopric or an abbey of such an income, and, as the Cardinal could bestow them as he chose, it always turned out that he was a certain winner.

As it was for me to obey all orders given on behalf of his Eminence, the Abbé de Beaumont had no sooner told me that I must become a hermit, than I had the dress of one made. He himself took care to furnish me with the stuff, which his brother had made up in his house, as if he was afraid that, did I procure it elsewhere, it would cause our secret to be discovered. I had the dress put in a bag, and having taken post to the army of the Duc de Candale[1] which was around Bordeaux, he sent it for me into the town, where it arrived before myself. I entered it in another get-up, just as if I had been a plain soldier, who was retiring to his province. The town was divided into several factions, one of the principal of which was the one called the "Ormistes." This was a mass of every kind of riff-raff such as had formerly risen against the King of Spain in the Kingdom of Naples,[2] which

1 Louis Charles Gaston de Nogaret de Foix, Duc de Candale, son of the Duc d'Épernon, 1627-1658.
2 The Neapolitan revolt against the Duc d'Arcos, the Spanish Viceroy, headed by Masaniello, which broke out on July 7th, 1647.

nevertheless had come near losing him this fine state.
This name arose from the insurgents having held their
first meetings beneath an elm.   Their number had at
first been very limited, as usually is the case at the
commencement of a revolt.   But it had so much
increased since, that it was now fully forty thousand
men.   They had from the first been obnoxious to
everyone alike, for they breathed but cruelty and
pillage.   They maintained themselves by their numbers
and the cleverness of their leaders, who made the people believe that they would never lower their arms, till
all taxes should be abolished.   From what they said,
they even aspired to change the form of government,
and establish a republic in the province after the
example of what had been done in England, and with
this idea they had sent to Cromwell to crave his protection in such a great undertaking; either because
they really did contemplate such a thing, or were
merely anxious to have it believed, because of their
interests being concerned.   However, this man, who
was a clever politician, had not wanted to embroil
himself in their business, nor in that of M. le Prince.
In spite of this, it was not on account of his not
having sent to entreat him just as they had done, but
Cromwell was of opinion that, whatever fine proposal
might be made him by either side, there was too much
danger attached for him to trust in it.   He knew that
he already had too many enemies in England, without
his drawing yet fresh ones upon himself in France,
where the populace would soon return to its duty.
He knew its affection for his Majesty, and that our
nation was in no way like his own, which thinks no
more of kings than of the humblest private individuals.

V

I LEFT the camp of M. de Candale disguised as I have just said. At a hundred paces from the town, I found a body of these "Ormistes," who were, at least, four or five thousand men in number. The Duc de Candale had got me a passport from one named Orteste, their general, as well as from the generals of the other factions; so, having nothing to fear from their brutality, I gave them an account of whence I came and where I was going, as they wanted it from my own lips, though they had already read it in my passport. One of their captains, Las Florides by name, before whom I had been conducted, then began to call me his comrade, and to declare that I must join with him. I appeared to be a good fellow, and he would make me benefit more by bearing arms in his company than I had ever done in the King's troops. Meanwhile, he wanted me to do away with my beard, because it did not at all befit a soldier. I replied that, as long as I had been a soldier, I had been turned out like one, but now that I thought of taking up another profession, I equipped myself according to the state of life I contemplated. He at once asked me if I wanted to be a capuchin, because only the capuchins wore long beards. I rejoined that I was eager to be one, since there was nothing better than to dedicate oneself to God, but, as it was necessary to have studied to be admitted amongst them, and I, so to speak, did not know A from B, I should content myself with being a hermit. I was anxious to tell him this, so that, if by chance he were to see me in the dress I had bought, I should not be an object of suspicion to him.

Hearing me speak thus, some Ormistes took to jeering at me. As they were heedless of their salvation by bearing arms, as they were doing, against their King, they did not understand that a man could thus dream of changing his life. Las Florides, who no more than they dreamt of doing the duty of a Christian (which consists just as much in rendering one's prince what is due as in rendering it to God), and who was a scoffer, told them they were wrong to be astonished at such a trifling thing. Did they not know very well that the Devil had become a hermit when he had grown old, and that everyone was eager to copy him? By this, he wanted to tell them that, when a man was laden with crimes, God sometimes was merciful enough to let him reform himself. However, either because they would not enter into the joke, or because they were inclined to make him chatter, they declared that, if the Devil had only become a hermit when he was old, I ought not to be allowed to do the same thing, as I did not as yet appear to be thirty years of age. This was giving up the world too soon, and, if he would take their advice, he would oblige me to make war in company with himself. Las Florides then told me that I must clearly perceive that everyone opposed my

idea, and that he would not let me go. I laughingly
retorted, as he was speaking in the same joking way,
that I would appeal to their general Orteste. My
passport was signed by him, and he would never permit
its provisions to be broken; in any case, were he to
oppose me as those about me now were doing, I would
at least ask him to make me the hermit of their troops,
so as in some way to carry out my oath. I had sworn
to be one, and mayhap he would not let me be a
perjurer. There were almoners in regiments, and
hermit or almoner was nearly the same thing. Las
Florides declared that I had no need to rely upon this
favour, for he would grant it me just as well as the
general, and I had but to speak. His real reason for
wanting me was, because he had observed in my
passport that I had served twelve entire years in the
Guards. It must be known that he had of a sudden
been made one of the chiefs of these rebels, without
having any other qualification than having killed a
number of oxen and sheep. He had been a butcher
all his life, but, because he had been used to shedding
the blood of these animals, his comrades had thought
that he would just as easily shed that of men. Nevertheless, whenever he had any order to give, he found
himself as much embarrassed as he had been the first
time he had to help others to kill an ox. For this
reason, he was eager for me to remain with him to tell
him what to do when there was need. He much preferred my telling him to one of his own people, because
he looked upon me as much less important than those
who had raised him to his present position.

His wishes and mine were pretty much the same.
His idea was to keep me by him, and mine to stay, so

as to find out anything which went on amongst the rebels. Accordingly, not standing out for the conditions I had proposed to him, I found myself unexpectedly in a position to render his Majesty great services. The rebels, though they knew nothing of warfare, did not fail to make themselves feared, and knew very well how to serve their own interests. They stopped all the vessels which went up and down the Garonne, and this brought them in great sums. Las Florides became my friend, because I would sometimes warn him against certain foolish things, into which he was about to plunge, and which would have made him a laughing-stock. Nevertheless, I did this only when the King's interests were not concerned. I also gave two or three pieces of information to M. de Candale, which were of great use to that general, and by which he did not fail to profit. The first of these was, that I indicated to him the spies of Las Florides in his camp, not that he should have them arrested, but to catch their sender in a snare. I had already adopted my hermit s dress, and was known by no other name amongst the rebels than as the hermit of "those of good resolve." Meanwhile, false information had been conveyed to Las Florides by his spies, whom the Duc de Candale had, owing to my information, deceived, and, trusting entirely in the reports made him, he took twelve hundred Ormistes to make an attack with. Las Florides took me with him without, nevertheless, letting me know any of his plans. Both of us, however, set out in a very happy frame of mind, he by reason of his great hopes, and I on account of mine. I was mounted as a regular St. George, Las Florides having lent me a Spanish horse, which was well worth a hundred good pistoles. I had my robe tucked up to my belt, and, as my eyes sparkled with joy to see him on the point of being defeated, my appearance pleased him so much, that he owned to me that, even had I not told him of my having been a soldier, he would have clearly perceived it.

In this way we discussed one thing and another, without my trying to ask him where he was going. I should even have been very sorry if he had volunteered the information. I wished him to go so far ahead that there could be no turning back, and so my advice to him must come so late that it would be useless.

When we reached the spot where the spies had informed Las Florides that he would be easily able to overcome a small body of the King's troops, he found eight hundred men instead of the two hundred he had expected. The first disagreeable thing which happened and made him suspect the truth of the reports furnished him, was the report of a piece of ordnance. To speak the truth, it was not a loud report, being but a four-pounder, but, small as it was, it did not fail to frighten Las Florides a good deal. It was a little field-piece, which the people of the duc had brought with them, to announce to the larger body of troops that they must be on their guard and they would soon see the enemy retreat.

Directly Las Florides heard the report he changed colour, and, observing that terror had already overcome him to such a degree that he no longer knew what he was doing, I asked him if the people of Bordeaux had not some garrison near the spot. He answered no, and, asking me in turn what all this meant, I replied, not wishing to flatter him, that it meant nothing else except that he was betrayed. I tried much more to further increase his fears than to allay them, and so, having hardly the strength left to answer me, I noticed that he was hesitating, and even stammering, as if he was already at the point of death.

In this way we proceeded in some sort of order to the entrance of the defile, which I knew very well was guarded. No sooner did Las Florides descry the enemy than he cried out to me that all was lost. I asked him if he would not try to assault it, but he took care not to answer, having already fled, and I soon lost sight of him. His men were in despair at seeing themselves thus abandoned. I now began to play the swaggerer, and told them they must rush to the assault, since there was no other way of saving ourselves. Some of them believed me and got themselves killed like madmen. Others laid down their arms, whilst others (but a very small number) were lucky enough to escape. Meanwhile, as there were some amongst these runaways who had thrown down their arms to be able to escape quicker and more safely, I picked up a musket, with which I fired a shot into my cloak which I had put against a tree at thirty paces distance. There were three balls in the musket, which each made a hole, and having next thrown it over my shoulders, I went back to the city quite proud of the reputation I should gain amongst the rebels for having run such a great risk, without meeting with any other accident than having my cloak shot through. Not a soul had seen what I had done; I had taken good care of that—and, as I was sure that no one would ever believe that these holes were my handiwork, I conceived that this would be useful to me to still further gain the confidence of the insurgents, and that not one of them would fail to take me for a desperate man.

Las Florides reached Bordeaux before me, having luckily for himself found a way guarded by no one. He was very much ashamed of his mishap, especially after having got out of the crowd, as he had done, without having dared to fire a shot. He was delighted that I had escaped as well as himself, perhaps as much from love of his horse, which he had thought lost, as from love of myself. He was one of the first to perceive the shots in my cloak. I had taken care to put them in a prominent place, and had been careful not to make them in the back part. I wanted to acquire the reputation of having shown a bold front to the foe, so as to further sustain the high estimation which I expected Las Florides would hold me in. Indeed, he did not fail to tell everyone, and Orteste amongst others, that I was a first-class man both for giving advice and carrying it out. That I had predicted everything which had happened, and that, had he been willing to believe me, he would not have made such a forward fight as he had done. Having thus the approbation of my general, I took care not to raise suspicions in anyone. Everybody wanted to see my cloak, so as to marvel at my adventure. It made the round of the city for four or five days, and there was no respectable house which did not desire to see it.

The Abbé Sarrasin,[1] secretary to the Prince de Conti, to whom the Abbé de Beamont had recommended me

1 Jean François Sarrasin, 1603-1654, a writer whose works are now completely forgotten.

to enter upon my negotiations, did not know how to reconcile everything reported of me with the part I had come to play on behalf of the Court. To negotiate on its behalf and fight against it, were two things which appeared to him incompatible. He spoke to me about it, begging me to explain matters. I did not think fit to do so, for I knew that there were things, the knowledge of which it was good to reserve for oneself alone. I merely told him that there were certain times, in which chance occasionally interfered, such, for instance, as my to-day finding myself amongst the Ormistes, which I had in no way anticipated when coming to Bordeaux, but, as I was now pledged to them, I must of necessity play my part to the end. It was for him to end all this when he liked, and the sooner the better.

This abbé was exactly the same man from whose pen we to-day have some works, which are valuable enough, and which he issued under his own name. M. le Cardinal had promised him money and a benefice, if he could detach his master, the Prince de Conti, from the side of the Prince de Condé. Sarrasin at once told me that this would be very difficult, because he drew a great pension from the Spaniards, and was, besides, fond of being in command, a thing he would lose once he returned to his duty ; in addition, he had a mistress in the town, who would oppose such an arrangement. She was clever enough to clearly perceive that he would proceed to the Court directly he had made his peace with it. He was fond of the ladies, and it was very much to be feared that at certain moments he might confide to her what was going on.

All this was literally true ; so, having informed the

Abbé de Beaumont of it, so that he might let the
Cardinal know, I warned him at the same time that, if
he wanted to overcome this obstacle, I thought it best
for his Eminence to send me some fripperies from Paris
to give to the lady. By these means, I should get
into her good graces, and then one might utilise her
to finish the work Sarrasin had begun. That meanwhile, so that the prince might be favourably influenced,
I thought a wife should be proposed to him. M. le
Cardinal had still sufficient nieces to marry off, not to
be embarrassed to find one for him. His ecclesiastical
state was not, I added, to his liking, though the cassock
served well enough to conceal the defects[1] of his figure.
Thus, this might perhaps be arranged as well as everything else, since he was of a disposition not to fall less
in love with the niece of his Eminence, than he had
done a year or two back with Mademoiselle de
Chevreuse.

The Abbé de Beaumont had returned to Court without my knowing anything about it. His Eminence
had seen fit to make him come back from Poitou from
fear of a more prolonged absence arousing some
suspicion. I was consequently much longer than I
thought in receiving an answer and at once concluded
that it was but because I had asked for some present.
I knew the Cardinal well enough to be aware that his
practice was to only give as little as possible. Nevertheless, no one could have been more mistaken. My
proposition of a marriage of his niece with the Prince
de Conti had so altered his ideas, that he had no
sooner scanned my letter, than he resolved to believe
me in everything. He had, therefore, at once given

1 The Prince de Conti was hunch-backed.

orders for the presents I asked for to be purchased.
He had them conveyed to me by means of the Duc de
Candale, and I received them from the hands of his
secretary, whom he had sent into the town to negotiate
about the ransom of some prisoners taken on both
sides.   It did not appear novel or extraordinary that
this duc should send some frippery into it.   He had
stayed there quite long enough, while his father was
its governor, to have some mistresses in the place.   It
accorded well with his age and inclinations, for he was
extremely liberal and was only twenty-four years old.
People even thought they knew for whom these
presents were meant, always supposing that it had
been the duc who sent them.   For there were others
who suspected it to be his father, because, whatever
age he might be, he was no more nor less given to
gallantry or love than his son.

Nevertheless, the arrival of presents in the parcel
coming to this secretary might perhaps not have been
discovered, had not the Ormistes, partly by force and
partly on account of the jealousy which prevailed
between the Prince de Conti and the Comte de
Marcin, got the gates of the city into their charge.

These Ormistes, having thus control of the gates,
would not let the parcel enter without inspecting it.
They had been afraid lest the Duc de Candale should
have put something prejudicial to themselves in it,
knowing him to be devoted, not only to the interests
of his Majesty, but also to those of the Cardinal.
They had, therefore, looked thoroughly into it to the
very least things, and especially into the presents sent
me.   For, as they were extremely avaricious of other
peoples' goods, everything precious or rare tempted

them in a way they could not resist. Accordingly,
an hour after the parcel had arrived, its contents were
known. This disconcerted me; I wanted to make my
gifts secretly, and I perceived my hopes shattered.
My grief, however, was not to be compared to that of
the wives of two conseillers of the Parlement of
Bordeaux, who expected that these presents were for
them. The duc had flirted with both of them, so
much so that, each thinking that her rival had received
them to her loss, they very nearly disfigured one
another at the house of one of their mutual friends
where they by chance met. At first they began to
mutually bicker over nothing; then, insensibly passing
to bad language, both were so indiscreet as to reproach
each other for having accepted these presents without
observing that the people present must infallibly take it
as a proof of their lack of virtue. I learned of this
dispute and was delighted at it, reflecting that I should
do no harm by fomenting the false reports, since
nothing could occasion a more favourable diversion
for myself. There were also some tiffs between the
mistresses of the Duc d'Épernon. They were under
the impression that these presents came from him and
that they had been distributed by the secretary to the
favourite, without their having obtained the smallest
share.

Whilst all this was going on, and everybody was
delighting, like myself, in setting these women one
against the other, I very softly insinuated myself with
the lady with whom I had to do. My cloak adventure
had procured me my first interview. She, like other
people, had been curious to see it; and either because
I flattered myself, or because I had some reason for

doing so, I imagined that I perceived in her eyes
something so favourable towards me, that I took it
into my head that, had I been able to appear before
her in a different dress from the one I was now in, I
might perhaps have made some impression upon her
heart. It was on the occasion of my first conversation
with her that I thought I perceived such goodwill
towards me. I built up on all this a plan, which
should have frightened me, considering my great beard,
but which I did not cease to try and carry out. I
resolved to play the lover. Nevertheless, I did not
want to do so openly. I deemed that a little mystery
would become me better, especially as I had to do
with a woman who must feel proud of seeing herself
loved by a prince of the blood. I had adopted the
expedient, the better to play the part I was taking, of
entering every house to ask for alms, not that I had
need of doing so, for, thanks be to God, I did not lack
for money. I had two hundred pistoles in a purse,
and, in addition, I had as much as I liked to eat at
the house of Las Florides. For this reason, he was
unwilling that I should thus go and beg, telling me
every day that it was neither seemly nor honourable
for a man who wanted for nothing. He even declared
that doing what I did was robbing the poor of bread.
My excuse was, that I was thus carrying out my calling.
I replied that mendicity should be the appanage of a
hermit, and pulled him up short with such a good
excuse, so, seeing that all his remonstrances were of no
avail, he let me do as I liked. Indeed, besides thinking
that this was the essence of my new vocation, I always
learned something new in the houses which I entered.
I tried to profit by this, and not always unsuccessfully.

I went very often to the lady's house, and even at hours when everybody was not allowed to go. I would even occasionally, from fear of meeting someone, catch her at the moment of rising. I wanted to take my time to advance my interests with her, or, to be more accurate, to advance those of the Cardinal. Be this as it may, taking care to call often, she began to delight in touching my heart. She suspected that it was already slightly affected, since I visited her so frequently. Accordingly, deeming it either a thing to be proud of or a real achievement, to be able to say that she had captivated a poor hermit, she made use of all the charms she possessed, and of all she could borrow, to place me amongst the number of her admirers.

I soon perceived her intention. It was not hard to divine, even had it been only from the flattering things she would say to me. Ten times a day she would talk of my courage, and, when I played the hypocrite to make her speak the more, she would declare that it was useless for me to pretend so much modesty, since my cloak showed well enough what I was! Eventually, I let her say what she liked, thinking that I should gain more by agreeing with all she said than by contradicting her as I had at first done. I was, indeed, eager to make her ponder over my vocation, almost giving her to understand that I was not what I appeared to be. With this end in view, I replied one day when she was again speaking to me in this strain, that she would cease to wonder, did she know all I knew. She was unable to make out what I meant by this, and, as to drop a word with two meanings is enough to strangely excite a woman's curiosity, this lady, who was even more inquisitive than others, would not let me alone till I had explained this riddle. To excite her the more, I said that I had let this slip by chance, and that she must pay no attention to it. I succeeded none too badly in my plan; indeed, far from taking this literally, she showed herself so assiduous in trying to get my secret out of me, that I was at last obliged to bid her take patience at least till the morrow. She had great trouble in consenting, but eventually, seeing that the space of time was not a long one, she made me promise to return the next day at the same time. I came even earlier than she had bidden me, so much so that, having found her in bed, she at once told me that I was a man of my word and that there was pleasure in having to do with me. I rejoined that my hope was always to be able to retain this good opinion in her thoughts, but that I was much afraid of losing it, once I should have satisfied her curiosity. For this reason I had not the strength to tell her anything, so that, if she wanted to know my secret, she must herself take the trouble to read it from a paper on which I had written it and which I was quite ready to give her, the moment she should command me to do so.

The lady was more inquisitive than discreet, so, though she much suspected that this could only be a declaration of love that I wanted to give her, she told me without ceremony that she would take everything I might present to her. I was holding a packet, quite ready to give it her or replace it in my pocket according to the answer she might give, but seeing her already stretching out a hand to take it, I gave her that which I had been holding, and at once went out as if nothing had happened. I took my time for her to undo it. She had plainly seen me leave and might have called me back, had she desired to do so. But, having felt that the packet I had given her was heavier than a letter, and not knowing what it could be, she wanted to examine it sooner than anything else. This packet contained fifty sheets of paper one upon the other, just as if I had been eager to keep her occupied till I had made my exit. At all events she believed that this had been my reason for having arranged such a number, that she thought she would never come to the end of them. Be this as it may, after having had the patience to turn them all over one after the other, and to examine them to see if there was not one with writing upon it, she found underneath a portrait in miniature which was on the lid of a box.

She could not divine what this meant, not finding that this portrait had any connection with what I had promised her. At first this made her form a strange opinion about me. She believed me to have more than one profession, and taking it into her head that I had undertaken to give her this present for someone else, she opened the box to see who my employer might be. She was wrong to entertain this suspicion as she did. I had never been the sort of man to work for another, and though at Court this kind of in-dividual is not very rare, such a thing had always been distasteful to me, so much so, that those who indulged in it had never passed as anything else in my estimation but as persons devoid of honour and undeserving of being even looked at. For this reason, no matter what other good points they might have, I esteemed them even less than mountebanks or quacks.

However, putting all this on one side, the lady, having done so much as to undo all these papers, went on to open the box, as she was not the woman to stop half-way. There she found my picture, not at full length, but from my belt upwards, as is usual in these sort of portraits. I was attired in a cuirass like a hero of the first rank. It is true, I had not copied Besmaux, who, having his full-length picture recently painted, mounted on a fine horse, a patch at the corner of his eye, and armed from head to foot, has also arranged that his hand should be adorned with a baton with *fleurs de lis* upon it, such as is given to generals in the army! Nevertheless, all his services reduce themselves to what I have before spoken of, and to having since kept watch over the prisoners at the Bastille! Be this as it may, not having been in a mood to imitate him, I did not fail to pass for quite another person in the lady's mind to the one I had described myself as being in my passport. Beginning in consequence to examine me more closely than she had yet done, she discovered that, were I to rid myself of my costume and my beard, I should be well worth her listening to me. I left her two days without returning to see her, so as to give her all the time necessary to adopt such a line of conduct as the circumstances warranted. Before committing myself, I was anxious to see whether she would be in a mood to inform the Prince de Conti of what had happened. Sarrasin, whom I had not only told that I wanted to play the lover, but who further had himself advised me to do so, had promised to let me know, in case she should have a desire to speak about it. His master had no secrets from him, especially in these kind of affairs. By pretending to

approve of all his follies, Sarrasin had found means of
having them recounted to him one after the other!
He even wrote most of the prince's letters about them,
as well as others of greater consequence. Sarrasin, I
repeat, having to warn me of everything which was
taking place, I could have got out of the business by
sounding a retreat in good time. All my measures
were already taken to that end. I knew of a place
where the Ormistes kept a bad guard, and whence it
would be easy to reach the army of the Duc de
Candale. However, I had no need of resorting to
such an expedient. The lady had never disfigured
anyone for murmuring soft things in her ear. As a
matter of fact, very far from wanting to begin with me,
she was, on the contrary, dying of impatience to see
me again, so as to learn much which she could not
make out. I seemed to her to be a sort of man much
more worthy of monopolising her heart than the
prince, who believed himself to possess it. Besides,
being an inquisitive woman, as I have just said, she
wanted to know who I might be and by what chance I,
who came from the Court, had fallen in love with her,
and, finally, whether she was the true cause of my
having exchanged my soldier's dress for a hermit's robe.

I had taken all the necessary measures with Sarrasin.
He had instructed me well enough; besides, I myself
was not too obtuse by nature, which had furnished me
with a fairly good tongue and sound enough judgment
to boot. True it is that it is not for me to say so, but
in short, what use is there in pretending modesty, when
truth is in question? Every kind of deceit is good for
nothing, and it is much better to boldly take the field
than remain a hypocrite for I do not know how long.

Eventually, the two days of which I have spoken having passed without my hearing any news, I returned to the lady's house. I chose a time at which she was still in bed. Without ceremony, I sat down by her bed-side and pretended to hardly dare look at her, the better to cause her to believe in my thorough earnestness. "Is it you, M. l'Hermite?" said she. "Will you not tell me how much longer your disguise is to last?" "As long as I can keep it up, madame," I quickly retorted, "since I have come from Paris expressly to see you, and would, indeed, have gone to search for you at the end of the world, had there been need." She told me laughingly that I must then be extraordinarily in love; so, perceiving that she wanted to laugh, I deemed that I ought to laugh too. I began to be enterprising, but the lady, being of opinion that it was a little too soon for this kind of thing, checked my vehemence and told me that, though I was a monk in dress only, I had assimilated all the monkish inclinations, when I had assumed the robe I now wore. Monks, at least, were accused of wanting to come to the point directly they could, in which, indeed, they were none too wrong, once they found women in a mood to humour them, but, as regards herself, who did not wish to be one of these, I must not only remember whom I was with, but also show her more respect. With a courtier's effrontery, I rejoined that, even were she not the lady for a monk, I could not show her more respect than by doing what I had done. Respect could only arise from great esteem, and one could not show a lady that one really respected her, except by desiring to enjoy her favours.

This seemed quite a novel kind of morality to her,

and she would have nothing to do with it. I thus had
to contain myself, in violence to my own feelings. For
very little was wanted to excite me, when I was priding
myself on taking the place of a prince of the blood.
Meanwhile, though she placed limits on my ardour, I
thought I discerned that she did so rather for form's
sake than from real decency. For this reason, without
wishing to put me out of countenance any more than
she had done when I had given her my portrait, she
enquired of me how long it was since I had fallen in
love with her and how such a thing had happened?
Indeed, unless I were to let her know, she could form
no idea. She knew that I had only come into the
city a short time back, that I had the same day
assumed the garb I now wore; so, if I had only
adopted it on her account, as I was now trying to make
her believe, my passion must have been already well
aroused before I left the place whence I had come. I
had plainly told her, when I had tried to enter upon
intimate relations with her, every sort of thing which I
thought likely to prove tempting, and, as this disguise
was not one of the least useful tricks in my bag, I had
taken good care not to be behindhand with it. Accordingly, it now being merely a question of satisfying her
curiosity, I declared that, if she would search her
memory thoroughly, she would remember a certain
painter, who had been with the Prince de Conti only
about five or six months before. This would be the
easier for her to do, because she herself had made him
paint her portrait. As a matter of fact, he had kept a
copy for himself at the same time, and, having seen it
in his workroom at Paris, I had thought it so beautiful
that I had endeavoured to obtain it at no matter what

price. I had, in consequence, given him all he had asked for it, and, from often casting my eyes upon it, I had fallen so much in love with the person it depicted, that I had determined to come and find her. I had learnt from this painter whose portrait it was and where I might find the original. He had, besides, told me that I was not the only one who had let himself be captivated. The Prince de Condé had given her his heart, and, as it was a dangerous thing to avow oneself the rival of a person of that rank, I had decided that I could do no better than conceal my passion from him beneath the garb I now wore. Besides, I imagined that it was absolutely necessary for me to adopt a disguise, for I might be recognised from having been seen at Court. I had, therefore, allowed my beard to grow, so that there was not a soul who to-day was not taken in.

Here is the account I gave her. It did not prove displeasing, as she was vain enough to take such a story seriously. She considered that her worth was doubled by it, and having asked to see the copy which I had just told her of, I showed her one which Sarrasin had had specially made for me by the best painter of the town. This I kissed thousands of times before her, to better and better persuade her that what I had just related was not a fable. I did not woo her badly by doing this, and as she was a woman, and there is none who is not weak enough to take pleasure in seeing herself loved, even though it be but by a groom, she told me with a gracious air that, whether all I had just told her was a fabrication or the truth, I had narrated it with so much grace, that she had derived almost as much enjoyment from it as when she was at a play. She next wanted to know who I was, wishing apparently to decide from what I might say about my rank, if I was worthy to fill the place of a lover of such consequence as hers was.

I was very near passing myself off for quite another person than I was, so as to further flatter her vanity. But, eventually considering that someone might recognise me, and that this could not happen without my being put to shame, I made myself out neither greater nor less than God had caused me to be born. Nevertheless, I was very much mortified at being yet a subaltern (though I was not yet as old as are now Servon and Soupir, who both held only the same rank I held then, and who have, all the same, already passed the greater portion of their life in it), and considered my reputation was affected by not being as yet a captain. In spite of this, as in the provinces it is thought that everything which approaches the King's person is rather worthy of envy than compassion, the humble individual that I was in no way disgusted the lady. I even made daily progress in her good graces, so much so that I perceived myself in a condition to shortly propose to her to make the Prince de Conti return to his duty.

It is true that what thoroughly served me to gain her confidence was my presenting her with everything the Cardinal had sent me. I began by the smallest object, because I had not yet told her that all this came from him. It was I who obtained the credit for it, so I was eager that my gift should appear proportionate to my means, or at least that, if it should seem in any way beyond them, she might attribute it to my affection. She was not ungrateful,

deeming that she ought to do everything for a man
who was doing more for her than he really could. I
was just as well treated as she treated the Prince de
Conti. But, before deciding on this, she did a very
peculiar thing, so as not to embrace me with my
beard, and one which even deserves to be detailed.

This beard displeased her as beards usually displease
all ladies. She did not dare to tell me to get rid of it,
because she would have been afraid of my accusing her
of being more solicitous for her own pleasure than for
my safety. Such being the case, she told Las Florides,
whom she had protected with the Prince de Conti at
the beginning of the rule of the Ormistes, that she
thought me very comical for a hermit. I must be
made drunk, and have my beard cut off whilst asleep.
I should be very astonished when I awoke, and there
would be fun in seeing the face I should pull, when I
found myself caught in such a way. Las Florides,
who asked nothing better than to humour her, and
whose line besides it was to amuse himself at other
people's expense, at once promised that he would
satisfy her before three or four days should have
elapsed. Not a day passed by that a boat laden with
wine of Langon[1] did not come by the position which
he was holding. He had had a cask given to him,
being of opinion that it was excellent. He had already
made me taste it, to see if I found it just as good as he
did. I should have had to have been extremely fas-
tidious not to have shared his taste, so, even outbidding
him, instead of declaring it excellent, as he had done,
I told him it was *excellentissime*. He replied, that he
was delighted at my finding it so good, and this being

1 Langon is a town which produces, or did produce, wine of
a very alcoholic and strong nature.

so, declared himself anxious that we should have a drinking-bout together, directly the wine should have settled itself.

Nevertheless, the King's troops did not give him too much time for such a thing. They were beginning to press the town very hard, especially since they had found means of winning over a certain foreign colonel, who was in one of the principal forts which the besieged still held on the Garonne. This fort even defended the mouth of that river, so much so that the loss was one which could not be repaired. M. de Candale had himself drawn up the agreement, and had then sent it on to me to give it the finishing touch. This colonel was an Irishman, and was called Islan, a man of rank of that country. All the same, his appetite had not been proportionate to his nobility. He had treated us very gently, though, had he known his business, he might have extracted a sufficient sum from the Court to have procured the finest estate in the whole of Ireland. He had been satisfied with two thousand pistoles as the price of his treachery, a sum which I caused to be advanced to him by a banker to whom I had letters of credit. I had donned another dress to go and visit him, and, although he was very surprised to see me with such a great beard, he had no idea I was "the hermit of the people of good resolve." If he had heard speak of me, he had never seen me. He only left his house to go to the Bourse; from the Bourse he returned to his counter, and, though he was more than sixty years of age, he had never done anything else.

Such was the state of affairs outside the city, while within there was even more danger. Most of the members of the Parlement and the chief citizens, who

had always hated the tyranny of the Ormistes, began
to be more than ever weary of it: so they each had
their plot to return to that allegiance which they owed
to their sovereign.   All this was very capable of
alarming Orteste and all his accomplices, and consequently, of preventing Las Florides from amusing
himself at my expense.   However, at last, his liking
for the lady and the bent he had for pleasure having
led him to omit making any reflections on the state of
affairs, he invited some of his friends as well as myself
to the opening of a great duck pasty which he had
received as a present.   This pasty was well accompanied.   He had provided himself with everything
excellent the season could provide for a great banquet,
and, as he had told these guests that he would wash all
this down with the best wine they had ever drunk,
everyone came thoroughly determined to drink deep
and heartily.

It was now so long since I had lost the habit of
drinking the wine of Langon (which is full of liqueur
and potent) that, in consequence, it went to my head
more than to other people's.   Wishing for this reason
not to overload my digestion with it, I frankly told the
company that the poor hermit wanted to go and lie
down.   If Las Florides had not desired to play me the
trick he wanted to do, he would never have allowed
me to be found wanting in public in this way, but,
having his plan, he told one of his servants to take me
to a room he mentioned.   A quarter of an hour later
(perhaps a little less or a little more) he sent to see
what I was doing.   I had lain down on a bed, on
which I had no sooner thrown myself than I had
fallen asleep.   I was even snoring in as loud a manner

as if I had been asthmatic, either from being in an uncomfortable position, or from the wine producing that effect upon me, and I might have been heard at the end of the street.   Las Florides, without informing anyone that the lady in question had begged him to have my beard shaved off, told the people that I ought to be played the trick in question.   Like myself, they had drunk a good deal, so, as there is no devilry which people do not think of when in that condition, they did not tarry long between the proposition and its execution.   Las Florides had ordered the best barber in the town to hold himself in readiness with some good razors for such time as he should send for him. Such an order had slightly embarrassed this poor man. He had been afraid that it was only to carry out some more dangerous and more criminal operation than the one he was wanted for.   Las Florides possessed a pretty enough wife, and, as she bore the reputation of not contenting herself with her husband, this barber thought that, having discovered some gallant with her, he wanted to put him into such a state as never again to divert himself with his neighbour's wife! Perceiving, however, on his arrival at the place where I was, that the thing wanted of him was not of the nature he anticipated, he became quite reassured, from having before been all of a tremble.   Accordingly, when he was asked if he could shave my beard com-pletely off without my awaking, he made reply that he could not absolutely swear to such a thing, but, at all events, he was very sure that, were he unable to succeed, anyone else would do no better than himself. He was told to begin, and, having first cut my beard with scissors, he then proceeded with the razor.   I felt

neither the one nor the other—in such a deep slumber
was I plunged. I even slept half the night through at
a stretch, but, waking eventually towards the middle,
and having by chance raised my hand to my face, I
was quite astounded to perceive myself no more nor
less than are those who are accused of bringing bad
luck. I at once suspected that this was a joke which
had been played me, and, not being able to attribute it
to Las Florides, I had not the very slightest suspicion
that the lady had had any hand in it. My condition
upset me, as, indeed, it must have upset every sensible
man. I was afraid lest it should serve to cause me to
be recognised, and that, as there were around the
Prince de Conti a number of people who had been
at Court, there might be someone to tell him that
I had been but a hermit in dress alone. Besides, it
was certain that the rumour of this joke would no
sooner have spread round the city, than I should be
mobbed like a bear-tamer by every kind of small child.
This was in no way pleasant for an honourable man.
Besides, the people who might be too wise to run after
me like the rest would not always be able to help
staring at me, and, in consequence, must recognise me,
if they had ever by chance seen me, though before
they would not have dreamt of doing so.

These reflections, which appeared to me sensible
enough, stopped me from closing my eyes all the rest
of the night. Those who had been present at the
banquet had slept at the house of Las Florides and
got up early, like himself, to be present at my rising.
They were delighted at being about to see the face
I should pull and amuse themselves at it in my very
presence. However, they were very surprised to see

that I was the first to burst out laughing, just as if I had been in no wise affected. I had taken my line, after having thought well over the matter. This line was, to abandon my hermit's dress, so as to avoid the affronts and inconveniences which I foresaw might arise, were I to think of putting it on again. Las Florides wanted to give me one of his suits. Both of us were about the same height, so that it would have fitted me very well, but I did not think it opportune to accept it, because I deemed it too magnificent for the position I wished to maintain in this part of the country. I was not eager for my costume to draw attention to myself. So, far from wanting to wear gold, I would willingly have put a sack over my head, had such a thing been permissible. Las Florides was wont to wear gold stuffs, since he had changed his knife for a sword, for he had previously been but a shoemaker and even one of those who do but little business.

As I had retained the soldier's dress with which I had arrived, it seemed to me the right moment to adopt it again. This spared me a good deal of embarrassment. For, as the news about my beard had already spread in the neighbourhood, everyone was only waiting to catch sight of my dress to call out "il a c—— au lit," as is done at Shrovetide. Indeed, there were already more than two hundred persons at each corner of the street in which Las Florides lived. They were even now quite ready to shout out their jokes after me, so, being afraid lest they should have been warned that I had changed my dress, and that they would greet me in the same way in the soldier's garb as in my former costume,

I said to a groom of this Ormiste, who was a good sort of fool, that I would bet him a pistole that he did not dare to put on my hermit's robe, and go in it only through three streets from where we were. He had not, like myself, seen the crowd of people, and, even had he done so, would not have had the sense to divine the reason of their assembling. Accordingly, being eager to win my pistole, he replied that he would make the wager whenever I liked. I answered that it should be that very moment, if he was ready, and at once taking me at my word, he immediately put on my monk's robe. The populace, which is clever enough in this part of the country, would not at first attack him. On the contrary, it withdrew into the other street, to make him pass right into the middle, before he should have discovered what was on foot. The groom, who was quite ashamed, had not only lowered his hood for concealment, but held besides his hand in front of his face, to avoid recognition. His appearance alone sufficed to make these people believe that it was I; so, no sooner had he passed, than they took to setting up a terrible clamour after him. At the same time, the crowd was increasing from every minute, and as I had suspected what was going to happen and already perceived that those at the corner which he had not as yet passed were running after the others, I passed right through the middle of the people and so extricated myself from the crowd. The poor groom was very embarrassed as to how to get out of the mess. Nevertheless, he kept calling out at every step that a pistole was a good thing to win, and that this was the reason of his having donned my costume. But as, in addition to the noise which this riff-raff made, he

had bawled himself hoarse before being able to make
a single word of what he was saying audible, he was
eventually obliged to stop, because he found himself
surrounded on all sides. There he told the people
that it was a question of his winning a pistole by
going as far as a certain street. He had made the
bet with me, and he would beg them not to stand
in the way of his success. They opened their eyes
at these words, and there were men present who knew
me and who began to perceive that this was not the
man they wanted. They were carried away with rage,
the wisest amongst them pointing out that I had
cleverly deceived them. They would have immediately
revenged themselves, had they dared, and would have
gone to besiege the house of Las Florides, in which
they still thought I was. However, the respect in
which they were obliged to hold him, or rather, fear
of his ferocity acting as a curb, which pulled them up
short, they had to champ their bit, for lack of doing
what they wanted to do.

When Las Florides learned what I had done to avoid
the insults prepared for me, he thought I had behaved
like a clever man. Meanwhile, he did not know what
had become of me, because, instead of returning to his
house, I remained four whole days without giving him
any news of myself. He tried to obtain some from
every quarter, because at every moment things occurred
in his new-found profession which made him want my
advice. For this purpose he addressed himself to
persons who could easily have enlightened him, had
they cared to do so. He applied to the lady who had
originated the joke played upon me. I had gone to
her on leaving his house, but she told him that she

had heard no more about me than himself. She had been quite astounded to see me in my present state. Although, as a matter of fact, she was not expecting me to arrive at her house with a long beard for some time, she was not at all prepared to see me appear without my usual dress. She asked me the reason of this change, and, as I was a long way from imagining that she herself was the cause of my having been rendered beardless, I was innocent enough to describe what had happened. She found it very amusing, and, thinking me even more to her taste than before, though my costume was not too becoming, she indulged in some pretty little ways which made me understand that, what she had not been willing to accord me before, she would grant me now. I did not need to be told twice, and, becoming at once good friends, she enquired, to keep up the conversation, who was it, did I think, that had played me the trick I had just spoken to her about? As I was beginning to be on good terms with her, I replied that there she was asking me a merry question. My intelligence was not so limited as to accuse anyone else but Las Florides. It was he who had tried to amuse himself at my expense, but I would not forgive him for it, either in life nor death.

She burst out laughing at this speech, and even so heartily, that I was quite shocked. For this reason I should at once have asked her in a very rough way where the joke lay, had it not been that she might have thought that I was taking such a liberty, only on account of the other one she had just let me take. Meanwhile, the more annoyed I appeared, the more she made game of me. She called me dupe more than a thousand times, and, not understanding what she meant by this, I was very nearly getting seriously angry with her. Nevertheless, I did not think such a thing would be wise for many reasons, so, begging her once again to let me know why she was thus jeering at me, she answered in a pleasant and bantering way, that I was to look well at her and afterwards say, whether a pretty woman such as herself would ever consent to share her couch with a monk. These words were not yet sufficient to thoroughly enlighten me. Indeed, I think that I should have there and then obliged her to have explained herself in some other way, had she not immediately added that, further, there was more pleasure in admitting a soldier to one's bed as she had done, than a beard an ell long.

I must not then blame Las Florides, but herself, for my adventure, for she it was who had not been able to endure my great beard. Nevertheless, I ought not to regret its loss, for, if all those who wore one knew that they had but to get rid of it to enjoy her favours, she presumed enough on her own attractions to flatter herself that no capuchins would be left in their convent!

She said this to me in such an agreeable way, that I at once proceeded to show her that, if I did not sport a monk's garb, I yet possessed all his best qualities. She was extremely pleased with me, and, as I could go nowhere where I should be more comfortable, and was, besides, afraid of descending into the street, for fear of the mob and the small children, who would not have again failed to try and make me their plaything, I begged her to keep me in her house. She resolved the quicker to do this, as she had no husband who controlled her actions, and besides, she flattered herself that I should make good return for her hospitality. Not that she was a widow; on the contrary, she had been married but two years ago, and, in addition, had a husband who had not as yet any desire to die. However, she had found means to get rid of him some days before, at the instigation of the Prince de Conti, who had bothered her a good deal on the subject. As it was his opinion that to possess a mistress was nothing at all unless one could pass the night with her, he had been desirous that the man should set out on a journey, so as to give him time to do everything he wished. He had sent the husband into Flanders to his brother, to carry some complaints against Marcin. The Prince de Condé, who knew all that went on at Bordeaux, just as well as if he had been there himself, listened placidly to the man. Meanwhile, as he had adopted the plan of telling everyone home truths, even including women, for whom one usually has some sort of consideration, he at once replied that his brother had not desired his words to be believed, since he had chosen him to come and speak of his affairs. He should have despatched a less suspicious person, in order to incline his mind to listen, for he was too interested a party not to add something of his own. He (the Prince de Condé) was sorry to have to speak so plainly to him, but it was his fault rather than his own, since he should not have undertaken such a disagreeable service. He was not the cause of his imprudence; he was bringing all this upon his own head. The emissary did not at first understand what was meant by this, either because he was not quick-witted, or that he was ignorant of the intercourse of the Prince de Conti with his wife. Accordingly, he entreated the Prince de Condé to

consent to tell him in what way he might be an object
of suspicion, since he had never had anything to do
with Marcin and was, consequently, just as ready to
do him justice as anyone else. " Will you swear to
it," retorted the prince, who wanted to divert himself,
" and not be afraid of being accused of falsehood ?"
" No, no, my lord," replied the poor cuckold, " I am
ready to swear any oath you like, begging you to
believe that I shall only speak the truth."   The prince
pretended not to be willing to accept his word, so
as to oblige him to take the promised oath: then,
softening of a sudden, as if he had only just begun to
be disabused of his suspicions, " I believe you," continued
he, " since I see you taking an oath; but, if you can
clear yourself of this, I am very certain you cannot
clear yourself of other things.   Your wife is too good a
friend of my brother's for you to warmly espouse his
interests.   You are, in consequence, unable to bear
witness against his enemies: you know this better
than myself, since you are not only a lawyer, but,
further, cause those who pass as masters in that profession to come and plead before you."   The poor
husband nearly fell to the ground when he heard these
reproaches.   He knew nothing about his wife's goings
on, or, at least, pretended not to, but, dissimulation
being of no further use after this, he went off very
sorrowfully to return to his own part of the country.

I still remained with his wife during this time, and,
as every minute we were becoming better acquainted,
I thought I had the right to say to her, but merely as
my own idea, that, were I in her place, I should try
and profit by the present moment; that things might
not always be so propitious for her as they were

to-day. She was in the good graces of the Prince de
Conti, and were she willing to employ the influence
she had over his mind to lead him back to the obedience
he owed his Majesty, I would take it upon myself to
obtain a recompense for her proportionate to this
service. She might by such means even procure some
position in Paris. The Court would give her husband
occupation, especially if he would buy the office of
Maître des Requêtes. A mere nothing was sometimes
needed to make one's fortune. A good example of this
was M. le Tellier, who, from having caused a report to
be drawn up, favourable to one of the children of the
late M. de Bullion, whilst he was Procureur du Roi at
the Châtelet, had afterwards been so well received that
he had concluded that he could rely upon him to
make his fortune. Selling his office, he had bought
one similar to that which I advised her husband to
purchase. He had done no harm, since he was now
not only Secretary of State and one of the richest men
in all Paris, but, further, on the way to one day
become chancellor.

The lady listened to me with pleasure. She had
heard say that Paris was the paradise of women; the
hope with which I inspired her, of being able to some
day take up her abode there was then so agreeable, that
she at once told me that, after having given herself to
me as she had done, she abandoned herself entirely to
my guidance. Nevertheless, she wanted me to be
grateful for such great confidence. Accordingly, she
immediately added that, if she thus easily gave up her
native place and her relations, I must be assured that
she did so only from love of myself. I could not
always live at Bordeaux. The bonds which bound me

to the Court by reason of my office would soon force me to return. True it was that I had declared that my leave was for four months, but already one of these had flown, and the others would pass just as quickly, even were the time a longer one than it was. We must therefore think of placing ourselves in a position to see one another continually. She was not as clever as I, and even a long way from it ; nevertheless, she did not fail to perceive that the expedient I had proposed would so greatly facilitate our plan that, if she wanted to succeed, she must look for no other. At the same time, she begged me to consent to write to the Court, adding that, by reason of any goodwill and gratitude I might feel towards her, I would use all my influence, and all that of my friends, to conduct this affair to a satisfactory termination.

I was enchanted at the warmth with which she received my proposition. Love, nevertheless, had no share in my satisfaction. Debauchery and policy had originated our intercourse rather than any attachment of the heart. Not that she was not pretty enough for that, and there would even have been many people in my place who would have considered themselves in luck's way. However, either because one is not made to love everybody, or because I did not love a mistress who divided her favours with another, I approached her no more than was sufficient to keep up the reputation of being a dashing gallant, which I had acquired with her. The need I had of her to assist me with the prince also caused me to humour her. Sarrasin had found the matter difficult on account of the prince being afraid of his brother. Though he had been enchanted with the portrait of the Cardinal's niece,

which this secretary had shown him as if by chance
(for he had not as yet spoken of my scheme of a
marriage with her, and wished first to see what he
would say about her portrait), the Prince de Conti was so
afraid of the lady's rage, were he to give her up, that
he could not make up his mind to do so. In spite of
this, Sarrasin, who was a clever man, had made use of
every reason which could sway him. He had pointed
out to him that his brother had a thousand times more
confidence in Marcin than in himself, so that, in
reality, all authority was in the hands of the former,
whilst he held it but in appearance. Were he to speak
the truth, he knew in his heart of hearts that the
prince dared do nothing at all without having first
consulted him : that all those really devoted to him
observed this only with indignation and prayed to
Heaven every day that they might see him escape from
this slavery. He added that all his brother's property,
which was very considerable, had been confiscated,
and there was no likelihood of its ever being returned
to him, since the bonds he was every day contracting
with the Spaniards were of such magnitude as to
appear indissoluble.

The portrait which Sarrasin had shown the Prince
de Conti was a rather flattering one, as ladies' portraits
nearly always are. Nevertheless, as it had not as yet
produced all the results we had looked for, either
because one had failed to speak cleverly to the prince
or that his fears still continued so great that he could
not surmount them, I thought myself obliged to produce another, which his Eminence had sent me. This
was a full-length one and looked very well indeed. It
was much more flattering than that which Sarrasin

had shown, so that one might call anyone very unsus-
ceptible who should resist the original from which it
was painted, always supposing it to be a good likeness.
I gave it to my accomplice, who put it in her room,
after having had a magnificent frame made for it.
This portrait was like the other, which was not very
strange, since both had been made from the same
person. The original indeed on the whole resembled
them, though in detail she was far from being as
good-looking or from having the same features.

The Prince de Conti, having gone to the lady's
house, at once recognised the person whom it repre-
sented. In spite of this, he was afraid that he was
deceived, since it was rather odd to hang up a picture
of this kind in a town like Bordeaux, in which the
Cardinal was hated like death itself, and thus, to
ornament one's room with a portrait of his niece was
a piece of boldness which seemed out of reason. He
therefore enquired of the lady, whose portrait it was,
as if he did not know, and even had no idea whatever.
The lady replied, that it was the picture of the most
beautiful, the most virtuous, and the most accom-
plished person in France. This was praise in a few
words, but what was the best thing about it was, that
it was true. Of the seven nieces of his Eminence, she
was not only the most perfect, but also appeared to
have epitomised in her own person the virtues which
all the others should have possessed. The lady,
having biassed the mind of the prince by such admir-
able and well-timed praises, almost immediately added
that the original of the picture was ready to be married,
and would just suit him. At the same time she told
him her name, whilst declaring that, if he wished to be

happy and also to succeed to the property and offices of his brother, he should seek for no other wife than her. His fear of his brother faded away before her praises of the Cardinal's niece and his inspection of the portrait. He fell in love as violently as is possible under such circumstances. He had never seen the lady, who had nearly always lived in a convent outside France, when he had been at Court. Accordingly, really believing that she was as beautiful as her portrait declared, he had no sooner returned home than he sent for Sarrasin to his closet. He there asked him the donor of the picture he had shown him, enquiring if it was not the Cardinal, and bade him speak the truth. This prince was too clever not to perceive that all this had been arranged, and that the girl was being thrown at his head. Sarrasin owned this without in any way mentioning me. Such a thing was not as necessary as to let his master know what the Cardinal's plan was.

The Prince de Conti, to whom he once more pointed out afresh the advantages he would gain by returning to his duty, having thought the matter over, at once commanded him to go on with this business and report the progress he should make. Meanwhile, wishing to discover from him his mistress's share in this affair— she who had a portrait of the lady, and had spoken quite frankly of her,—Sarrasin told him that it had been necessary to tell her about it, since it was quite evident that he would not agree, were he not urged on by some power stronger than his own. It had been believed that she would have more power over him than anyone else, and that otherwise, she should have known nothing about it. The prince gave orders, as this was

the case, that she should be told nothing more.
Sarrasin let me know this, and I was not too displeased,
because I felt sure that a secret could be in no worse
hands than those of a woman. Besides, I concluded
that the prince was the more firmly determined in his
intention, since he was importing mystery into this
intrigue. Indeed, when one cares about anything, it is
not agreeable for it to be known everywhere, whereas,
when one is indifferent, such a thing is of no consequence whatever.

Be this as it may, this prince, having gone the next
day to see the lady, very nearly surprised us together.
Her lady's maid, whom she trusted, and whom she had
ordered to admit no one without first informing her,
having amused herself by making love, instead of
attending to her orders, we suddenly heard the foot-
steps of several people in the ante-chamber. It was
the prince and his suite, and, expecting such to be the
case, I quickly jumped into a closet near her bed. I
had not the time to shut the door upon myself, and,
not being able to go back to it after his entrance, my
uneasiness as well as the lady's became great. She
indeed was completely upset, and could not recover
herself. The prince, who was not a handsome man,
and who consequently mistrusted his own appearance,
asked her what it was which was so extraordinary as
to make her appear in the state in which he now saw
her ? This enquiry completed her embarrassment, so
much so that, his suspicions increasing more and
more, he looked to right and left, and perceived the
door of the closet which was ajar. This made him
curious to come and inspect it. He was extremely
surprised to see me there, although he should have

expected such a thing, after the confusion he had noticed the lady to be in. In a tone which would have caused me to tremble, had I been wont to give way to terror, he demanded of me what I was doing in such a place? I had had time to think matters over, in case he should approach my hiding-place, so, being quite ready with an answer for him, I declared that his secretary would go bail for my behaviour, for he knew why I had come into the town, and he himself should know it also, at least from what had been repeated to me. This should be enough to let him know what I was now doing here, and that this was all my business with the mistress of the house.

The lady, who had been near fainting, when she had seen the prince enter the closet, recovered herself a little at my words. I had thus given her an opening to excuse herself, which she had before not thought of. The Prince de Conti clearly perceived what all this was worth. His orders to Sarrasin not to admit the lady any more into his secret did not coincide with my excuses. Nevertheless, as he had already determined to marry the person proposed to him, he did not desire to make all the fuss which at another time he might doubtless have done. In spite of this, he told me very drily that I must leave the town within twenty-four hours, otherwise, once that period of time should have elapsed, it would prove no safe place for me. Having thus manifested his anger in a few words, I do not accurately know what he said to the lady. He made me leave the house at once, and I did not think it prudent to return and see what had happened to her. I let Sarrasin, who was in despair, know of my disguise, and he sent me a passport directly he had returned home. As he always had blank ones by him, he had no need to speak to his master of the matter to obtain one for me. I did not go to bid good-bye to Las Florides or anyone. My valise had remained at one of the friends of the secretary of the Duc de Candale since the day of my arrival. I sent to fetch it, and having at once set out, for fear of some fly passing in front of the prince's nose and making him change his mind, I arrived at the camp of M. de Candale, whom I found already informed of what had happened to me.

I do not know how and from whom he had been able to hear of it. It appeared to me that both the Prince de Conti and the lady were, one as much as the other, concerned in not boasting of what had occurred. We three alone had taken part in this scene, and it seemed to me that, if there was one of us who might tell the story, it should be myself rather than anyone else. Knowing very well that it was not myself, it must, consequently, have originated from one of the two. I admitted the truth to the duc, but kept back anything which might sully the honour of the lady. The Duc de Candale laughed a little at me for playing such a discreet part, telling me that I had cause to reckon this as a piece of good luck, because, being accustomed, as a Musketeer, to only have mistresses who were in the habit of seeing twenty-four men a day, I was apparently to-day contenting myself with one who had seen but twenty in her whole life! He would cite them all to me, if I liked, by their names and surnames, and, were he to be discovered lying, it would be at most about one or two of them. He knew for a certain fact that the Prince de Conti was the seventeenth of her favoured lovers, from which circumstance one could draw one's own conclusions as to the worth and appetite of the lady.

The duc liked joking so much and was besides so fond of scandal, that his words made little impression on my mind. Nevertheless, being afraid lest the Cardinal should be set against me, and that I might receive only ingratitude instead of the reward which I had a right to expect for my services, I begged him to consent to write to him on my behalf. He professed himself quite willing to do this, but instead of writing to him in strong terms, the letter he gave me ruined my interests more than it assisted them. He sent word to his Eminence, wishing to amuse him, that the Prince de Conti was right to want to marry, since he was not lucky in the matter of mistresses. His last one was the seventh who had proved false. Luckily, a wife was being selected for him whose virtue was proof against coquetry, and in this lay his safety, because, personally, he was so very unfortunate that he would be cuckolded by his wife as he had been by his mistresses, were it not for the precautions which were being taken.

VI

ON my arrival in Paris, M. le Cardinal, who was eager to avoid the importunities for a captaincy in the Guards, which he foresaw I should pester him with, told me that he had not reckoned on sending me to Bordeaux to make love, but rather to look after the affairs of his Majesty. I clearly perceived the reason of these reproaches: so, as everything I had done had been but with a view to serving him, I replied, without being surprised, that I was ignorant as to who had discredited me to his Eminence, but that, had he heard the truth, he should have been told at the same time that my love affairs had been described to him, that there was just as much credit in playing the lover in the way I had done, as in the most difficult matter in the world. An envoy, it appeared to me, should transform himself into all sorts of things to bring his negotiations to a successful termination. Indeed, I had done nothing without first consulting with Sarrasin, whom his Eminence knew to be a clever man, and, as he had been of opinion that I ought to act as I had done, it did not seem to me that I ought to be blamed.

My firmness silenced him. One had to contradict him to carry one's point. He reproached me for nothing more, but I was no better off for all that. Having tried to speak to him of the reward for which he had so long made me hope, he replied that, now he had returned to France, he did not want to get himself expelled all over again. He was well aware that he had promised me a company in the Guards, but, as it could not be bestowed without causing me to pass over the bodies of twenty lieutenants senior to myself, far from asking him for it, as I was doing, I ought not even to dream of it, if I had the slightest friendship for him. To speak like this was to declare himself terribly opposed to me, so, concluding that I had nothing more to hope for at Court, I resolved to sell my commission and retire to my own home. I told M. de Navailles this, that he might speak to the Cardinal about it, and that the latter might allow me to look for a purchaser. M. de Navailles tried to alter my resolve, telling me that it was, at all events, better for me to be what I was than to be reduced to go and plant cabbages! It appeared as if I did not know how bored a man who had retired became, since that state of life did not frighten me! Once one had had anything to do with the Court, one could do nothing else. Not a day passed that one did not long for death, and he did not advise me to personally try such an experiment.

All these reasons, however good they might seem to him and, indeed, might really be, did not affect me. I persisted in my resolve the more firmly, because the assistance I had for some years received from gambling now failed me entirely. From the first day I had begun to lose I had always continued to sustain fresh losses. For this reason I occasionally found myself so bereft of everything, that I thought there was no one in the world more unfortunate than myself. So much so was this the case that, if I have mentioned that I had at Bordeaux a purse of two hundred pistoles, it must be understood that I had procured it from one of my friends. Seeing me ordered to leave, apparently on account of something serious, he had brought them to me without my having asked for them. I had made no bones about taking them, because I had imagined that the worst thing which could happen to me would be that I should be reimbursed for what I had spent. But the Cardinal, after having tried to pick a quarrel with me as I have just described, thinking he had a right to give me nothing at all, had ordered Servient to let me have a bill for but two hundred crowns, and even to tell me on his behalf, when I should come for it, that I did not deserve that, and so, if he was giving it me, it was only because I was not rich and stood in need of someone's assistance. I do not know why he did not further add in definite terms that he only acted as he was doing by way of charity, since that was the sole thing lacking to complete his kindness: indeed, I am ignorant whether he did not say so, since such words were quite of the same kind as those which he caused to be conveyed to me.

This it was which made me so out of temper and caused me to want to retire from everything. Perceiving that all he could say to make me stay was of no use, Navailles eventually promised to speak to his Eminence. He did so in very kindly terms as regards myself, and even in a way which was well calculated to make him change his mind. For, after having told

him that I was a man without reproach, who had
always served him faithfully and with zeal, he added
that my retirement would make a good many people
think over things, and it might be thought that there
was no longer any profit or honour to be got by serving
him. For this reason, if only for his own sake, he
ought not to let me depart without some recompense.
He further told him many weighty reasons for this, so
much so that, having quite upset him, his Eminence
replied that my demands must then be satisfied, since
there was no other way of keeping me. I must, however, assist myself, if I wanted that post (a captaincy
in the Guards), since it was well worth my doing so.
Navailles perfectly understood what he meant by this.

The help his Eminence asked for was that I should
give him some money.

Upon this, so as to make him realise in good time
that he must not expect any, Navailles, who still
wished to be my friend, rejoined that I did not possess
one sou, and that, had I to return to Bearn, he knew
from a good source that I should have to borrow the
wherewithal to get back with. Eventually, after a
good deal more talking, one side always making a
thrust at me and the other parrying it, the Cardinal
and Navailles separated without it being certain whether
I should be given what I asked for or allowed to
depart. For, although the Minister had declared that
I·was to be satisfied, since otherwise I could no longer
be relied upon, as he had immediately added that I
must help myself, it was a question of knowing whether
he would abandon this last stipulation. He was as
grasping as a Jew whenever his interests were concerned, so much so that those who knew this were

accustomed to declare that he would have been much more fit to keep a shop than to be a minister of State.

I was awaiting the answer of Navailles with all the impatience imaginable, when I was very surprised to hear that he did not know what to say to me. At the same time he described what had occurred, and, still continuing to show himself my friend, advised me, were the Cardinal to try and sound me on the subject, to make myself out even poorer than he himself had done. Indeed, it was a shameful thing that he should try and extract money for a thing which cost him nothing, but it was all very well to say so, he went on in just the same way. His Eminence had, on his entry into the ministry, introduced this custom of giving nothing without money, and firmly intended to keep it up to the end. I thanked Navailles for his good advice and replied that, even had he not given it me, I should not have failed to put it into practice myself. I was forced to do so by necessity, and, as necessity knew no law, the Cardinal would have great trouble before making me produce any money. He was all powerful in a good many things, but in this I defied him to make himself obeyed. Navailles made reply that he was well pleased to see me in this state of mind, and that I should take care to keep myself in it.

For some days M. le Cardinal said nothing to me, although I took care to present myself before him evening and morning. I did not know what this meant, deeming that it was he who should speak first : however, seeing him do nothing of the sort, and thinking that I should very probably have to wait some time before he did so, I would not delay any longer without having a personal explanation with him. I again snatched my opportunity, as I had done on many occasions, to address him just as he was coming from the gaming-table and had been winning. I knew from experience that he was never in such good humour as at such a moment—indeed, one might have said that he had seen the heavens open, so serene was his countenance and so delighted his look. He clearly perceived that I wanted to speak to him, and, as he was aware that it was to ask him for something, and not to give him anything, he tried to avoid me. He was successful, and, having thus escaped once, believed that he had got rid of me for good and all, when, one day that he least expected to do so, he found me at the house of Madame de Venelle.

This lady was the companion of his nieces, and I was paying her a visit on the pretext of bringing some truffles which had been sent me from Dauphiné. She was extremely fond of them, and I had observed that no present was more welcome to her. The nieces of his Eminence were much of her way of thinking, too. They always had their pockets quite full of them, and, though this lady was aware that they were already sufficiently inclined towards gallantry not to need this spur[1] to urge them on to it, she did not dare to take the truffles away, because they would have been in a mood to retort that it was bad taste on her part to blame in others that which she herself approved of.

The minister was surprised to find me there, without my having been sent for, and on his enquiring what I

1 Truffles had, and have still, in France the reputation of exciting the passions. It is improbable, however, that they are really an incentive to gallantry.

was doing in a rude way (and behaving as if he was inclined to believe that I had only come there for the purpose of leading his nieces astray), I answered that, having intended to make a small present to Madame de Venelle, I had come with it myself, from fear lest any bearer I might send should by chance be tempted to pilfer. At this word "present" he softened, so accustomed was he to be pleased when one was made him! Accordingly, at once adopting another tone to that in which he had spoken to me, he rejoined that he had for a long time known me as a cautious man, and one not easily caught. I was none too wrong to be suspicious of my neighbour, for the world was at present so corrupt (and especially in France) that there were a hundred rogues to one honest man. I did not dare tell him what I thought about the reproach he was making against our nation, to wit, that, if to-day it was so corrupt, it was only since the bad example he had set from the first day he had entered the ministry. At least, this is what most honest folks declared.

Be this as it may, not daring, as I have just said, to show my resentment and having, on the contrary, kept a respectful silence, as if agreeing with what he said, the Cardinal enquired of me what the present I had mentioned might be? Apparently, he wanted his share, if he could have a finger in it. If I was a cautious man, as he had declared, he for his part was a good manager. He let nothing escape through any fault of his own, and had this in common with some other people, that he never missed turning everything to account. Nevertheless, when he learned that the present was only truffles, he became as grave as if he was eighty years old. He then at once asked me if

14—2

this was not making fun of people, bringing such things into a place where there were young girls. The fire was already nearly alight, without trying to set it ablaze. I ought to be more discreet, and he would have never have believed this of me. He immediately asked to see these truffles, and, either from fear of what he had spoken of, or because he was eager to get hold of them, ordered a gentleman of his who was in attendance to call one of his men to take them back to his house. Madame de Venelle, who did not like seeing them disappear under her nose, after having been their possessor, then told him that, if it was dangerous for young girls to eat truffles, there was no danger in a woman of her age partaking of them. His Eminence retorted that, if there was no danger, as she declared, there was also no necessity; besides, she was too good-natured to refuse them to his nieces, were they to chance to ask for some. The minister having thus taken sole possession of them, without letting her have the least share, I was afraid of having selected a bad time to speak to him, though I had carefully chosen my words as I have just said.

Nevertheless, this did not stop me from persisting in my resolve, which was to discover, once for all, whether I was to return home or stay with the Cardinal. Accordingly, my mouth was open to have an explanation, but, being beforehand with me, he said, in a considerably softer voice, that I was then about to leave him, without remembering that he had always reckoned me amongst his most faithful servants! Navailles, who had spoken to him on my behalf, knew very well what he had always said about this. There was a kind of ingratitude in this conduct, especially in my pressing him, as I was doing, with my sword at his throat, to give me a company in the Guards. I should at least have some patience, and choose a time which would not make my comrades raise a regular outcry against him. I, better than anyone else, knew how impatiently they bore cadets being made to pass over their heads. For this reason, some pretext was requisite for such a thing, and it was this for which he was searching so as to content me. With such an end in view, he had caused enquiry to be made as to my assisting myself, for, could I do so, he might point out to my comrades, when they should come to complain of the favour bestowed on me to their own prejudice, that it was not so much a favour as a civility which he was doing me. They would have no answer to this, since, indeed, it would have cost me something to obtain it. On this account, he would once again advise me to see if I could not do something, either through my endeavours or through friends. His only wish was to do me good, but, to be brief, it was not right that he should ruin himself to oblige me. I should place myself in his position, and in that of other people, and I would soon admit, if I wanted to be at all truthful, that matters could not be arranged in the way I desired without thoroughly compromising him.

Thus, so as to deal me another blow, did he pretend to only desire my prosperity! Another person, who might have known him less well than I, would doubtless have fallen into the snare and moved heaven and earth, rather than not agree with his idea. But, as I was up to his tricks, I continued to fall back upon my poverty, which did not allow me to do everything which I wanted. The Cardinal was annoyed at not being able to get me to agree with him, and either because he was anxious to get rid of me without obtaining the reputation with which Navailles had threatened him, or that he really was afraid of making enemies by favouring me more than my comrades, he told me that, as I could not raise a sou, I must do something which would make my comrades hold their tongues, when they should see me pass in front of them. The King intended very shortly to take back the fortresses which M. le Prince had captured when passing over to the enemy. I must distinguish myself beyond others, and I would soon obtain the fulfilment of my desires.

This speech did not please me,—not that I valued my skin, as one might perhaps think. I had always done my duty everywhere, at least I flattered myself that no one had any other opinion about me. But, deeming all this but a rebuff, I found myself very embarrassed as to whether I ought to speak or remain silent. For if, on the one hand, I did not like to be played with further, on the other, I was afraid that, were I to persist in asking for leave to depart, I should be accused of having degenerated from that which up to that time I had always appeared to be. So, after having well thought over the matter, I resolved not only to remain, but besides, to do everything in the campaign which might put his Eminence in the wrong. In spite of this I was afraid that, though I might do my best, I should never succeed. There did not seem to me much probability of our doing anything considerable in that year.

The rebellion was still going on in Bordeaux, and,

since I had left, the Comte de Marcin, who had perceived that the Prince de Conti was quite ready to
play his brother false, had been watching him so
closely, that it was impossible for him to accomplish
all he was anxious to do. Meanwhile the people of
Bordeaux had been for some time suffering from the
miseries which civil war usually brings in its train.
Commerce was at a standstill, and the town was so
closely invested that nothing could enter the walls.
The sufferings of the populace caused them to cry out
for either peace or bread. The Ormistes, however,
who were afraid of receiving the punishment they
deserved, adopted a different tone. Marcin, who had
judgment and experience, sent word to the Prince
de Condé that, unless he should find means of quickly
succouring the town, everything would be lost for him
in that part of the country. The Ormistes, indeed,
still continued in a state of rebellion, but, as they were
hated by everyone, he did not dare to appear on very
good terms with them from fear of incurring the hatred
of the public. Everything depended upon the help he
was asking for and its speedy arrival.

M. le Prince, who could no longer amuse himself
with the ladies of Paris, who had made him let a good
many favourable opportunities slip, did not go to sleep
on this occasion. He sent a confidential man to
England to make representations to Cromwell (who
was still reigning there since the sad death of the late
King), to point out that his interests lay in taking the
city of Bordeaux under his protection. Cromwell,
who had other matters to attend to, would not en-
cumber himself with this as he had formerly done. He
had just declared war with the Dutch, because he had

observed that such a course was agreeable to his
nation, which was secretly jealous of that Republic,
and did not like to see it in the flourishing condition
which it was then in.   England would willingly have
given up everything to abate its power and force it to
bend to its sway.   For it is a characteristic of the English
to think no one their equal: so much so is this the
case that, had they as much ambition as they have
vanity, they would either soon render all nations sub-
servient to their own, or meet with the fate of Phaëton,
who met with destruction, as the fable tells us, for
having presumed too much on his own powers.   Be
this as it may, M. le Prince, having but wasted his
time in this quarter, had recourse to the Spaniards to
make up for Cromwell's unwillingness to help him.
Marcin had already sent as far as Madrid to obtain
the same assistance as the prince was now asking of
the archduke.   However, all these efforts came to
nothing; for, although a fleet was sent to succour
Bordeaux, it was eventually compelled to retire, after
having several times tried in vain to assist the besieged.

M. le Prince fared no better in what he did in
France.   Nevertheless, he had hoped to accomplish
marvels, on account of people still continuing to be
discontented with the Cardinal.   However, M. de
Turenne, whom the Court had sent against him,
having limited all these great plans at the taking of
Roye, which he even had to at once abandon, we
followed him to the Somme, where it was feared he
had an understanding with some governors of that
district.   Most of them indeed did not have many
scruples about betraying their master, so much so
that, had the Prince de Condé had any money to

bestow, many of them would have made no great difficulties about siding with him. But he was so poverty-stricken that, very far from being able to give others anything, he had not even enough for himself. The archduke gave him as little money as possible for some reason of his own.

M. le Prince did what he could to entice the Vicomte de Turenne to engage in battle. He calculated that, were he to be successful, he could re-enter France. The Cardinal had brought the King into our army and was wont to show him to the soldiers, to animate them against a rebel who was the more guilty because he was in duty bound to do just the opposite of what he was doing. M. de Turenne, who was very clever, did not think the time an opportune one to risk a battle; he told his Eminence so, and added that it was useless to promenade the King along the ranks as was being done. This was a good thing only when one wanted to animate people to accomplish, so to speak, the impossible. It would accordingly be much better for his Majesty to return to Paris than to stay any longer where he was, for his presence would be much more likely to produce a bad effect than a good one.

The Vicomte de Turenne was none too wrong to speak like this. The ardour which his Eminence had inspired the troops with by his tactics was so great, that they had already engaged in two or three skirmishes, which had seemed likely to be followed by a general engagement. The Cardinal had been much alarmed at this, and, if the Vicomte de Turenne had been less clever and careful than he was, I do not know what would have happened. I seized this

opportunity to distinguish myself, as his Eminence
had recommended me to do, but, either because he
was only trying to pick a quarrel with me, or that his
fright of things resulting in a battle was still power-
fully affecting him, instead of being pleased with me, I
found myself terribly abused. He reproached me with
not being at all the man he had thought me, and
declared that, had there been but two dozen men like
myself, we should have been followed by the whole
of the army. In reply I urged that, provided everyone had done their duty like myself, there would have
been no great danger in such a thing taking place: far
from it, we should soon have driven the enemy over
the Somme, for they were still this side of it, the
Prince de Condé making as if to attack now one
fortress and now another.

His Eminence took care not to agree with me, and,
having continued to abuse me more and more, I was
so pained that I resolved this time to go away without
even looking behind me. I told this to my most
intimate friends, and, not thinking he would be so
unjust as to refuse to let me sell my post, I sought
for a purchaser without speaking to him further on the
subject. Everyone agreed with me, so reasonable did
my resentment appear. His Eminence, meanwhile,
left the army, and hardly had he gone from our camp
than we were informed that the Bordeaux arrangement
had been completed. The Prince de Conti did all he
could to conceal from his brother's friends that he had
any hand in it. Finally, however, he raised the mask,
for further dissimulation would have availed him
nothing. His marriage was one of the clauses of the
treaty, and even the one which pleased him most, and

which was, as it were, its seal. He thought he could never have a wife soon enough, and, though he had already had too much to do with ladies—at least, whispered rumours said so, he had, all the same, a strange desire to try this one. To speak the truth, she was well worth it, and, though not quite as beautiful as her portrait, she was yet sufficiently so to thoroughly rouse his desires. He retired to Cadillac, where we were told he was undergoing treatment, to prepare for the amorous encounter which he was soon to wage with her. This made me tremble. I knew that there was one woman who had been common to both of us, and that, whether it was she who had made him the present, the effects of which he was now experiencing, or that it was he who was the giver, I ran a great risk of one day repeating the proverb: "For one pleasure a thousand pains."

Nothing reassured me in my alarm, except that I still continued to enjoy perfect health. Besides, the more I called to mind the complexion and face of the lady in question, the more it seemed to me that a great many rumours were fabricated, and that, though the whole of our army was filled with nothing but reports of this prince's malady, there was a great likelihood that all this was but slander.

I found a purchaser for my post as I had desired. An ensign of our regiment, who was one of my friends, knowing I wanted to get rid of it, informed a captain of the regiment of Rambures, who had a wish to serve in our corps. He was a long way away from us, and was serving in Italy. Nevertheless, having discussed the matter by letter exactly as we might have done if we had been in one another's presence, we agreed that

he should betake himself to Paris directly the campaign
should have ended. I was to present him to M. le
Cardinal, and, if he had any friends about him, he was
to make them speak in his favour, so that he might
approve of what he had done. He felt sure of obtaining
what he wanted, because he had served a long time,
and, besides, a captain in a regiment like his was
something in those days.

Both armies continued to pursue the campaign in
their different ways, M. le Prince being eventually
obliged to retreat across the Somme. Two regiments
of reinforcements, which came from the army of the
Duc de Candale, arrived at our camp and described
the surrender of Bordeaux, and how Orteste had been
captured while trying to escape. He had expiated his
crimes by the most cruel death which could be devised
for the most guilty of men. I asked for news of Las
Florides, being very much afraid that he had shared
the same fate. Both men were equally guilty, the only
difference being that one had been chief of the rebels,
and the other had not. However, he had, they said,
not been quite as unfortunate as his associate. Search
had been also made for him to kill him, and he had
very nearly been caught in a house to which he had
retired, but, having had presence of mind enough to
hide himself under the skirts of a dropsical woman, he
had escaped notice, because the enormous appearance
which the woman presented had been merely attributed
to her disease. He had then gained a ship which had
carried him to England for two hundred pistoles, and
was believed to be there now.

He was, as I have just said, quite as guilty as the
other man. He had committed a thousand robberies

and a thousand crimes just as Orteste might have done; but, however criminal he might be, as it is impossible, when once one knows anyone,. to wish him to end in such a way, unless all sentiments of humanity are totally discarded, I was in no wise vexed that he had thus found means to escape the punishment he deserved.

Meanwhile, M. le Cardinal made us cross into Champagne, and increased the army with troops under the Maréchal du Plessis and most of those who were returning from Bordeaux. We besieged Mouson, but M. le Prince as a set-off captured Rocroi. Eventually, Mouson was taken by our forces, and M. le Prince contented himself with giving the command at Rocroi to the Seigneur de Montal who had embraced his cause, and who was not one of his worst officers, both as to courage and discipline. This ended our campaign, and, as I now served only so to speak with regret, perceiving clearly that we were under a ministry which set more store on money than worth, I at once took post, more resolved than ever to retire.

The captain of the regiment of Rambures, with whom I had treated, had already arrived in Paris more than three weeks ago. He had his money quite ready to give me, and had sent me word to that effect on his arrival. We agreed together to see M. le Cardinal the Thursday following. This was still three days off, and we thought it best not to hurry more than this, so that the captain might have time to set his friends to work. One of them had a good deal of influence with the Cardinal : this was the Maréchal de Clérembaut,[1] a clever man, and who was as clever as he was skilful in his profession. Be this as it may, my captain having

1 Philippe de Clérembaut, Comte de Palluau (1606—1665).

begged him to be good enough to say a word to his Eminence in his favour, the maréchal replied that he was sorry that he did not ask for anything more important than that, so as to show him how delighted he would be to have an opportunity of doing him a service.   He went about it with much straightfor-wardness and fervour, unlike most courtiers, who promise things every hour and every minute, without having any intention of keeping their promise at one time more than another.   He spoke of it that very day to the minister, telling him that, however good a subject the individual might be whose place he was taking, the King would certainly not lose by the exchange.   For this he would go bail, and he was ready to answer for it himself, should he find that he had not told the truth.   M. le Cardinal received his petition not only with a gracious air, but with so many marks of favour, that the maréchal was quite delighted. The minister's answer was exactly similar to the one the maréchal had given the captain, to wit, that he was sorry that no greater opportunity of serving him presented itself, so that he might give a proof of the esteem he held him in.   He had but to hand his notes to M. le Tellier, and present to him on his behalf the person he was recommending.   He would at once settle the matter, and, as he knew his high opinion of him, he was certain it would be done with much pleasure on his part.

The maréchal withdrew, feeling the happiest man in the world on account of these fine words, and, having announced to the captain that M. le Cardinal had granted his request, arranged a time to take him to M. le Tellier.   The captain let me know this, thinking

to please me greatly by the news. He had observed
me very keen to resign, and did not believe I had
changed my mind since. I did not think so myself,
so much reason had I, did it seem to me, to complain
of the way I had been treated, but, eventually hearing
the thing was done, and that M. le Cardinal had made
not the least pretence of regretting me, I felt quite
differently at hearing this news than I should have
imagined. Nevertheless, I tried to hide my confusion
before the officer. I did not want him to be able some
day to repeat this weakness of mine to his Eminence,
and give him further this new subject for triumph,
after having already had so much reason for complaining of his behaviour. Accordingly, as I still pretended
to be of the same mind, the captain pressed me to
receive my money. He had deposited it with Le Cat
the Notary, and, enquiring whether I should like him to
bring it in an hour or two, he added, at the same time,
that he did not think he would have to wait for his
commission, because, provided I gave him my resignation, he reckoned that the affair could not fail to reach
a successful issue. I replied that he might have his
money brought me when he liked, and that, as to my
resignation, it was of no consequence. I was going to
pass the afternoon at a lawyer's, and would bring it
back with me, so, if he would return and see me about
seven in the evening, or the next morning, it would be
a settled thing and one requiring no further thought.
He had but to choose his time, and he would find me
at home at the hour I should appoint.

Directly he had left my house, I duly went to a
lawyer whom I knew, to arrange what I had told him.
I deemed that, as I had to swallow this cup, I had

better do so with a good grace than reluctantly. I
was too haughty and too proud to do otherwise:
besides which, I should have been acting in an un-
gentlemanly way, were I now to draw back, since it
was myself who had petitioned for my retirement. My
captain did not fail to return in the evening, though
he had not yet been to the house of M. le Tellier.
Some work had prevented the maréchal from going
with him. He had put the matter off till the next
morning, and they were to go together. He brought
with him twelve thousand crowns, which was the
price we had both agreed on, and, having shut them
up in a coffer which was in a cabinet which stood not
far from my bed, I placed my resignation in his hands.
The next day, I took a thousand crowns from this
coffer to go and pay my debts, so that, directly it was
done, I might leave Paris and take the rest with me
to Bearn. This was settled in the course of the
morning, and, having gone in the afternoon to bid fare-
well to my friends, I did not forget M. de Navailles.
He was quite astounded at the speech I made, telling me
with an air of friendship that what I had done was a piece
of gross stupidity, and that, had I come to him for
advice again, he would (had he any influence over me)
have dissuaded me! I replied, that the thing was
settled, and one must think no more about it ; besides,
M. le Cardinal did not value me enough to cause me
any regrets at leaving him. This indeed was not
what he had sometimes promised, but one ought not
to rely on the promises of great people any more than
on a winter's sun. Both were apt to be soon obscured
by clouds, and of that I was now having a sad proof,
without having to draw upon the evidence of others.

Having parted thus, he thinking never to set eyes on me again, and I for my part being of the same opinion, I went to complete my visits. I spent all the remainder of the afternoon doing this, and, one of my friends having begged me to sup with him, I only returned home about eleven at night. The landlord with whom I lodged told me on my arrival that M. de Navailles had twice sent for me, and that, his lackey having found me on neither occasion, he himself had just been to tell me to wait for him the next morning. He had something of consequence to tell me, and he had given him strict injunctions to let me know. I was not, I confess, unmoved by this news; I was going away, but regretfully, so, flattering myself that the important news he had to tell me was, that I was to stay, I lingered agreeably on such an idea. I imagined that M. le Cardinal was about to do something for me, and that he must have informed me of it. I did not sleep a wink the whole night, so impatient was I to learn whether I was deceived or not. The night, nevertheless, seemed very long to me, for there is nothing more wearisome than not to sleep when one has gone to bed. Nevertheless, it having passed just as any other might have done, before it was yet six o'clock M. de Navailles was announced. I was stretched out in my bed, and, having got into an arm-chair near my couch, he told me that M. le Cardinal did not want me to depart. He had never been so surprised as when he had learnt of my selling my post, for he had not thought that it was mine that the Maréchal de Clérembaut had asked to dispose of. For this reason, he had at once sent to M. le Tellier to forbid him to

deliver the documents.   M. de Navailles added that all
would be well for me, unless he was much deceived,
and that was why I must appear at the morning
audience of his Eminence, to thank him for the
interest which he seemed to take in my affairs.   He
had called upon me the previous evening, so as to
let me know this good news, and had again returned
this morning for the same purpose; for, although no
one was up at the present hour, it had been his
opinion that, had he even been more matutinal than
he was, I should have found no fault, because one
could never be too early to announce such news as
this!

I thanked him to the best of my abilities for the
warmth with which he still continued to manifest his
friendship.   He then went to his work, and scarcely
had he left when my captain entered with a sorrowful
face, and one on which it was easy to read his grief.
He told me he was bringing back my resignation,
because M. le Tellier had sent to tell the Maréchal
de Clérembaut that M. le Cardinal had forbidden him
to issue the necessary documents.   He had been
astounded to the last degree, because this was not
only inconsistent with his word which he had given
to the maréchal, when he had spoken to him on his
behalf, but also contrary to the assurance which M. le
Tellier had also given him when they had been to see him
together.   It was true that the latter had appeared
very much surprised, when the maréchal had told him
that the discussion was concerning my post.   But
eventually, he had not failed to be as civil as possible,
and to promise him as well a thousand fine things on
account of the influence which had been employed.

He could not divine the origin of this change, but most likely I could let him know, were I to trouble to do so, since it seemed impossible for me to know nothing about it.

I answered him quite sincerely that all that I could say was, that I had been informed that M. le Cardinal would not consent to my giving up my post; that I had just heard this from M. de Navailles, who had that moment left me; that this change surprised me just as much as himself, because it seemed to me that this minister ought not to change his mind so soon concerning me, after the little attention he had a thousand times bestowed on the matter. M. le Maréchal de Clérembaut must, I added, have told him that it was my post he was discussing, whilst he was asking to have the disposal of it, so it was surprising enough, and even incomprehensible that, after having consented in the way he had, he should now be unwilling to give his assent.

The captain rejoined that, when the maréchal had spoken of it, no one had been mentioned by name. He had only asked the Cardinal for the disposal of a lieutenancy in the Guards, without specifying the person from whom he was going to purchase it. There lay his mistake, and the apparent cause of the Cardinal retracting his word. Nevertheless, I must take consolation, since, if this minister did not want to ruin me, as seemed likely, he might not be so considerate towards everyone else. One of my comrades would some time be discovered, who would be willing to get rid of his lieutenancy, and, as he now knew how to manage matters in a way to encounter no obstacles, he would, on another occasion, when desirous of pur-

chasing the post, not fail to do everything necessary.
At the same time, he asked me for the return of his
money, as it was right that I should give it back, but,
having used up a thousand crowns of it, I replied that
for the present all I could do was to return eleven
thousand crowns, because, as I had believed I was to
depart in less than forty-eight hours, I had made use
of the rest to pay my debts. I added that I was now
very sorry for this, but, not having been able to foresee
what was happening to-day, he must give me a little
time to meet the situation.

This captain was rather a hard man, so, instead of
receiving my excuse civilly, he retorted, roughly enough,
that he did not understand how I made this out. One
ought never, it appeared to him, to dispose of money
which was not one's own and his did not belong to me
till such time as he should have been established in my
post. This was the custom of good society, without
it being permissible in any way to pass its limits. I
replied (without taking either a higher or lower tone,
for, had I spoken more haughtily, it might, perhaps,
have seemed as if I was trying to pick a quarrel with
him, because I owed him money) that I agreed that
such was the custom about a deposit, but his money
had appeared to me to be my own property, and, consequently, I had been able to dispose of it as I had
done, without violating the most strict rules of honesty.
I was, however, sorry for it to-day, since things had
turned out differently. This was all I could plead in
my own justification, always supposing that I had
made a mistake, for which excuse was necessary. In
spite of this, I thought there was no need of any, and,
doubtless, he would form just the same opinion as

myself, were he to be willing to think the matter over a little.

The captain was so uncivil, or, to be more accurate, so brutal, as not to be satisfied with my answer. He was beginning to irritate me terribly. I was not at all long-suffering by nature, so I felt my gorge rising more than once. Nevertheless, having again mastered myself, so as to make no retort, because, as money was concerned, I feared that, however right I might be, people might perhaps not be willing to forego applying that proverb to me which says, " he who owes is in the wrong," it appeared as if my patience was making him even more insolent than before. At last, having bitten my lips several times to stop my saying that which my resentment brought to the tip of my tongue, one of my friends chanced to enter my room without in any way knowing what was going on. He had only learnt how my affairs had turned out at Court, and had come to congratulate me. This he thought himself the more forced to do, because I had always held him in particular esteem, and because he had never been willing to approve (any more than had M. de Navailles) of my giving up everything, as I had been desirous of doing. I was delighted to see him, as I had need of a witness who could give an account of my behaviour, especially were the captain to oblige me to resort to force, to protect myself against his insolence. Accordingly, making no difficulties about at once telling him what was occurring between us two, he raised his voice to tell this captain that, in his opinion, he was wrong. There was no likelihood of my running away on account of a matter of a thousand crowns, and, even had I spent the whole of his money, no one could have blamed me for it, since, as I had

very excellently told him, I had had good reason to
deem it my own.

The captain, who was a good deal more selfish than
reasonable, rejoined that the speaker was too great
a friend of mine for him to consent to share his views,
and, still continuing to upbraid me as he had begun
to do, my friend ended by not having as much patience
as I had had. He told him that he must certainly be
paid without a moment's delay, since he was not the
man to grant a respite. He himself would go and get
the thousand crowns, but would take care, whilst going
to find them, to furnish himself with a friend who
would help him to prove to both of us that his sword
was as good as his tongue was evil. The captain
answered that, if that was the only thing needful to
restore his money to him, the matter should be soon
settled. He had but to set out to get it, and he for his
part would prepare to act on his proposal. Both my
friend and myself really believed that he was speaking
sincerely, and just as we might have done, had we
been in his position. However, instead of carrying
out what he had told us, he betook himself to the
house of the Maréchal de Clérembaut, before whom he
laid his demands. He told him that, instead of returning his money, I admitted having spent a part of it.
This the maréchal believed, not knowing that the
captain was an ill-bred fellow ; so, a moment later, I
received a visit from a guard, who brought an order
for me to appear before MM. les Maréchaux de France,
to account for my actions. Never was man so astounded
as I at the appearance of the guard ! I at once suspected on whose behalf he had been sent, and he
himself admitted the truth of my suspicions to me.

Meanwhile, my friend returned with the thousand
crowns he had promised. He had just sold his silver

plate to get me out of this mess. He was nearly as astonished as myself, when he perceived the guard, and would hardly have believed that he had come in connection with the captain's business, had I not told him that the man had been the first to admit it. However, even had he not been willing to do so, both of us would not have failed to have known it : for, far from the captain returning as he had promised, he did not show himself again to us, except at the meeting of the Maréchaux de France. The Maréchal de Clérembaut caused this meeting to be held the same day by his personal influence, and, having been notified to attend, I previously took my guard to the house of M. de Navailles, whom I wished to tell that I should not be able to go and thank M. le Cardinal at his morning-audience, as I had been recommended to do, on account of the unfortunate occurrence which had happened to me. I did not find him at home, and, having written a note to let him know, my servant was never able to deliver it to him, although I expressly sent it to the house of M. le Cardinal, where I was well aware he would be. He was, indeed, there, but a guard, who disliked me, and who was at the door, having been malicious enough to refuse my man entrance, the latter had not the sense to complain either to Besmaux or to some other officer of that company,[1] so as to have the soldier called to order. As all the officers were friends of mine, or, at least, acquaintances, they would certainly have procured him access to M. de Navailles, for whom he was searching. His stupidity having duly caused this mishap, M. le Cardinal was very much scandalised at not

1 Cardinal Mazarin's Musketeers, afterwards the 2nd Company of Musketeers, known as "Les Mousquetaires noirs" from their black horses.

seeing me. It had been by his orders that Navailles
had come to visit me, though he had made a mystery
of it ; so, believing that I might, perhaps, have taken
post to depart, as it had been reported to him that I
had received my money, he told Navailles that, if I
had done such a thing as that, after having received his
message, I might rely that he would have me arrested
wherever I might be. Navailles made answer that his
Eminence would be doing just the right thing, but
added that he did not think he would be put to that
trouble. He knew me too well even to impute such a
thing to me. It was true I did not belie my birth in
the way of being proud, but, whatever pride I might
have, I was wont to always moderate it by reason. If
the Cardinal wished it, he would set out that very
minute, to discover the cause of my having failed in
my duty, and would immediately bring back the
answer.

The Cardinal was too diplomatic to consent to such
a thing as this. He would have been afraid of my
getting too much the whip-hand of him, and of my
thinking that he could no longer do without me. It
was for this reason that he had instructed Navailles
not to tell me on his visit that he had come on his behalf. Being therefore intent on pursuing the same
policy for the present, he told him that it must not
be he who should go, it had much better be Besmaux,
because his going would seem of much less importance.
He would merely have to pretend that he had heard of
my having wanted to depart, and had consequently
come to congratulate me on matters having turned out
differently.

Navailles agreed with him that he was right, and
would even have done so had he not been, to such an

extent was he wont to give way to all his wishes!   He
went to tell Besmaux, who was in the guard-room,
what his Eminence desired of him.   Besmaux set out
to go and see me, and as an hour had already elapsed
since I had returned from my ineffectual visit to
Navailles, he found me quite alone with my guard.
My friend had gone away, and had strongly insisted
upon my keeping the thousand crowns, though I had
tried to force him to take them back.   I had alleged
as a reason that, as the man we were dealing with had
failed to keep his word, it was no longer necessary to
make a point of paying him so soon.   MM. les Maréchaux de France would listen to reason better than he,
and would thus not refuse me the time I might ask
for.   At the same time I had tried to oblige him to
return to get his silver plate, offering to myself give
the silversmith whatever he might ask as the price of
returning it.   However, after having scoffed at my
offers as being unworthy of being made to a friend,
he had told me that he desired me to keep this money,
because he had an idea in his head, which did not
accord with the reception which I intended giving
this captain.

Besmaux congratulated me with a much heavier
heart than Navailles had ever had.   Being a man, as I
think I have already said, who knew nothing about
friendship when his own interests were concerned, far
from telling me, or making me realise by well-chosen
words what was going on, as sometimes is done
amongst people of the same province, and those who
have some mutual bond, he made no mention of
the Cardinal on one side or the other, and I did the
same thing, not alluding to the reason of the guard being
with me.   However, he could not be deceived on the

subject, as the man was in a decent dress. He bore on his back the signs of his occupation, as that sort of man usually does. In spite of this, Besmaux was curious enough to ask me what could have occurred to have gained me such a companion. However, as I desired that it should be Navailles who should describe this affair to the Cardinal, I contented myself with making reply, that it was a question of money which had involved me in a dispute with an individual, and not having been able to arrange it in a friendly manner, we had to have the affair settled by MM. les Maréchaux de France. I had but spoken the truth in telling him this; so, deeming it a true account, he left me a moment later to go and describe to his Eminence both what he had seen, and what I had told him.

Before allowing him to depart, I entrusted him with the letter which I had written to Navailles, and which my lackey had brought back to me. This letter appeased the anger of M. le Cardinal, when Navailles had shown it to him, and when he had told him that my not appearing at his audience had been through no fault of my own. At the same time, Navailles told him that I was very unfortunate, since trouble overcame me when I least expected it. The Cardinal broke off the conversation, being afraid that he merely said this in order to make him understand that he ought to pay the liability for me, whilst awaiting an opportunity of doing me some good turn. Navailles came to see me about the matter, and declared that he was very much put out at not having the ready money handy to offer me on this occasion. I thanked him, not for his good will, but for his kind speeches. Indeed, I knew that he might not only have lent me this sum had he liked, but even thirty times as much, had it been needed. Of all the courtiers of his Eminence, there was not one whose affairs were in such a good state as his were. He had obtained an infinite number of favours from that minister, so much so, that it might be said that, avaricious as he was with regard to others, Navailles had found means to change his character as far as he himself was concerned. Meanwhile, as one must take the good with the bad in one's friends, I took care not to show that his words annoyed me. On the contrary, I was as civil as I could possibly be, to that degree that he left me in great good humour.

My friend, who had lent me the thousand crowns, came to dine with me. He had bidden me wait for him, and, having drawn me aside when we had risen from table, he said that, when I should appear before MM. les Maréchaux de France, I must not make any mention at all of him, unless my opponent should speak first on the subject. Should he not do so, I could pay him off in due time, and declare that I had found my thousand crowns in the purse of one of my friends. Were he, however, to speak of him, I must ask for time to pay these three thousand crowns. This he deemed necessary, to do away with the suspicion that the captain might have been called out for being such a coward as to lodge a complaint about this affair. Accordingly, I must deny it like "murder itself," for I might, perhaps, not be aware that edicts existed, which threatened heavy penalties against those who might challenge others to the prejudice of the law.

My friend stayed with me till three o'clock, and, as this was about the time that the meeting of the Maréchaux de France was to take place, I entered a carriage with three or four of my friends, who were desirous of accompanying me, for it is the custom not to allow those called before this court to go there quite alone: so, the more friends one has, the better company one goes in. The Maréchal de Clérembaut was there, and though, perhaps, this was the first time that he found himself the sovereign judge of the nobility, (for it was but a very short time that he had been honoured with the baton of a Maréchal de France), he did nearly everything he could to prove that my conduct had not been straightforward. I asked him, with all the respect which was his due, and which I should not have owed him six months before (for he was of no better family than anyone else), in what respect I could be accused of bad faith, as he urged? I, who had disposed of money which I deemed to legitimately belong to me! He was extremely surprised at my firmness, and even more so at my reasoning being just as fair as his own.[1] As he spoke a good deal, and even spoke very well, he had thought to at once overcome me by his cackle! The other maréchaux listened to me, and could not disapprove of the liberty I was taking by contradicting my accuser. Nevertheless, as there are no judges who do not support one another, especially when they see that one of their number is attacked in their own tribunal, the Maréchal d'Estrées, who gloried in overriding everyone, asked me what I expected to gain by all my

[1] D'Artagnan here speaks ironically. The Maréchal de Clérembault stammered and expressed himself only with great difficulty. Madame Cornuel, with whom he had a liaison, after a final interview, said: " It is a pity he is going away, I was just beginning to understand him."

arguments, and whether I thought they would get me off paying?

Though he said this rudely enough, I was delighted that I was asked for nothing more but payment. I was afraid that something further might be brought against me on the score of the challenge made to my adversary by my friend, and that both of us might be sent to prison. My opponent was present at the whole of the proceedings, and I tried to irritate him, so as to make him blurt out all his grievances. I tried after this to defend myself, according to my friend's advice: but, having remained silent for a long time, I no sooner perceived that he had been wise enough not to implicate others from fear of losing his own reputation, than I told the Maréchal d'Estrées, by way of answer to the piece of rudeness he had just favoured me with, that neither he nor the other Maréchaux de France would ever have seen me before them, had I had to deal with a man with sufficient patience to wait merely twenty-four hours. As a matter of fact, I had already procured the thousand crowns which I lacked to complete his money, and it but lay with him to now come and get them. I was very malicious in speaking thus. I wanted to frighten the captain, knowing from experience that he was none too bold. My adversary at the same time, raising his voice, replied that there was no need for him to go: for, since he had brought the crowns to my house, I ought to have them returned to his, or, at least, to his lawyer's, which was half-way. This lawyer lived quite close to St. Eustache, the captain near Ste. Marie,[1] and myself close to the Palais Royal.

[1] Sainte Marie-l'Égyptienne at the corner of the Rue Montmartre and the Rue de la Jussienne, which last word is a corruption of Égyptienne.

Upon this, the Maréchal de Clérembaut spoke, declaring that, after this gentleman's having cited me before the court, he did not think it very fit that we should meet each other face to face before our dispute should be completely adjusted. So, if his advice were followed, I ought to carry this money to the lawyer, who would return me my resignation. His views were those of the other Maréchaux de France, and, all being of the same opinion, I took these twelve thousand crowns to the house of Le Cat, where the captain did not dare to be to receive them. This did not prevent my giving them to the lawyer, and, he having returned my resignation to me, the affair would have ended there, had not all which had passed lain heavy on the hearts of myself and my friend. Accordingly, we longed to obtain satisfaction: this is why my friend, having gone to find the captain, the next morning caught him while rising from his bed, so that he could not get out of the affair, if he were a man of the slightest spirit. However, as he was not, no sooner did he hear what my friend had to say (which was that he would always show him up as being a coward, unless he gave us satisfaction), than he answered that, please God, he would never make such a mistake as that. He knew that MM. les Maréchaux de France had forbidden us not only to resort to any violence, but, further, had reconciled us both. Accordingly, as it would be making himself doubly guilty to break their decrees, since it would be wanting in respect to them and to his Majesty, he had taken care to do nothing contrary to his duty. My friend was an extremely violent man, so, not parleying with the captain in any way after this reply nor restraining himself, he told him so many

offensive things, that the man made pretence of being
offended. Declaring that honour was concerned, he
appointed a meeting-place in the Bois de Boulogne for
us to fight, two against two. My friend came to tell
me all this, and how he had had to provoke my
adversary to render him sensitive. I deemed all this
augured none too well, and, telling him at once, as
if by inspiration, that perfidy was in the air, and that
I would advise him not to keep this appointment, he
replied that he would not prevent me from failing to
go, did I feel at all suspicious. For himself, he would
take care not to miss it, even were his existence at
stake. His honour was dearer to him than his life,
and, as it would suffer if he did not keep this appointment, it was his firm intention to be the first on the
spot.

Such words as these were calculated to make me forget
the remembrance of the obligation I was under to him !
No man had ever been told, as he was telling me, that,
were I afraid, I had but to go and hide myself. True
it is that he had not exactly used these terms. He had
seen fit to conceal what he thought beneath other
phrases not quite so harsh, but which yet meant but
the same thing to those who knew French well. In
consequence, I was so outraged that, had I been able
to engage in combat with him on the spot, without
having exposed myself to censure, I should have done
so with all the pleasure in the world. Nevertheless,
as I was afraid that the world might dub me as being
a mere monster of ingratitude, I adopted a more con-
ciliating tone with him. I pointed out that, if reason
showed me that some danger existed, there was on
that account no cause for saying that my courage was

impaired thereby. He had but to lead me where he liked, I would follow to the end. He might repent of it just as much as myself, but it should make no difference to me, since such was his wish.

My friend pretended not to hear my words, and, having the next morning made me mount horse, we took the road called the Chemin des Bons Hommes, to enter the Bois de Boulogne by the gate which lies on that side of it. The meeting agreed on was to take place between seven or eight o'clock in the morning, and, having betaken ourselves to the gate, we found it shut, at which I was surprised enough. It is true that we were then in the shortest days of the year, which made me, after some reflection, think that it arose merely from laziness having overcome the porter, and that he had not yet risen. We knocked, in order to have the gate opened, and the porter, having at once appeared, told my friend, who was the first to approach him, that he must return to Paris without losing a moment's time, for he would inevitably be lost were he to advance but a quarter of a league into the Bois. It was full of archers ready to capture him on account of information received, that he was coming to fight a duel of two against two.

The porter had been my friend's servant fifteen or sixteen years before, and, as he kept a wine-shop, he had obtained this information from an archer who had slept at his house and had given him a description of what was on foot, after drinking without knowing his connection with my friend. This had been the cause of his having shut the door, from fear of our making our appearance without his perceiving us. My friend was much surprised to hear him speak like this, and

told me that I had been more in the right than himself; for this reason, he now thought that we should
not be far wrong, were we to retrace our steps without
even having the curiosity to look behind us. I was
delighted that he should take this line of his own
accord, both because our safety was concerned, and
because it would make him repent of his having insulted me as he had done. We immediately returned
to Paris, and my friend having on the way asked my
pardon for his angry behaviour to me, I made reply
that it was very necessary to put up with certain
things from one's friend, when one knew, as I had
known in his case, that their intentions were not
malicious.

The captain, after having waited for us some time in
the Bois, had the insolence to come and look for my
friend at his very house in company with his pretended
second, to ask him the reason of our not having made
our appearance on the ground. He intended apparently to invest himself with a good deal of glory at
having caught us in fault, but my friend, who had not
allowed me to say one word, without getting angry
at its not having been to his taste, was up in arms
directly he heard the man speak in this way. At once
drawing his sword, and without giving him time to
utter any more similar speeches, he taunted him with
not contenting himself with being a coward, and
further declared that it was no fault of his that he had
not added betrayal to his lack of courage. The captain pretended not to understand what he meant by
this and asked for an explanation, so that he might
answer it. My friend would give him no other than
that which he was presenting to him, that is to say,

a chance of fighting.   But as, when once a man is full
of feebleness, nothing can spur him on to do a good
deed, my friend might well present the point of his
sword at his stomach ; the captain could never make up
his mind to put his hand to his own weapon!   His
second did just the same before me, so much so, that
it seemed as if he had been chosen as being the double
of his principal, so that neither might reproach the
other.   I also held my sword in front of his stomach,
but, perceiving that he was just as callous as his
comrade, I began to give my friend the signal as to
how we ought to treat these two worthies.   My signal
went beyond the usual ones and even beyond ordinary
practical demonstration, for I set to to give my unwilling opponent a series of blows on the head with the
flat of my sword, a thing he bore with a patience
which surprised me.   This did not all the same occur
without his at first making some move.   He attempted
to get to the door, and having happily reached it, shut
it on himself to save me, as it seemed, the trouble of
escorting him any further.

The captain was at once treated by my friend in
just the same way as his second had been by me, and
exactly followed his example.   He allowed himself to
be beaten without making even the least show of
revenging himself, and, having tried to run away just
as the other had done, made an effort to open the
door.   It but lay with my friend to run him right
through.   The man's back was turned towards him,
and could not have been in a better position, but, as
an honourable man never sullies his hands with the
blood of a wretch who, far from trying to defend
himself, seeks only to escape, my friend himself opened

the door, so as this coward might reach the staircase. He did not need twice telling, and, having run down it with quite unusual agility, the point of his sword caught in the banister-rails of the staircase, and nearly broke his neck. He fell on his nose, his sword having broken in two owing to the resistance it met with while he was rushing down. The landlord of my friend, who had already heard the noise on the stairs, when the second had taken the trouble to make his exit, came up to see what this fresh disturbance might betoken, and found the captain, who had not, so to speak, the courage to get up again. Although he had as yet but received some blows from the flat of a sword, it seemed to him every minute that my friend was going to run him through, because he had enjoyed following him, to observe the state of fright he was reduced to. He consequently set up a howl that he was dead, and the landlord, being afraid that he had some sword-thrust in his body, because he noticed that my friend was seeing him out, sword in hand, placed himself in front of him to prevent his being finished off. Seeing this rampart, the captain seized the opportunity to rise, but, as the end of his sword was in its sheath, and this sheath, which was also broken, hanging between his legs, he tumbled down a second time, which strangely alarmed the landlord. This second fall broke his nose, and the blood at once running down his face, he immediately believed, not only (as he had already done) that he was wounded, but further, that his hurt was mortal, since he had not been able to take two steps without falling down afresh. The fear the landlord was in of his dying in his house, and that a guard would at once be placed there, as usually

16—2

happens in such a case, made him immediately call
out to his wife to quickly send for some chairmen, so
as to put the captain in a sedan-chair. There was
a stand of chairmen at the corner of the street, so, the
chair having not been long in arriving, the captain,
who had his handkerchief to his nose, was placed inside. So confused was he as to not say one word.
Nevertheless, as fear still overcame him, he was as
pale as a freshly disinterred corpse. His silence and
general condition, therefore, made the landlord more
and more certain that his end was not far off, and
fearing the results of such an affair, he told my friend
that, to guarantee him against the effects of this
assassination, and also for his own safety, he should
take the necessary legal steps. My friend, who knew
that his sword had not been nearer than half a foot to
the captain's body, clearly perceived that it was fear
which made him speak thus. He was eager to cure
him of it, and having replied that he should calm his
fears, since all the blood which had been spilt could be
but the result of the hurt the captain had sustained
from his fall, the landlord's spirits began to revive.
My friend even gave him a description of what had
happened, so as to further reassure him. The landlord enjoyed this account by reason of the interest he
took in the whole affair. Nevertheless, as he was a
sensible enough man, and from a province besides,
where people understand legal quibbles to the tips of
their fingers from their cradle up, he told my friend
that, though there was no one killed nor even wounded,
he must not, all the same, fail to take the proper steps.
The more cowardly the man he had to deal with, the
more likely he would be to serve him some other dirty

turn. The trick he had tried to play him in the Bois de Boulogne was a specimen of his methods. He should be careful, and, added he, there was no better piece of advice than this that could possibly be given him.

I do not know for what reason my friend had wasted his time in describing to this man that we had wanted to fight, and, in addition, that we had taken horse expressly for this purpose. As for myself, I should have behaved differently, had I been in his place; but, as he was hasty, and as vivacity has the bad quality of very often making people do things thoughtlessly, he had, no doubt, begun his story without having thought over the matter in any way whatever. Be this as it may, not despising such a warning as this, he resolved to follow it, after having asked my opinion. I disliked everything which goes by the name of legal proceedings, good and bad alike, a circumstance which usually inspired me with much aversion for everything which tended in such a direction. But the captain's behaviour showing me that more careful precautions should be taken in respect to him than with other people, I agreed to all my friend wished to do. We sent to find a commissaire, and, having lodged our complaint, setting forth that this captain, in company with one of his friends, had come to challenge us, the landlord, who was from a district where no law-suit has ever been lost for want of false witnesses, confirmed our statement by his evidence. In spite of this, he knew nothing except what my friend had told him; but, as he would have belied his birth-place, if he had testified only what he knew, he did not trouble himself with such a detail. He did far more, being afraid that

what he had said would not suffice; he further furnished
us with two other witnesses, who were from the same
part of the country and were no more scrupulous than
himself. They declared that they had been at his
house when this challenge was made, and, having
testified to our unwillingness to accept it, they signed
their evidence just in the same way as if it had
contained only what was true.

The captain was not from the same province as
these people; whereas they were from the city of
Mans, he was from Montpellier, but, as cowards such
as he always take crooked paths, he was no sooner
outside my friend's lodgings than he deliberated how
he might avenge the insult he had just received. At
first, this seemed to him difficult enough, because he
had himself gone to court his misfortunes, and there
was a likelihood that he would, without fail, be asked
what he had come to do there. Nevertheless, maliciousness possessing this especial quality, that it soon
smoothes away all difficulties which may lie in its path,
he for his part betook himself to a commissionaire,
with whom he lodged the following depositions:—
"Having found in the sum of money which I had
returned to him some false pieces, and ones which
had not been among those he had given me, he had
gone to find me at my house to return them. Not
wishing, however, to go there quite alone, on account
of his having caused me to appear before MM. les
Maréchaux de France, he had begged one of his friends
to accompany him. They had not found me at home,
and, discovering that I had gone to my friend's house,
they had both proceeded to look for me there, but not
only had I had evil conscience enough to deny that

I had ever given him the money in question, but, further, the boldness to insult him in my friend's room. My friend himself had done just the same thing to please me, so much so that, having snatched up his pistols, he would certainly have killed him, had he not attempted to escape. For this purpose he had thought it best to make for the stairs, but, before reaching the bottom, my friend had called out to his servants to lay hands upon him and to break his sword. Three or four of them had assaulted him with their sticks and any other arms which had been first to hand. He had received several blows, and his sword had been broken in its scabbard."

As he had hurt himself in the fall, the blows he spoke of seemed real enough to the commissaire, but all the same, as the most necessary thing of all was lacking—which was to have witnesses—this captain had the landlord sounded, to find out whether he would not be inclined, in consideration of a certain sum, to do a portion of what he wanted. The land-lord might, perhaps, have been the man for him, had he set about bribing him earlier in the day, but, after having testified against him as he had just done, he did not think he could carry out his wishes with any safety as regards his own conscience, or, rather, his own person.

He let us know of the proposal made him, so that we might be grateful to him for his fidelity. Notwith-standing this, we did not value it very much more, for, though we were obliged to him for having done what we wanted, as false witnesses are held in no esteem (although they are occasionally employed), this seemed as a proof that, very far from repenting of his behaviour, he was further ready to stick to his evidence like grim death.

The captain, perceiving that he could find no witnesses, and that his declarations would, in consequence, vanish into thin air, adopted the course of setting out for his own province, to there go and conceal his infamy. He no longer thought of entering the Guards, in which corps there was reason for thinking I should not give him too good a reputation, as long as I continued to serve. Meanwhile, it only lay with my friend and myself to press him terribly, and we were strongly urged to take this course by the commissaire who had taken our depositions. As he resembled the surgeons, who cry out only for wounds and bumps, he came himself to find us, to enquire if we would allow our proceedings to remain where they were. He pointed out that we ought not to stop after making such a good start, for, had the captain the same hold over us as we had over him, he would not let it slip through his fingers. Apparently, he had heard speak of the declaration which he had caused to be drawn up, and he tried to irritate us by mentioning it, but, as what we had done had been only to guard against his maliciousness, and, as we had been fairly successful, since we had obliged him to decamp, we did not think fit to give this blood-sucker a chance of exercising his calling.

After the events I have described, I went to thank M. le Cardinal for what he had done for me. He declared that I had not been deserving of his goodness. I had wanted to leave him without letting him have a single word. My reply was, that he did not then remember that I had before spoken to him on the

subject, and begged him to refresh his memory. He
rejoined that he perfectly recollected everything which
had passed on that head, but that, as he had since
spoken to me, and as my last exploit was a novelty
which I could not excuse, the best thing I could do
was to make no further mention of the matter. His
liking for me was greater than I thought, and he would
give me proof of this before long. He had already
spoken in this strain, so, after that, though he appeared
on this occasion to be doing so more sincerely than
ever, I was not sure whether I ought to repose any
more trust in his words. Time alone, however, being
the only thing which could instruct me as to this, I
left matters to him without troubling any more about
them.

At that time he was in fairly high spirits. He had
just retaken Mouson and St. Menehout, and, though
we had lost Rocroi, he hoped to recapture it without
striking a blow. His ideas about this were based on
the opinion he had once expressed to me, that the
French were greater slaves to money than all the
other nations of Europe. There had, indeed, been
some truth in such a statement of late, either because
we had been taking lessons from him, as I have before
said, or because there is no people which is not eventually corrupted, when one takes to tempt them by their
own gain. His Eminence had tried this not long ago,
that is to say, when it was a question of making the
cities of Paris and Bordeaux return to their duty. The
Cardinal de Retz had facilitated the surrender of the
one on account of obtaining a Cardinal's hat, and the
promise of some money to help him pay his debts.
It is true that he had ulterior objects in view, having

flattered himself that he might himself become Prime
Minister, but, as he had thought of this only as a last
resource, it was clear that, by his conduct, he had in
no way falsified the opinion which Cardinal Mazarin
held regarding the whole of our nation.

The same thing applied to the Prince de Conti;
though the desire of exchanging his priest's robe for a
wife had much contributed to his going over to his
brother, there is much the same likelihood that he
would have held out more firmly, had it not been for
the splendid promises made to him.   Meantime, he
awaited their fulfilment at Cadillac without seeing the
least appearance of its taking place.   The Cardinal
cunningly threw difficulties in the way, so as to manage to marry off another of his nieces at the expense
of the one promised to the Prince de Conti.   Prince
Thomas, who had married the sister of the late Comte
de Soissons, had suggested his son to his Eminence as
a husband, stipulating that he should be given back
the post of grand master of the King's household,
which he maintained belonged to his wife.   It had
been given to the Prince de Condé, the father of
the duc, and the rebellion of the present prince seemed
to serve as a pretext for its return.   The young Comte
de Soissons appeared an acceptable enough suitor to
the Cardinal, so he continued to trifle with the Prince
de Conti, thinking that, once he should have married
La Martinôzi, he would find means to appease any
irritation he might feel!   Be this as it may, having
made himself master of Paris and Bordeaux, he
thought he could do the same thing with Rocroi,
which was nothing in comparison with these two
towns.

What further raised his hopes was, that its commander, Montal by name, was but a poor gentleman
who had not a thousand crowns in the world; so, as
princes of the blood and of the house of Savoy were
governed by self-interest, his Eminence did not imagine
that such an insignificant personage would resist their
example. The puzzling thing was, through whom and
how to make proposals to him. There was no one
who could be trusted in the vicinity of Rocroi. The
governors of Mézières, of Charleville and also of Rhetel,
the three nearest towns, were to be regarded with great
suspicion. To employ Fabert would have aroused
attention, and besides, he and Montal were none too
friendly.

I chanced to present myself before the Cardinal one
day that he had been pondering over this matter, and,
observing his pre-occupation, told him that I was very
unhappy at his not entrusting me with some mission of
importance, by which I could prove my devotion. This
speech gave him an opportunity of confiding in me,
and he spoke of his plan and the obstacles to its
accomplishment. In reply, I declared that it appeared
to me that he was worrying himself over a small
matter, and, if he would send me as part of the garrison of Rhetel, with three or four companies of our
regiment, I would soon see what stuff this Montal was
made of. His Eminence answered that there were
many difficulties in the way; Montal was somewhat
scrupulous, and besides, M. le Prince had spies everywhere, who informed him of all that took place. He
was right as to this; many of the King's officers were
in communication with the Prince de Condé, whom
they admired for his great deeds. They only served

the King on account of the pay they received, and
abominated the Cardinal, whom they wished as far
from the Court as he was at present near it.   Accordingly, not being able to contradict this minister, I said
that I had hoped he would have had a sufficiently good
opinion of me to have believed that I should carry out
such a mission with the discretion and diplomacy it
required, and added that it would be through no fault
of my own were I to fail.   He listened attentively, and,
being well pleased at my talking in this way, told me
that there was some sense in my words, provided I
could find means to satisfy him as to another objection
which he could not help raising.   I was well aware
that captains in the Guards did not like to be sent to
do garrison duty.   Perhaps I remembered that there
had been nothing but complaints from a battalion of
that regiment, which had been sent to Sedan by the
King's orders.   The officers had written to him sometimes even as many as two or three letters in one
single day, so, had these letters been sent to a poor
man and he had had to have paid the postage, more
would not have been needed to ruin him.

I deemed this expression more worthy of the Cardinal
than dignified in its tone.   But, as this had nothing
to do with the matter now under discussion, I rejoined
that I had not meant that a whole battalion should be
sent to Rhetel, though it was for his Eminence to judge
if the service of the King required it.   One or two
companies would be enough, and the captains might
be excused from going; indeed, this was necessary to
the success of my plan.   The company of which I was
lieutenant should be one of the two sent, and the
lieutenant of the other one should be my junior, so

that I might hold the supreme command, and thus meet with no obstacles to my scheme. His Eminence replied that all this was very complicated, and that he knew a shorter way. The King should give me one of these two companies, and the other would have no captain, or rather, he should be absent. He should be either governor of some fortress, or have something else to do. Accordingly, I should, in the natural course of events, be in command, and there would be no need for so much mystery.

I did not feel at ease on hearing him speak thus. He really intended this time to make me a captain in the Guards, and, as human prudence is nothing in comparison with what men of the world call luck, and what wise and pious men term Providence, he had formed this resolve for a reason which was much more calculated to hurt than to serve me. Owing to my affair with the captain of the regiment of Rambures, his Eminence, whilst becoming aware of the bad state of my finances, had at the same time learnt that it had taken me but an hour at most to obtain the money I lacked to make up the sum for which I was in debt, and, accordingly, he had an idea that, were he to bestow this post upon me, I should find money to pay him a fine just as easily as on the previous occasion. This is why he determined to do justice to my merits. I was accordingly made a captain in the Guards, without his having told me his secret, but, two days later, I received a letter from M. de Bartillac, the Queen's Treasurer, in which he informed me that he had orders from M. le Cardinal to let me know that I must bring him twenty thousand francs in twice twenty-four hours. Such news came as an extraordinary wet blanket upon

me. All my friends had come to congratulate me on
my promotion to this post. It had been given me
without M. le Cardinal or anyone belonging to him
having mentioned a word as to the money which I
was now asked to pay. All I had known was, that
I was to give up my lieutenancy to him for him to
dispose of to whomever he liked. I would even have
assisted his Eminence to sell it advantageously, so
grateful was I for what he had done. But his present
demands altering all this, I went to find him, to point
out my inability to produce the first sou of this sum of
money. The Cardinal answered me that it was not
for himself that the money was wanted. The needs of
the State required that one should draw some help
from the posts which chanced to fall vacant. I was
wrong to complain of the very moderate sum demanded.
The custom was to always pay half the just value of
the post one received. A company in the Guards was
worth forty thousand crowns, so sixty thousand livres
might have been demanded, and to ask me for but
twenty thousand was treating me so gently that I
ought not to appeal against it.

It is true that the Cardinal's plan had for some
time been to make people pay about the half of the
value of any post they received or thereabouts. Nevertheless, though he wanted me to be so grateful, I did
not perceive that he was treating me more favourably
than others. My old post, which was his to sell, and
the twenty thousand francs which he now asked for
were about the half of what my present one might be
worth. I did not fail to tell him this, for, if one did
not dare to answer him back, he would willingly have
trampled upon one's body. He then asked me a nice

thing, to wit, what my lieutenancy had cost, and if I
had ever given much money for it ?   I replied no, and
that it had been given me for nothing, upon which he
retorted that I must not then say that I was not better
treated than anyone else, since it cost others at least
twenty thousand crowns to obtain, and myself but
twenty thousand francs !   He added that I should not
make myself very ill by giving that sum, and I must
not say that I could not find it, for I had found another
in a minute, when such a thing had not been necessary.

I should have argued a long time with him, had
he been willing to let me, but, having left me quite
alone without saying anything more, Debor came up to
me and asked me what was the cause which made
me so sad, that my face itself showed my state of
mind.   This was a very ill-timed speech of his, for
he knew the reason just as well as myself.   The fact
was that he had been sent by M. le Cardinal to find
out exactly when I was going to pay the twenty
thousand francs, and he had specially selected Debor,
with whom at one time I had been friendly enough, to
make these enquiries.   However, as it is not a good
thing to be too clever, especially with people who
know how to take care of themselves, his Eminence
gained so little thereby, that he was no wiser than
before.   Nevertheless, either from the instigation of
the minister, as I believe, or from the good-will of certain persons, I received in less than twenty-four hours
five notes setting forth that I had but to speak, and the
sum in question would be at my service.   There were
four of them, which were, one from M. de la Basinière,
paymaster of the treasury, one from M. de Lionne, one
from M. de Servient, and yet another from M. Hervart.

These were four good enough purses to draw upon,
except that of M. de Lionne, who was none too rich,
but, as all the four were on terms of the greatest intimacy with the Cardinal, I thought that it was he who
had set them to work, and nothing has ever been able
to disabuse me of this idea, in which I do not think I
was wrong, as I leave everyone to judge. His intention apparently was to at all events obtain my acknow-
ledgment, under the name of him whom I might
secretly consent to deal with, calculating that this
would always be better than nothing at all, especially
as I was resolved to marry, and was more than ever on
the way to making a good match.

The fifth of these notes was of quite a different kind
from the four others. It came from a woman of easy
virtue, and she herself did not deny this, which is rare
enough in the present century, when everyone wants to
pass for something quite different from what they really
are. After having congratulated me on my promotion,
she informed me that I knew her by reputation only,
a thing which would not cause me to think her letter
of much account. There was nothing in this world
like the possession of wealth. She had even discovered
that it was a necessity, when no more than fifteen
years of age. This had made her form a resolve to
never die a beggar, and she had succeeded none too
badly. It was true it had cost her a little kindness to
people, for whom at bottom she had no great esteem,
but they had paid so well for it that she had no regrets.
Her income exceeded twenty thousand livres, and it
was well invested in Paris, without counting a quantity
of valuable furniture and silver plate. She had besides
ten thousand silver crowns in ready money in her

closet. All this was more than sufficient to pay what
M. le Cardinal was asking of me. It would cost me
but a yes before a priest, and though she could only
offer me the leavings of two great financiers, they had
seemed so fair to a number of people of the Court,
that they had not scrupled to propose the same bargain as she was to-day suggesting to me. She sincerely
owned that she had a fancy for me, and at the same
time admitted her way of living: so that, were I to
take her at her word, I should not afterwards be in the
position of a man who could tell her that she had
deceived him.

This note might have tempted a good many people
more than the four others. The lady was very pretty
and was as yet in the flower of her age. She was no
more than twenty-five years old, but, as she had taken
to her profession betimes, as she herself made no
scruple about saying, her reputation was so widespread
in Paris, that she was just as well known as the wife
of the First President might be. This was the reason
that I did not hesitate for a moment as to the course I
should adopt. Nevertheless, being anxious to discover whether the fancy she had declared for me
would not be capable of making me obtain a share in
her wealth without its costing me the word she asked
for, I told the bearer of the note that I would go myself and give my answer in the afternoon. I took care
not to miss this appointment, and, doing my best to
not only sustain her goodwill towards myself, but
further increase it, so that she might refuse me nothing, she said, observing that I was beginning to make
great professions of gratitude and love, that all this
might be well and good with a dupe, but for herself she

would have nothing to say to it, without the assistance of a lawyer and a priest. She wanted me as a husband and not as a lover, and for this reason she advised me, as a good friend, to put aside all my compliments, unless I at the same time clothed them with the forms she had mentioned. This answer was not that of a stupid woman, but, as I thought myself as shrewd as she was and hoped to insensibly lead her to my point of view, were she to give me a little time, I replied that it seemed to me a good thing to make one another's acquaintance before concluding the bargain she had proposed. Madame de Miramion had once told me the same thing, as I think I have mentioned, when I had wanted to make her my wife.[1] I therefore could not fail to follow her example, though it was with another end in view. My intention was to persuade her to see me in spite of all her shrewdness, for I knew that, when once a woman has a fancy for anyone, he has but to be attentive to her and murmur sweet things in her ear to make a good deal of progress in a short time. But she was cleverer than I thought; accordingly, either because she saw through my plan, or because she had formed the resolve of beginning where other people end, she rejoined that she had no need to know me any better to settle her course of action; as for myself, she did not know my intentions, but it appeared to her that all I had to wish for was to be enlightened as to whether she had the property she had informed me of, or whether she had not. If this was the reason I wanted to know her, she thought it no bad one, but, if I had any other, as it could not but be disadvantageous to herself, I need only not take the trouble to come and see her again.

[1] See Vol. i., p. 416.

It would not have been honourable for me to make use of the pretext, which she herself was furnishing me with, to carry out my plan. A man always looks awkward if he appears self-seeking, especially on those sort of occasions on which it is a question of making a favourable impression. For this reason people always leave these kind of enquiries to their relatives or friends, whilst they themselves do nothing else but make protestations of love, respect and unselfishness. Being therefore extremely embarrassed as to what answer to make, because, indeed, I saw nothing which I could say likely to content her, "Ah!" cried she, perceiving my discomfiture, "I pity you for being so sincere; you wish to lie to me, but dare not do so. This is extraordinary enough in a courtier, whom it usually costs nothing to say everything he has never thought of. As regards yourself, however, I divine your thoughts very well without your being obliged to tell them to me. My property would suit you admirably, were I willing to give it you to become your mistress, but if, like me, you in your turn also perceive what my ideas are, you must clearly see that you have no reason ever to hope to touch my fortune, except on the conditions I have proposed to you." At the same time, she asked me what kind of a woman I took her for, when I had got it into my head to try and get the better of her? She added that I had not thought over things much, when I had asked her for time. M. le Cardinal would give me none, and all Paris knew, like herself, that I had but twice twenty-four hours to find my money in, and, therefore, if I wanted hers, I had not a moment to lose.

Seeing her so clever and so resolute, I deemed that

17—2

I should only be losing my time by protracting my dealings with her any longer. She wanted someone to marry her, and I was not the man for that, so I withdrew in silence. Notwithstanding this, to do everything politely, and without giving her cause to complain of my behaviour, instead of telling her my reasons for not being willing to think of this business, I told her that I would return to see her immediately. I do not know whether she really believed this, or whether she did not rather perceive that it was but an excuse. Be this as it may, keeping my word was the last thing I dreamt of, when I had left her house. If I was to become one of the great confraternity of cuckolds, as only happens too often to most of those who marry, I was at least desirous that it should not be with my own knowledge. I deemed a thing like this unworthy of an honourable man. I was not of the disposition of certain people whom I see in the world, snatching up their swords and gloves, when they see their wives' gallants coming! It is true that I did not believe this girl to be of a character to cause scandal, once she should have obtained a husband ; much rather did I think that her idea was to live as a respectable woman. But it was enough for me that she had not lived in this way whilst she was unmarried, to have no regrets for her riches. Accordingly, though I well knew that I had lost them, only because I was much more delicate in my feelings than a number of other people would have been, had they been offered a chance of this kind, not a moment was necessary for me to console myself in.

VII

Y speech to M. le Cardinal was calculated to make him leave me in peace. Twenty thousand francs were to him as a drop of water in the sea, so to speak; instead of which, to me it was like Peru itself. But, as he understood no one, when his own interests were concerned, hardly had the forty-eight hours, which he had given me to make my payment in, elapsed, when he asked M. de Bartillac if I had taken care to satisfy his demands. I think he did this more for the sake of form, and that he knew just as well as I did what the real state of affairs was. The people who had offered me money had apparently let him know that I had declined it, or I am very much deceived. Bartillac, who was a good man and a benevolent one, replied that I had not produced one sou, and had contented myself with demonstrating to him my inability to pay. I had nothing in the world but my post, and, as no money could be raised upon that, he had not pressed me to let him lend me money.

It was not true that I had seen him; he merely told the Cardinal this to assist me, and without knowing of the offers of the four people, or rather of his Eminence.

M. le Cardinal shook his head at hearing him speak
thus, meaning to express that he was not at all pleased,
and that I was not so much in want of friends as he
thought.   Fearing, however, that M. de Bastillac was
not the man to divine what he meant by this, he proceeded to tell him in plain language that it had but
rested with myself to make this payment.   This he
knew for certain.   Several courtiers had come to tell
him that a man was very lucky who received any
favour from the Court, for all the best purses were
immediately open to him.   Whether one had much
money or none, friends immediately appeared.   Of
this I was a good example,—an individual who, having
but a mantle and sword, had no sooner obtained a
company in the Guards, than four men of importance
wrote to lay their purses at my service!   All this
behaviour of mine but arose from my disinclination to
pay the money!   M. de Bartillac must therefore see
me again and inform me that I would be given but
twenty-four hours more to liquidate this debt in, and
were I to fail, the King would know what to do.   He
added, that I was to be told that I had only to accept
the money which had been placed at my service.
This would much surprise me, for I might not perhaps
as yet be aware of his knowledge of what was going on.

This speech of his Eminence, which M. de Bartillac
repeated to me word for word, thoroughly confirmed me
in my idea, that it was the Cardinal who had procured
me so many friends, who on another occasion might
perhaps have been behindhand.   Perceiving eventually
no way out of all this, I resolved to go and see M. de
la Basinière, who was one of my friends.   I preferred
him as a lender to the three others, because I knew,

whether it was his own money or the Cardinal's, he
would not be a hard creditor to deal with. I had
noticed that, though an extremely selfish man, as are
nearly all financiers, he had besides a greater weakness
than that. He loved flattery to an incredible degree,
so, as it would cost me nothing to bestow this upon
him, I determined to in this way pay him the
interest on the sum I was going to borrow. Fool-
ishly enough, I believed that this would content
him, and my reason was that I had seen numbers
of people at his table, who paid him in no other
coin. I reached his house before dinner, and, as
his conceit led him to take pleasure in letting every
sort of person see him eat, he at once told me that one
knew one's friends by the trouble they took to come
and keep one company at supper. I replied that this
was partly the reason of my coming, but that there
was yet another ; the fact was, the Cardinal had shown
himself a regular Turk with respect to myself, and so,
being obliged to change my mind, I had come to beg
him to let me have the money I had before refused.
M. de la Basinière very obligingly replied that his
purse was at my disposal now, just as it had been
before, and the twenty thousand francs should be
counted out to me after dinner. He added that
he was much flattered at my preferring him to
MM. Servient, De Lionne and Hervart, who he
knew had written to me on the same subject, the
moment they had known my need. I was indeed
doing him justice in deeming that he was much more
my friend than any of these gentlemen.

This speech would have further confirmed me in my
idea, that all these four men had done had only been

by the orders of M. le Cardinal, if I had really had the
slightest doubts on the subject. However, as my mind
was made up, it made no difference to me whatever.
Nevertheless, chancing to mention to M. de la
Basinière (without having any idea that it could any-
way affect me) that neither he nor the other three
gentlemen had been the only people who had offered
me money, he pressed me so much to explain myself,
that I did not think I ought to make any further secret
of the matter. I told him frankly of the offers of the
woman, and informing him at the same time that I
should not have scrupled to accept them, had she not
insisted upon some conditions which were too severe
for me to accept, I had no need to say more for him to
at once guess what these conditions were. On my
admitting the truth of his surmises, he at once said
that, now I had told him this, he would have something to say to me directly we had dined. He would
indeed have spoken at once, so eager did I perceive
him to become, had not dinner been announced, and
a great company of people been awaiting him. We
were then in his study, and, having both entered the
dining-hall, we sat down to table and indulged in such
good cheer that, had one been at the King's, one could
not have been any better served than we were. A
quantity of subjects were discussed, and amongst
others, the exploits of Montal, who was beginning to
make a great stir throughout the whole of Champagne.
It was Hervart who opened this conversation, and, as
he was entirely devoted to the Cardinal, a thought
flashed across my mind, which perhaps may have been
false or may have been true. I conceived an idea that
the Cardinal had confided to him that I was to go to

Rhetel and had bidden him speak of this governor, so as to discover whether I was likely to embark in some indiscretion, and be communicative from a too great desire to show my importance.

An idea such as this was more than enough to make me cautious, even had I been a great talker, which, thanks be to God, I was very far from being. I had learnt from my father, whilst in the cradle, that one never repented of having kept silence and that, on the contrary, one nearly always repented of having broken it. For this reason, nothing was wont to escape my lips without my having first of all weighed it well, a fact which had sometimes made my friends say, when they saw me so reserved, that I should have suited the ancient times, when there was a temple of idols, for I should have not done badly in the way of speaking as an oracle. Hervart was very much surprised to see me so reserved, either because he really had orders to make me speak, or because the subject under discussion was more one for a military man than for business people, which most of the company were. It seemed quite odd that I should hold my peace, whilst others let themselves go, without knowing whether what they said was sense or not.

Dinner being over, M. de la Basinière, who, after the fashion of the Court, affected to be on familiar terms with all who came to see him, proceeded to say that he had something to tell me and we should return to his study. I believed this was in order to give me the money, or, at least, an order to receive it from one of his clerks. However, after he had again made me repeat the offers which the woman had made

me, he declared that he was too much my friend not
to blame me for having refused them. Accordingly,
so as to oblige me to return to her and thereby cause
me to recover a fortune, he no longer had any money
to lend me. Notwithstanding this, he intended to
demonstrate by such a refusal that he was a thousand
times more my benefactor than if, by misplaced kindness, he was to make me master of all the wealth which
was at his disposal. What he would do for me
besides, was to mention this matter to M. le Cardinal,
so that, in place of the twenty-four hours he had given
me to produce my money, he might accord me just as
much time as would be necessary for me to complete the
marriage which was proposed to me.

The person surprised was myself, when I heard him
talking in this way. I retorted that surely he did not
think of wishing me to marry a prostitute. I called a
spade a spade, being thoroughly angry at his having
dared to propose such an infamy. M. de la Basinière
burst out laughing at my reply, at once rejoining that
I might perhaps marry one who, very far from enrich-
ing me as this one would do, might be just as much a
beggar as myself. He asked my pardon for his blunt-
ness, but, in short, one ought to speak frankly to one's
friends, for to flatter them was not giving proof of
being really what one said one was. He told me,
besides, much more of exactly the same nature,
so much so that, hardly knowing whether I was
dreaming or awake (so much did his words surprise
me), I eventually told him that, if he wished me to
believe that he was one of my friends, as he was
taking pains to make me think, I would beg him to
give me better advice than that. Everything which

tended to impair my honour could only arise from an
evil source, or, at least, from people who did not care
about making me lose all which I held most dear. I
was about to tell him a good deal more, so moved was
I, when he interrupted without letting me say anything
further. He said that he clearly perceived that my
case was like that of those people who had to be
bound, to have an arm or leg cut off, when necessity
required it; so, as I was like them in wanting to ruin
myself despite my friends' advice, I must be treated in
exactly the same way. Binding not being requisite, as
there was no question of amputating an arm or a
leg to save the rest of the body, my hands must yet
be tied so tightly, that I should be forced to do what
reason and my prosperity demanded. A chance was
before me of attaining a comfortable position, and it
must not be missed by any foolish tenderness for my
feelings. He reiterated that he no longer had any
money to extricate me from my difficulty, for it would
not be acting the part of a friend to waver on an
occasion like this. I might obtain what I wanted
from the purse of the woman who offered it, if I chose,
and not have to return it. This was the best advice
he could give me. To this he added that, should I
deem his words a little rough, a time would come
when, very far from entertaining such a thought, I
should praise him and bless him for having forced
me against my own will to choose the course of action
which was best for me.

This is all the answer I could obtain from him; so,
being quite shocked at his behaviour, I could not help
saying that I had up to this time thought that all
those who called themselves honourable men shared

the same ideas, but that, after what I had just heard, I clearly realised that I had been deceived. Financiers must certainly have quite a different morality from military men, since I did not believe that there was a single man, who wore a sword, who would be of a humour to follow his advice. Nevertheless, he was giving it me not only as being passable, but further praised it as most excellent. For myself, I took quite a different view, and one of us two must be wrong. He might keep his money, since he valued it so much as to wish to persuade me to purchase it at the expense of my honour. I would never in my life ask for it again, especially when he wanted to put such a price upon it as this.

I left his house in such a rage that, instead of going straight to M. Servient or to the others, who had made the same offer as M. de la Basinière, I returned home to let my anger cool a little. There I thought well over the matter, and decided I should only have to declare to M. le Cardinal or Bartillac, in order to avoid paying the money or at least defer its payment, that the man I have just spoken of had refused to lend it me. As I was extremely irritated at his rudeness, I rather desired that his Eminence should discover his bad faith, indeed, I intended to bruit it abroad everywhere. I did not fail to tell everyone I met of his behaviour, and, as he was none too civil, which caused him to have enemies, and possessed great riches, for which he was envied, within twenty-four hours the whole of Paris knew of the fine advice he had tried to give me. M. le Cardinal was the only one who did not know it, or, at least, pretended not to, for he sent Bartillac to me to say that he did not like my laughing at him like this, and would for the last time request me to do what he had ordered, for, should I fail to do so, he would know very well what course to take in order to be obeyed.

These threats did not astonish me, for they were usual with him in such cases. I told Bartillac, so that he might repeat it to his Eminence, of the bad faith of M. de la Basinière, and also described the pretext he had alleged as its cause,—a pretext which appeared to me so extraordinary, that I could not help thinking that he was of an evil disposition. Bartillac replied that he shared my views. He had already heard all the details of this affair, and begged me to except him from the number of those who preferred money to honour. He had, he said, a son whom he wished to marry as soon as possible, but, rather than he should marry a woman such as the one I had been advised to take, he would himself drown him. I was delighted to hear him speak words like these, which confirmed me in the high estimate I had already formed as to his character, ever since I had known him. Meanwhile, he advised me, as a good friend, to settle this matter with the Cardinal as speedily as possible. I might, he said, avail myself of what I had told him as an excuse. He himself would let him know of it, but he much feared it would avail me but little, for he appeared as bent upon getting this money as if it had been a million. I must do what I could, because the sooner it was settled the better for me.

In consequence of this advice and the minister's avarice, which I so well knew, instead of going at once to see him, I went to M. Servient. As he held the keys of the treasury, I could think of no better man;

besides, he had promised me the money. For this
reason, being ushered into his study by one of his
clerks in a very confident frame of mind, I made
exactly the same speech to him as I had done the day
before to M. de la Basinière. I took good care however to avoid mentioning the woman in any way, lest
he should take to giving me the same advice as the
other, but, as M. de la Basinière had himself told him,
I found him not only fully aware of it, but also so
imbued with his ideas, that he told me that, when one
possessed resources such as I did, one should not
resort to one's friends. Although twenty thousand
francs were a mere nothing, they were sometimes
harder for him to find than a large sum. He was at
the moment overdrawn to the extent of five millions,
so that he had not one sou in his house. This was
putting me off just as rudely as his colleague had
done, and showing also as little right feeling; so, being
as ill-pleased with the one as the other, I betook myself to the house of Hervart, to see if he was like these
other two. He was closeted in his study with his
secretary (Debi by name), who was an honest enough
man, and who had always shown me much good will.
They were, I was told, engaged on an important
matter, so, thinking that I ought not to interrupt them,
I determined to wait till they had finished. There
were some people in the waiting-room with whom I
discussed different matters. At last, after half or three-
quarters of an hour, Debi came out of his master's
study, and having noticed me, came and asked what I
wanted done. I described my business as briefly as
possible, and though he was from a province where
people are not usually afraid to burden themselves

with a woman of easy virtue, always providing that she has something whereby to lighten the horns which she brings as dowry to her husband, he could not help at once shrugging his shoulders from impatience. He proceeded to express his surprise at people of such weight and reputation having advised me to enter upon such a marriage, and declared that, for himself, he very much approved of my repugnance, since I was a man of honour and a man of honour never forgot what was due to himself. He added that, if by any chance I did not find the twenty thousand francs of which I stood in need in his master's purse, I should do so in his, but he would give me a piece of good advice, whomever I borrowed the money from, which was, to ask for a "brevet de retenue"[1] on my post, which I should try and get made out for forty or fifty thousand francs, or even more, if possible ; it would always be of use, and besides, serve as security for the money I might borrow.

Though I perceived he was looking after his own interests, in case I should accept his offers, I could not blame him ; for I might die or be killed, in which case any lender would run a great risk of losing his money. However, I did not care to involve my friends in any way for my sake, so I thought it best to address myself to those who had offered me their help. There were two of these left—his master and M. de Lionne. I entered the former's study, to see if I should be greeted in the same way as I had been by Basinière and Servient. I ought to have expected no better reception from Hervart, for he was of Swiss nationality, and he would have had to have belied the usual reputation of his countrymen, if he had been willing

---

[1] *Brevet de retenue* : A kind of charge which could be used as a security for borrowing money upon.

to help me. I duly set forth the object of my visit, and, having done so, he was unable to reply, like Servient, that he had no money. Debi had just counted out fifteen thousand louis d'or which lay outside their bags, though the custom was to weigh and not to count them, and I do not rightly know why this usage had been broken. Be this as it may, not being able, as I have said, to give this reason for being untrue to his word, he made use of the same excuse as La Basinière to get rid of me. He asked me straight out, which was the most hurtful to a man's figure,—to be made a cuckold, or a sword-thrust in the water ? I saw what he was driving at and consequently replied in a way which should have dumfounded him, had he not apparently been animated by the same sentiments as his colleagues. I said that neither a sword-thrust in the water nor a man's making love to a woman really spoilt the figure of him who was interested ; but, as the one upset the mind in a dreadful degree, whereas the other did not deserve the least thought, he must allow me to tell him that no comparison was possible. Upon this he retorted, that only fools and people of unsound judgment worried about what I spoke of. A cuckold's leg was no worse made, because his wife amused herself. In his idea, the only thing which should give one a headache, was to have an affair on hand, without money to extricate oneself from it ; and, as I was in such a plight, I should be able to give him an answer on the subject. He proceeded to advise me, as a friend, not to lose the chance I had, and a proof of his friendship was, that he had no money to lend me. I ought to take what was offered and put myself in a comfortable position for the rest of my life.

From this answer I clearly divined that all three had agreed on a given course of action to annoy me; so, thinking that it was useless to say any more, I went to see M. de Lionne, whom I found out. Discovering on enquiry, that he would not return till the evening, I went for a walk, in order to decide on some course of action and pass the time between then and now, calling at my house to see if anyone had been to visit me. My landlord told me that no one had called, except a servant with a letter which he proceeded to give me. No sooner had I cast my eyes upon it, than I perceived that it came from the woman. I opened it to see what more she might want, after what I had told her. I thought that I had shown that there was nothing to be hoped for from me. Be this as it may, having opened this letter, I perceived that she expected nothing—far from it, she merely reproached me for my behaviour, and said that it was a strange thing that her good will towards me should have but drawn my slanders upon herself. I had been quite at liberty to take her or not, there was nothing to be said on that score; but, if this was permissible, to cruelly bruit her name abroad, as I had done, was not.

From the style in which her letter was couched, I saw that she did not like my having boasted, as I had done, of the offers she had made me. Indeed, all Paris was talking about it, and, as she had said nothing to anyone, and it could only have become known through what I had confided to La Basinière having become common property, more was not needed to make me admit that I had been wrong. I went to see her to apologise and frankly own in what spirit I had

acted.   My conduct had in no way arisen from a spirit
of slander, and I could have taken whatever oath she
might have desired to that effect, but I was not troubled
to do so.   She refused to see me, either because she
did not want my civility, or was outraged at the contempt I had shown for her, by refusing the proposal
which she had not herself scrupled to make to me.

This refusal delighted rather than pained me.   After
what La Basinière, Servient and Hervart had done, I
had reason to be afraid of De Lionne following their
example, but now, neither M. le Cardinal nor any of
his creatures could again tell me that I ought to
have recourse to this woman to procure the money.
For, being enraged, which she could show in no
better way than by refusing to open her door, as she
had done, she was at present very far from wishing to
give me any.   I should, therefore, have heartily desired
that M. de Lionne should, like the other three, have
given me a refusal, for I flattered myself that, once
M. le Cardinal should really be convinced of my inability to pay, he would leave me in peace.   However,
De Lionne, who was a more honest man than the
others, having taken care not to break his word once
it was given, told me that very evening that, though he
had not the money by him, he would not fail to find it
for me by the next morning, but he must, he added,
ask me for certain reasons to let no one know that he
was the giver.   This was a more important thing than
I could imagine.   He would ask me for an oath to
that effect, and I ought not to refuse it, so as to let his
mind rest in peace.

The oath he wished to exact more than ever convinced me that it was M. le Cardinal who had set all

four to work, when they had offered me money. I also
concluded that M. de Lionne, being more honourable
than the others, did not wish to lay himself open to my
accusing him of having broken his word, and so was
about to lend me the money, in spite of the Cardinal's
having now forbidden such a thing. I assured him
that I would do all he wished, adding that I would be
sincerely grieved to inconvenience him in any way, and
would not permit him to borrow for me, since he had
no money at hand. He most honourably rejoined that
it was of no consequence whatever ; he had, he said, a
purse at his command, which never failed, but, even
were it to do so, he would not fail to extricate me from
my difficulty. I might not know that there were some
subjects on which the Cardinal did not understand
joking. For this reason I ought to settle this matter
at once, and he thought he need say no more. A mere
word was needed to send me back to my province, and,
as no greater misfortune than that could ever happen
to me, especially to-day, when I was beginning to see
the way to making a fortune, there was nothing I
ought not to do to guard myself against such a fate.

By this he meant becoming a captain in the Guards ;
indeed, once one had obtained a post of this kind, it
was rare that one left it without a governorship, and
he looked upon the governorship of a fortress much as
a fat abbey, in which also he was not far wrong. Be
this as it may, having made an appointment the next
morning at nine o'clock for me to come and get my
money, he sent to beg the treasurer-general of the
states of Brittany to send him this sum. It was a
man named Harouis who then held this post, and still
holds it to-day. No man was ever more obliging than

he! He had never known what it was to refuse anything to an honourable man, so much so that, had one
asked him to give himself, I think he would at once
have done so. He had, besides, none of the ways of a
business man, having much more those of a prince, so
generous was he! Apparently this came to him from
descent, for, regular financier as he was, his was no
low origin, as is usual with all the people who take up
this profession. His ancestors had always held a
prominent place in Brittany, and his father had been
First President of the Chambre des Comptes there.
He sent M. de Lionne the twenty thousand francs
which he had sent to ask for by letter. They had just
come as I arrived, and, finding them still quite warm,
I did not give them time to get cold. They were in
beautiful double pistoles, and, having taken them away
to the Cardinal's house, the first words he said when
he saw me were, had I complied with the order he had
had conveyed to me by Bartillac?

Though he asked me this, I was sure that he did
not think that I had been able to do so; for, from
what M. de Lionne had said, and on account of a
thousand other circumstances, it was clear to me that
he it was who had forbidden all four to advance me
the money they had promised. I must say, however,
that, far from the Cardinal wishing me evil, I really
believe that, putting his own interests out of the
question, he wished only to do me good. Knowing
me to be a pauper, which to him seemed the most
miserable thing possible, he would have desired me
not to have shown so much delicacy and only spoke as
he did, or, at least, I thought so, to be able to again
repeat that I must marry this woman, since she alone

could make a certainty of my obtaining a company in
the Guards.   His Eminence was very much surprised,
when I had told him that I had brought the money to
him, adding, that I had not taken it to the house of
M. de Bartillac, as he had ordered me, because, it
being rumoured that he was on the eve of setting out
on a voyage, he could not furnish himself with finer
pieces and more portable ones than those I had now to
give him.   They were quite new double louis, so much
so that one would have said that not two days had
passed since they had been minted.   He enquired who
had given them to me, and as, after what M. de Lionne
had said, I took good care not to tell him, I made
answer that there he was asking me a thing which I
would not confide to my confessor himself, were he
ever to ask it.   The giver did not want to be known,
and the best thing I could do after such a kindness
would be to comply with this wish.

My story made him believe that the money came to
me from the woman who had made the offer.   He
asked to see the pieces, and, having turned them out
upon a table, wished to know if I had counted them
before putting them in the bag.   I replied yes, and
that I had found their number correct.   The minister
believed my word, and, having wanted to himself
replace the coins without allowing me to help, they
were no sooner collected together than he put his nose
to them.   I did not understand what he meant by this,
having never heard of people smelling either gold or
silver.   Nevertheless, I had formerly read in Roman
history that the Emperor Vespasian had once made
his son act like this, because he had opposed an edict
of his which dealt with certain sanitary matters.   I

had read, I repeat, that, after his son had replied that
he could detect no smell in this money, he had rejoined that, notwithstanding that, it was produced by
the edict in question, which he had declared to have
such a bad odour. Be this as it may, not happening
to think of the same thing as the Cardinal, I hardly
gave a thought to what he was doing when, after
having smelt the bag, he bade me smell it also. I at
once thought that he had detected some smell, and,
having put it to my nose and finding none, I told him
what I thought, because he had asked me if it did not
emit an unpleasant odour. I had no sooner let him
have my opinion, than I clearly perceived that he, as
well as myself, had read Roman history, and was even
trying to apply it to me. Indeed, he at once told me
that, since this money had no bad smell, everything I
could extract from the same source would have none
either. He added that he would not enquire whether
it had been given me under promise of marriage or as
a reward for some service already performed. I should
be too discreet to admit such a thing, but, in short,
wherever this present came from, he congratulated me
upon it.

The Cardinal was in an excellent temper, because
there was nothing more likely to make him so than
the sight of the metal I had just shown him ; so, after
some jesting, he asked me when I should like to set
out for Rhetel, adding that my voyage was very necessary, owing to the complaints made in Champagne of
the ravages of Montal, who was levying contributions
up to the frontiers of Brie. I answered that, if he
desired to stop these ravages, whilst I tried to arrange
matters with that governor, I would soon let him
know the way. This was to keep our own troops

under stern discipline, by which they were too little controlled at present. Indeed, they were as bad as the soldiers of the Prince de Condé in this respect, from whom they could not be[1] distinguished, as both sides belonged to our nation. Many complaints had been already made to his Eminence about this, but he had deemed the evil irremediable, because he did not know how to set about arresting it.

He was delighted at my words and at once told me that, if I could do the King such a service as this, I might rely upon a speedy reward. I thought of answering that all the recompense I would ask for would be the return of the two thousand pistoles I had just given him, but, reflecting that, in his present mood, he would rather give me the baton of a Maréchal of France than return this money, I repressed any inclination to speak my thoughts. So, instead of saying so, I declared that a good servant of the King, such as I professed to be, was not swayed by self-interest, but left his reward to his prince; so, without further ado, I would quickly let him know my views as to the repression of the ravages we had spoken of. We had only to fill our villages with soldiers and entrench ourselves strongly, for in this way our troops would not leave their entrenchments without the orders of their officers, and as these officers would perceive the danger of attacks taking place at any moment, unless a good look-out was kept, they would have to be the first to betake themselves to these villages, so as to supervise their soldiers, whereas, now that their companies were in towns which they knew

[1] Regular military uniforms had not as yet been introduced. A scarf or other similar emblem served to distinguish the different sides.

to be safe, this was not the case.   They came to spend
their time at Paris, because the neighbourhood suited
them well, as did the freedom in which they lived.
This freedom was so great, that all their actions had
nothing to do with the career of arms, which they
professed to follow; for, though it requires no less
order and obedience than exists in convents, everyone wanted to be master, so much so that, provided
one was a captain, one could go out on horseback
without thinking of asking the leave of a soul.   Only
the subalterns were compelled to observe some sort
of discipline, and they very often broke away from it ;
for a single lieutenant being constantly left in a
garrison, especially when safe from attack, the other
lieutenants or ensigns thought it shameful to go and
salute a man who only had the advantage of being in
command, because he belonged to a regiment which
took precedence over their own.

M. le Cardinal agreed with what I said, and told me
to prepare to set out the Thursday following, and he
would issue the order for my company to march to
Rhetel with the one which belonged to Pradel. Pradel,
who was Governor of St. Quentin, had gone to that
town by the express orders of his Eminence, so everything was arranged as it should be, in order that I
might have the command of these two companies.   As
they were to set out the same day as myself, I asked
M. le Cardinal to allow me to remain in Paris some
days longer, calculating that I could, by taking post,
rejoin them before they reached Rheims.   However,
his Eminence would not consent to this, because he
wished me to go and see M. de Voisins (who is to-day
a Councillor of State), and who was then Intendant at
Châlons.   He was uterine brother to La Basinière,

but, as there is more honour to be found amongst magistrates than financiers, I found him to be a just man, and one not to be corrupted like the other. I was ordered by the minister to lay before him a plan of my operations, so that he might give me every assistance in carrying them out. He agreed with me as the Cardinal had done, and, having stayed four or five days with him, I set out to join my company at Rhetel. M. l'Intendant gave me an escort to that town, which was a highly necessary precaution, until such time as my plan should have been carried out; but, once troops were marched into the villages, it was no longer needed at all. The reason for this was, that sentinels were placed in the bell-towers, and as this part of the country is very open, signals were made from one to the other, and sufficient soldiers sent out to cope with the enemy's forces. A chime, more or less, of a bell announced their number. M. Voisin told me when I went away, that he would soon come and see me, as I was the originator of this plan, and seven days later, he made his appearance, and we set out together with an escort to reconnoitre the villages which were to be fortified. I had lines drawn round those which were to be defended with palisades, and orders were issued for earthworks to be constructed, where I deemed them needful. Meanwhile, as all these precautions must fail, unless orders were sent out for all officers to return to their garrisons, these were duly promulgated and had to be obeyed on pain of being cashiered for disobedience. The Trésoriers de l'Extraordinaire[1] and their clerks were also instructed not to pay those who were on leave without a certifi-

[1] These were the officials who looked after additional expenses for " extraordinary " purposes, such as war.

cate from the intendant. By these means they were
obliged to attend to their duties. Montal at first
attempted to worry us, but, as we were sufficiently
strong to repel any attack, he was merely put to the
trouble of having to retreat without having effected
anything.

Meanwhile, so as to find means to communicate
with him, I made fifteen of my soldiers set out one
night on the pretext of reconnoitring. I instructed
them to return to Paris by devious roads, with the
exception of one, who was to act as I had previously
directed him to do. They all acted exactly in accordance with my orders, and the man who was not to
return to Paris reappeared the next morning, like one
terrified by some horrible catastrophe. He proceeded
to describe before a number of officers at my quarters,
how all his comrades had been killed one after the
other, the enemy (to the number of two hundred)
having surrounded them in a little wood and carried
out this fine piece of work in cold blood, without
heeding their prayers for quarter. He alone had by
good luck escaped, leaving the other fourteen men
lifeless on the ground. Only the governor and myself
knew this to be a fabrication. I feigned to fly into a
rage at this news, and asking the governor what he
now intended to do, without awaiting his reply, declared that my opinion was that, as the enemy had
granted no quarter to the regiment of guards, the
regiment of guards should grant them none in return,
and, as his jurisdiction extended only to matters within
the walls of the town, he at once said I might do as I
liked. I, therefore, immediately despatched a drummer
to Rocroi to let Montal know that my men would not,

if possible, let one of his soldiers escape alive, if any should fall into their hands. On his enquiring the cause of my rage and learning it from the drummer, he declared that I was trying to pick a quarrel with him, as no reason whatever existed for my indignation. He was sorry, he added, that I wished in this way to waste life in cold blood; but, as such was the case, he would give me back as good as I gave, when occasion offered. I pretended great anger, on the drummer's return, at this speech of Montal's, and said before everyone, that he did well to deny such a deed, because every bad action ought to be denied. Meanwhile, I sent out some bodies of men who spared none of the enemy, whether they were in force or not, whenever they chanced to meet. I should have been sorry for this state of affairs to continue long, but, as there are certain times, at least, in war, when it is permissible to make some individuals perish to save a greater number, I waited patiently till I should find means to stop the state of disorder the country was in. In addition to these measures, I began to mix other soldiers with my own. Montal did not fail to gain information of this, and, indeed, his men who were constantly fighting with us could not have failed to perceive it. It was as easy for them to distinguish the soldiers of the Guard from those of other regiments, as it is to distinguish a lame man from a well-made one. The former were well dressed, because their captains were obliged to equip them, whereas the latter were as naked as one's hand. Be this as it may, Montal, who could be humane or brutal as the circumstances required, being desirous, if possible, to arrest the flow of blood which was commencing, and which appeared likely to last, wrote to the governor on the subject, so as to devise some remedy for such a state of affairs.

The governor, who had orders to consult me about everything, let me know of this, and asked what his answer should be.   I asked him to send word to Montal for an officer's passport, so that this matter might be settled in a friendly manner.   Montal, who did not wish for anything better, at once sent back a passport with a blank space for the officer, in which the governor, by my instructions, inserted my own name.   I at once mounted horse, so as to lose no time, and, having reached Rocroi that evening, Montal, who had never seen me, was very much astounded when, on reading the passport, he perceived that I was the individual who had inaugurated this campaign against him.   Being a clever man, he immediately suspected that I had not come for nothing.   He took care however, to keep his thoughts to himself, and proceeded to express, in very polite tones, his regret at my having believed one of my soldiers to his prejudice, adding, that I must perceive that it was I alone who was responsible for the blood which had been shed.   However, as that was past, the best thing we could do would be to trust one another more, for the fact of our being enemies need not detract from our humanity nor our politeness; indeed, amongst honourable men, such a thing rather increased one's eagerness to gain the esteem of an adversary.

His looks did not at all coincide with the suavity of his words, for his appearance was more like that of a satyr than a well-bred man.   Nevertheless, as one must never judge people by appearances, and as I

knew that he was a redoubtable antagonist, I kept a
good watch over myself, lest I should let drop some
word which might give him a hold over me. I was
aware that flattery overcame most people, and therefore began to overwhelm him with it. I descanted
upon his vigilance and his activity, and laid stress on
the fact that M. le Prince had given him a signal
mark of his appreciation by choosing him for the important position he held, to the detriment of many
others who followed his fortunes. All this was but
meaningless talk, but notwithstanding, I proceeded to
keep up the same tone of flattery throughout our conversation. We next proceeded to discuss the matter
which had brought me, and as there were other
negotiations to be debated by me on behalf of the
Governor of Rhetel, we had several conferences
together. I found means during these interviews to
further compliment Montal, telling him that it was a
pity for a man such as he to waste his youth by serving
another than his King, and enquiring what he could hope
for from such a course of conduct; for, besides his honour and duty being at stake, it was certain that the King
could do more for him in a single day than M. le Prince
in his whole lifetime. To this he was obliged to agree,
and, having ceased to discuss anything else, I next
told him that, as he admitted the truth of my con-
tentions, he would be neglecting both his fortunes and
his honour, were he not to attempt to repair his faults
by some conspicuous services. By this I meant him
to understand that the giving up of Rocroi to his
Majesty would be the service in question, but, as he
desired to see what I was driving at, he listened very
attentively without making any interruption. He

assumed, however, a certain docile air, as if he was already half persuaded by my reasoning; so, perceiving this, I did not stop half way after such a good beginning, and added that, though he might perhaps address himself to others who had more influence than myself with the Court, my connection with M. le Cardinal was close enough for me to be of use to him, were he willing to employ me. I should be doubly pleased to do my best, since, in addition to the service I should be doing the King, I should further have the satisfaction of obtaining his friendship.

I do not know for what reason he allowed me to continue speaking without making any remark, but, as he could not always remain silent, he eventually said, intending to draw me out further, that my arguments were very good ones, but, after a step such as the one he had taken, no retreat was possible. The whole of his future was in the hands of M. le Prince, who had already done a great deal for him. He had promoted him from ensign to the governorship of such an important fortress as Rocroi. M. le Cardinal, who controlled all Court favours, was not the man to do the same for him nor anything like it. He was as hard as a nail when there was a question of giving anything away, and there was no need to tell me this, since I had passed through his hands. My answer was that, though I would not deny that his Eminence bore the reputation of being miserly, yet, in spite of this, when his Majesty's interests were at stake, his behaviour was of quite a different kind. True it was that there existed no chance of his bestowing a governorship upon him directly he should have left the service of M. le Prince, for time was necessary to obliterate the remembrance of his having been a rebel. Upon this he interrupted me, and said that, since his defection would always be remembered, he thought me too just and disinterested to counsel him to accept an arrangement by which he would always be looked upon with suspicion. As he was esteemed by the party he was now siding with, he would do much better to remain with them than join one by which he would be always regarded as a traitor; indeed, he must either lose his sense or his honour to let himself be seduced by my words.

Anyone else than I might perhaps have been puzzled how to meet his objections, for they were to a certain extent valid, but, as it is seldom that one who is fighting for justice and truth is stopped short, I protested that, from all appearance, he had not understood what I had wished to convey to him. When I had said that M. le Cardinal would not at once give him a governorship like the one he was holding, I had only meant that there would have to be an interval between his rebellion and his recompense. M. de Turenne, the Comte de Grandpré, Bussi Rabutin, and others, had all recovered the King's favour, after having borne arms against him, though at first it had not been deemed opportune, owing to public opinion, to show any signs of reposing especial confidence in them. I gave, besides, several other reasons to support my contention. He appeared more than half convinced by these arguments, so, continuing in the same strain, he eventually asked me straight out what the Cardinal intended to do for him, were he to come over to his side. At that time, the King was no more spoken of than if he had never existed. His name indeed was affixed to public documents, but only as a matter of form. The world was unaware that he would become one of the greatest Kings whom France ever boasted, and the most worthy to rule. Directly I perceived that Montal was reaching the point of making this enquiry, I deemed my negotiations to be going on well, but thinking it best to be more cautious than he, I determined not to put forward any offers yet, though I was empowered to do so, for I feared he might divine that these had been the express object of my coming. I replied, therefore, more reservedly than ever, that this was going beyond my powers. If he wished for any definite assurance, he must let me write to the Court. He made answer that I had done well to act so shrewdly, and he had expected nothing else from me, but nevertheless, it was totally useless in his case, because he saw through everything, and felt pretty sure that I had come into Champagne expressly to win him over, and I ought to admit this, if I were as frank as himself, and it would serve my interests more than I thought.

He failed to persuade me, though he held out such great inducements, for I knew that nothing was so dangerous as an enemy's advice; so, having maintained my reserve, he told me that I might tell him my secret, whenever I thought fit to do so. I asked him again whether he wished me to write or not and, on his making reply that I might do as I pleased, but it was unnecessary, I pondered over this somewhat ambiguous answer and determined to leave matters as they were.

In the meanwhile, we agreed that quarter should be given by the soldiers on both sides, a thing which was mutually advantageous, and besides, I was already

beginning to feel some qualms at having been the
originator of the horrors which had taken place.
After the discussion of some other matters, Montal
pressed me to leave, for he feared that, were I to
make a longer stay, he might become an object of
suspicion to M. le Prince. I did not think fit to
remain in defiance of his wishes and, telling him that
I might return to settle the question of " contributions,"
which was under discussion between us, he rejoined
that I must arrange matters so that that might be
my last visit, because he would not see me twice
more in his fortress. I thoroughly understood from
this answer that he was anxious to at once learn all
I had to say and, having informed M. le Cardinal
of the whole of my negotiations, his Eminence sent
me fresh instructions. The first offers he had made
were to promise him a company in the Guards and
twenty thousand silver crowns in ready money, on
consideration of the surrender of Rocroi. In the fresh
ones, there were added twenty thousand more crowns
and an abbey, together with an income of seven or
eight thousand livres for one of his children, when
old enough to hold it. My own opinion was that,
though the company in the Guards and the forty
thousand crowns were worth something, the promise
of the abbey in the future was but one of the Cardinal's
tricks.

I found means to return and see Montal, as I had
told him I would, on the pretext of settling the question
of the " contributions." He received me well enough to
give me some hopes of his accepting or refusing my
offers, according as they seemed advantageous or
disadvantageous to himself; but, on my letting him

know of the first proposal I had to make, he repulsed me so utterly that, though I had kept in reserve the abbey and the twenty thousand crowns, I felt at once convinced that I should do no good with him. I had thought it best to imitate those merchants who always keep their best goods for the last. Meanwhile, I sought a way to inform his Eminence how matters were proceeding. This was difficult enough, for I could neither despatch couriers nor receive any letters. Being in this pass, I played the part of a sick man and asked for a doctor. The physician sent me by Montal, either from ignorance or to have an opportunity of proving his own worth, told this governor that I was very ill. I complained of bleeding with violent internal pains—the truth of the one was self-evident but the other was more difficult, since what goes on inside one's body cannot be seen and my word had to be taken. Montal had allotted me a room at the house of a certain councillor, who was his friend and his spy. He used to report to him everything which happened in the town and he did this so cleverly as to excite the suspicions of no one. He was ordered to watch my illness and report how it went on.

It must be understood that, for one or two years past, I had been subject to the same ailment[1] which had so tortured the late Cardinal Richelieu; for this reason, all my linen looked just as if it had been plunged in the blood of a newly killed ox. This was a thing to thoroughly deceive this councillor, who was even more ignorant of medical than of legal matters, though indeed he knew little of anything. Accordingly, he no sooner learnt of this malady of mine, whilst feigning to visit me solely for compassionate reasons,

1 See Vol. I., page 182.

than he sent to tell the governor that it would be a
miracle if I ever recovered; consequently, having
succeeded so well, my looks were the only thing which
could betray me. I was very far from having the
appearance of a sick man. I looked much more like a
confessor of nuns, who is carefully given a good bowl
of soup in the morning, to keep his complexion clear.
This being so, I had all the shutters of my room closed,
on the pretext that the daylight hurt my eyes, and,
when I heard anyone entering, I began to cry out like
some wretch being broken on the wheel, so that I
might prevent anyone from staying with me. At last,
after having played this part for two or three days, I
sent word to Montal that I should certainly die, unless
I was allowed to send for a surgeon from Paris; that I
knew of one who had already cured me of the same
illness. Montal was neither a native of Le Mans, nor
a Norman, nor a Gascon, people who pass for being
the cleverest in the realm. He came from some district
near the river Loire, but was none the less shrewd for
all that; so, whether he suspected something, or was
careful to take precautions, he had my valet arrested,
after having given me permission to send him for a
surgeon. This took place in a wood which he had to
pass through, this side of the first village out of Rocroi.
At first, the man thought that his captors, who were only
three in number, were robbers, but was soon disabused
of this idea, because of his being merely searched and
not robbed. Montal apparently had some doubts as
to whether I was ill or not, and was afraid that, if he
had the man's money taken, it might delay his journey
and thus cause my death. Be this as it may, nothing
having been found upon my servant (for, suspecting

19—2

what would happen, I had told him with my own
lips all that I wanted the Cardinal to know), he
was allowed to proceed on his way. After this, Montal
believed me to be really ill, and, having come in
person to see me, as he had already done two or three
times before, I told him in a faint voice that, if it was
the will of God to call me from this world, I should
die content, provided that he promised to return to the
King's service. I must not trifle further with him;
besides, there was no time for that. I was empowered
to offer him up to forty thousand crowns with a company in the Guards. Besides this, an abbey should be
given to one of his children. An offer like this was
well worth considering, since he would obtain wealth
and reputation at the same time as he would be
enabled to recover his honour.

This offer of mine was received by the governor in
question in a way which showed me it was no more
acceptable to him than the first one I had made had
been. He soon convinced me of this by complaining
of the small esteem in which his Eminence appeared
to hold him. Far from treating him as he had the
the Comte d'Augnon, to whom he had given a baton
of a Maréchal de France and five hundred and fifty
thousand livres, he was offering him a paltry forty
thousand crowns and a post of about the same value
at most. Mayhap, he continued, he desired by this to
show that Rocroi was not worth Brouage, nor a
Montal as good as an Augnon;[1] but his Eminence
might be wrong, and, even were Rocroi not so valuable

1 Louis Foncault, Comte d'Augnon gave up Brouage in 1653.
Brouage, opposite the island of Oléron, has now entirely lost its
former importance as a seaport.

as Brouage, he would wish him to understand that a
Montal was the equal of fifty Augnons. He added,
however, that he did not wish me to tell the Cardinal
this, because he liked deeds much better than words,
and would very shortly show him what it was to
underestimate his capabilities, and this, it would soon
be seen, was no mere gasconnade. This he said in a
tone which showed me that this time he was perfectly
sincere, and that he was speaking his real mind.
I was vexed that my instructions did not extend any
further, because I clearly perceived that that was all
now necessary to win him over. Meanwhile, as I had
hopes of my valet bringing me good news from Paris,
I made use of all the best reasons I could find to soften
him. I succeeded but ill, so angry was this governor,
and, having left me mad with rage, as far as I could see,
with the Cardinal, I awaited my man's arrival with great
impatience, to know whether I was to return to Rhetel
or go on with my negotiations. I had not made direct
application to his Eminence. I had told him to speak
to Besmaux in the first instance, so as to discover if he
was to present himself to him. Besmaux had become
captain of his guard, Champfleuri having retired dissatisfied to a wretched house of his near Chevreuse,
where he still is to-day. I had instructed my man as
to what he was to say. He was first of all to tell
Besmaux that he had something to communicate to
his Eminence on my account, were he willing to listen
to him, and if this should not be the case, he himself
was to tell him that the horse his Eminence had
ordered me to buy would cost him much more than he
thought, so it was for him to judge if he would take it
at such a price, or give up all thoughts of it. Were he

however, to leave the matter to me, I would deal with
his purse as with my own.   My valet's instructions
were to say no more than this in case of his speaking
to the Cardinal, and he did not know the purport of
this message.   However, as he was no fool, he had a
good idea that these words concealed some mystery,
but what it exactly was he could never tell.   My man
spoke to Besmaux as he had been instructed, and the
latter having announced his coming to his master, his
Eminence at once ordered him to be brought into his
study.   He acted as I had bidden him, and the minister
at once grasping the meaning of his words, commanded
him to remain in Paris till further orders.

Meanwhile, I still continued to play the sick man,
whilst awaiting my valet's return with all the impatience
imaginable.   Montal no longer came to see me, letting
apparently his resentment against the master fall upon
his emissary.   Two days more than were necessary for
my servant to return in having elapsed, I became
puzzled as to the cause, which anyone might well have
been, but it was something which could not be guessed.
M. le Cardinal, being incensed against Montal for
holding out for such high terms, had no sooner left my
valet than he secretly informed M. le Prince that I was
at Rocroi for the purpose of making a treaty with him,
not a treaty such as had served as a pretext for my
voyage, but one to make him false to his allegiance.   The
Prince de Condé, who justly had great faith in Montal,
sent word to the major of the fortress, who was entirely
devoted to him, not only to keep watch over his
conduct, but further, to arrest everyone going to or
returning from Paris, and to search them, notwithstanding any passports they might be carrying.   If

anything suspicious should be found on their persons, he was to send them straight to him, without letting anyone know. The major duly carried out his orders, and would have placed me in a fine fix, as I will presently tell, had it not been that, perceiving that there was nothing to be done with Montal and the consequent uselessness of tarrying longer at Rocroi, I made a sudden recovery, and, suspecting what was about to happen, from my knowledge of the Cardinal, went off without awaiting my valet's return.

Montal, whose eyes were everywhere, had already perceived how matters lay, and wrote an account of my visit to M. le Prince, adding that he had not done so before, because the matter seemed too trifling to trouble him with. However, as I had eventually proposed to him a company in the Guards, forty thousand crowns, and an abbey for his children, in consideration of the surrender of his fortress to his Majesty, he thought it his duty to let him know. The Prince de Condé deemed this news to have come rather late in the day, and was not too well pleased, thinking that it was sent him only because no arrangement had been come to between us, but in spite of this, he dared not show what he thought, from fear of hurrying on the treaty with the Court. Accordingly, he contented himself with sending word to Montal that he had known of all this for some time past, but had always felt sure that the Cardinal was wasting his time, a reply which surprised the governor. He concluded that this was some trick of the Cardinal's to make him an object of suspicion, and fearing lest he might send some spy into his fortress with letters addressed to me, as if I were still there, he adopted all possible means to prevent them falling into his major's hands. With this end in view, he set one of his friends, Mauvilli by name, to work, with orders not to re-enter Rocroi without having dispelled his fears. Mauvilli, who was a determined man, chose nine or ten soldiers as brave as himself, and having provisioned them for four or five days, prepared to carry out his orders. However, they had not to stay away as long as that; for the Cardinal, having deemed that, after his warning, M. le Prince would not fail to take his measures, sent off my valet with a packet addressed to me, hoping he might fall into an ambuscade. As he had reason to believe that I had gone back to Rhetel, he was afraid lest my man should learn of my return on his way and not proceed.to Rocroi, so he sent off another courier three hours before his departure from Paris, to wait for him at a hostelry at Fismes, at which the post made a halt. This courier pretended to my valet when he arrived, that he was the commander of a village two leagues from Rocroi, and after having learnt that he was my servant, declared himself delighted at falling in with him, because he had a letter to give me from M. le Cardinal, which had been in his keeping for three days past; he would therefore beg him to take charge of it, when he should proceed on his way.

My valet believed all this, and, the sham commander having prevented him from discovering if I had returned to Rhetel or not, set out with both letters concealed in one of the flaps of his saddle, without the slightest idea of the trouble in store for him. Hardly, however, had he gone another league when he fell into the hands of Mauvilli, who arrested him with his postillion. The poor man wanted to show the passport given him by Montal, but Mauvilli took not the least notice of it, and led him into a neighbouring wood. Both the postillion and my man thought their last hour had come, and that they had fallen into the hands of robbers, but they changed their minds when they perceived that, after having been searched without their money being taken, search was made everywhere for some letter. Mauvilli, seeing the extreme state of agitation my valet was in (for he feared the letters being found), began to threaten to kill him if he did not point out where they lay hid. He had looked everywhere in vain, and had not as yet thought of looking in the saddle. Eventually, however, having ordered the two horses to be unsaddled, my valet confessed everything. Directly he saw Mauvilli beginning to rip the flaps open with his knife, he threw himself on his knees before him. Mauvilli had both men bound to trees, and having taken these letters to Montal, this governor found them to be in cipher, and had them deciphered by Mauvilli himself, who was very skilled in such matters. The first letter was one from the Cardinal, urging him to come to terms quickly for his own sake, and was written for the purpose of falling into the hands of M. le Prince. The second was for me and promised me great things, did I succeed in that which I had begun so well.

It is impossible to describe Montal's rage at the sight of these two letters; he sent Mauvilli back to the wood with orders to release the postillion and bring my valet into the town. He had been confined in a dungeon, and had I been in his hands Montal would, I think, have served me the same way, so enraged was he.

After some deliberation, it was determined that my valet should be sent to M. le Prince and, under the

escort of Mauvilli, he was taken across the Ardennes
beyond Philippeville to Namur ; however, the Prince de
Condé not being there, Mauvilli was obliged to proceed
to Brussels. M. le Prince expressed his pleasure with
Montal for the course of action he had taken, and
declared that nothing could have more clearly demon-
strated his innocence. He would, he said, take
measures to extract the truth from the lips of the
prisoner, who might not prove so obstinate when about
to be hanged. However it was not necessary to put this
man to the torture, for, directly M. le Prince interro-
gated him, he made a clean breast of everything, and
was near being allowed to go scot free, had it not been
urged that, were this valet released, it would prove an
incentive to spying. The Prince de Condé, though
he usually cared as little for a man's life as if he were
not his fellow creature, was inclined in this instance
towards clemency, but, yielding eventually to the advice
given him, he sent back the valet to Montal, so that
the latter might act as he thought fit. The governor
in question deemed that his honour demanded the
hanging of the prisoner, so, having carried out this
execution in full daylight in the presence of all his
garrison, he no longer felt afraid of this poor wretch
saying anything against him, now that he had gone to
another world.

I learned this news in Paris, to which place I had
thought it best to return when nothing more was to be
done at Rhetel. I was much grieved, knowing that I
had been the cause of this poor man's death, but, not
being able to mend matters, I had prayers offered for
his soul, which was all which could now be done for
him. I found that the Cardinal had completed the

marriage of his niece with M. le Prince de Conti after having come across many obstacles both from M. le Prince himself and from Rome. M. le Cardinal had not yet abandoned his idea of obtaining the company of Musketeers for one of his nephews ; the eldest had died two years before. His Eminence had wept like a woman, and could even now not keep the tears out of his eyes when he spoke of it. Although the younger one was not so fitted for the career of arms as his brother, as he hoped that he might become a living proof of the proverb which says, "that practice makes perfect," he declared one day, that he was so pleased with me that, though I had not been a captain in the Guards for long, he did not intend me to grow old in such a position. He wished to do something more for me, and as I was a friend of M. de Treville's, I should try and get him to consent to the company of Musketeers being re-established for someone else to command, so that the eldest of his nephews might obtain it. As the latter was still a youth, he could not take up such a post just yet, so the future sub-lieutenant would be its master, and he had chosen me to occupy that position.

I was the more delighted at this scheme, because I had a worse opinion of his nephew than his Eminence. He was idle and lazy beyond belief, and liked only loafing and carousing. He was not stupid however, nor badly built, except for his legs, which were too big. My own interests being concerned, I arranged to dine with Treville before much time had passed, so as to try and make him more amenable than he had previously been. He was in his house at Grenelle, which he had bought specially to use as a pleasure resort.

It was really but a nice farm, and entirely devoid of luxury. However, its being close to Paris made up for everything to him. On my first visit, a good many people were there; so, not having been able to discuss matters, I returned at the end of the week. I told Treville that, as he was now quite used to living away from the Court, the loss of his post ought not to trouble him at all; he should however try and obtain some compensation for it. His children were too young for him ever to hope to see them at the head of the Musketeers, but still something might be arranged. I knew for certain that M. le Cardinal would listen to any reasonable propositions, and, if he would confide matters to me, he might rely on my doing well.

M. de Treville was unlike anyone else. My words were enough to make him think that M. le Cardinal had instructed me to speak to him. He made reply that his opinion of my friendship for him had greatly lessened, by reason of my thus attempting to be mysterious with him, and, when I sought to justify myself, would have nothing more to say to me than if I had been a Suisse! We then separated mutually irritated with one another. It was easy to perceive which of us two was in the wrong, but as it is rare that justice is done, we turned the cold shoulder upon one another, from that day forth, till such time as M. de Treville thought fit to abate his irritation against me.

It was just about this time that the King resolved to strip M. le Prince of a post he had formerly bestowed upon him as a recompense for his services. Stenai, Dun and Jamets, which had always belonged to the Duc de Lorraine, had been conquered by him, and had formed part of the reward given him by the Court, and measures were now adopted with a view to bringing these places under the domination of his Majesty.

During the course of these operations, the Vicomte de Turenne displayed such great qualities that the Court bestowed upon him the post of colonel-general of cavalry, which was vacant by the death of the Duc de Joyeuse. A thousand people had wanted to obtain it, who were totally unworthy of holding such a command. Bussi Rabutin had even put in his claim, though his only credentials lay in having purchased the post of Maistre de Camp Général of cavalry. Indeed, no one could tell how he had attained his present position. He had borne arms against the King after the imprisonment of the Prince de Condé, and if he had desisted from doing so, it had been because the Prince himself had not appeared to value his services sufficiently to make him wish to follow his fortunes any longer. He had therefore returned to his allegiance in spite of himself, so he was not, as may be imagined, held in any great esteem as a servant of the King. Be this as it may, his conceit, which had already caused him to buy a post beyond his capacity, making him think that he had a right to the one the Duc de Joyeuse had held, not only did he ask for it as I have just described, but further, began to sulk when he saw that the Court took no notice of his demands. He did not however dare to show his resentment, but, as the Vicomte de Turenne understood fighting better than making fine speeches, he determined to direct his attacks against him. The general in question had had some love affairs. This was a passion which was natural to him like other people, though it seemed to suit him ill enough. He was always the dupe of all his mistresses, and indeed, having a short time back tried to make love to a certain princess, she had jeered at him so much, that he had been very much hurt—a circumstance which had made him slander her with the result of entangling him with her relatives.

Anyhow, either because he perceived himself unlucky in love, or because, once in one's life, it is as it were impossible to stop oneself from committing the folly of marrying, he had just married Mademoiselle de la Force, the only daughter of the maréchal of that name. She was a very good match both in birth, property, and appearance, nor was she one of those Court coquettes, whom it is so dangerous to burden oneself with. She had been brought up under the wing of her father and mother, who were both good Huguenots, and, as people of that faith do not willingly let their children do what we often allow ours to do, everyone who wanted a virtuous wife cast their eyes upon her, to join her fortune with their own. The sister of the Vicomte de Turenne had thought of Mademoiselle de la Force for her son, who is to-day Duc de Duras, but, having let slip a word on the subject to her brother, she by so doing gave him the idea of taking for himself what she wanted for her own son. Be this as it may, Madame de Duras and her son, having not been able to keep from complaining, the one of her brother, the other of his uncle, Bussi, hearing of this, took occasion to attack the Vicomte de Turenne. The latter heard of these attacks, and was so displeased that he spoke very strongly to him on the subject. Bussi took the course of denying everything, and the Vicomte de

Turenne, who understood no joking and well knew the state of affairs, replied that he was satisfied, since he disclaimed to his face what he had said behind his back, but for himself, were he ever to circulate any stories of people, he would support them even at the cost of his life. One would have thought that, after this lesson from the general, Bussi Rabutin would no longer have dared to do anything further of the same kind, but nevertheless, he attempted to meddle with military matters, so as to annoy M. de Turenne. The latter, however, who was of such a modest disposition, that one would never have thought, to look at him, that he was commander-in-chief of the army of the first Crown in the universe, left the settlement of this affair to the Court, and Bussi had no cause to be pleased with its decision. His claims were set aside, so much so that, perceiving himself chaffed on all sides, he tried to save himself by the slanders which he still secretly continued to circulate.

VIII

THE campaign of 1654 being ended, M. le Cardinal sent me once again into England *incognito*, so that I might give him an exact report as to the state of affairs in that country. Although there were but a hundred leagues between Paris and the capital of that realm, one would have said there were ten thousand, so different were the reports which came to hand. Some insisted that Cromwell was looked upon only as a usurper, and was so hated by the populace, that he kept his position by violence and cruelty alone. Others, on the contrary, declared that he was adored to such an extent that there was no one in the three kingdoms who would not willingly have sacrificed himself for his sake. It was important for his Eminence to know for certain which of these two parties spoke the truth. This was nevertheless not so much because of affairs of State, as on account of his own private matters. Indeed, I think that these latter affected him far more than anything else, and as, since M. le Prince had gone away, he had found means to appease the Parlement by bestowing pensions or favours upon those of its members who were most influential, he now saw nothing further in the way of his schemes. He had got such ideas into his head about his nieces, that he intended to create as many new sovereigns as there remained to him nieces to marry! At all events, the Crown of England seeming to him not one of the most insignificant of those which might fall on anyone's head, he was anxious to know to whom he should offer a niece—to the King of England, or to a son of Cromwell? His Eminence had, besides, a far more ridiculous fancy than this. I have it on good authority, and know it from the Bishop of Fréjus, his confidant. He proposed, in the event of succeeding in making a Queen of England of the girl, to soon after make another niece Queen of France. He also told the prelate in question, as I have heard further from him, that, this once done, a plank would have been laid down which would make him speak much more boldly to his Majesty. He would have no scruple about proposing that he should marry the sister of a queen, and the King himself could have none, since another would have shown him the way. Indeed, from that day forth, he began to look upon all the nobles of the realm as unworthy of being allied to him. He even became vexed at having bestowed a niece upon the Duc de Mercœur, deeming that, when one had hopes of marrying her sisters to two such great kings as were those of France and England, the son of a bastard was too insignificant to be connected with.

His Eminence showed no knowledge of the King when he thought him capable of such baseness. Never had prince finer sentiments than he! However, what had originated this idea of his was, that he had observed that the Queen of England, an aunt of his

Majesty, had not herself scrupled to have proposals made for the marriage of her son with the eldest of the Mancinis yet unmarried. She had nevertheless, felt much repugnance to doing this, still retaining a royal heart in her misfortunes, and one which secretly reproached her with this alliance, being in no way suited to the grandeur of her rank; but, as she was surrounded ˈ by people who sought but to pay court to the minister, so as to obtain some of his favours, she had let herself be brought to believe them, the more so on account of their having maintained that, otherwise, her son would never remount his throne. As this affair had been dragging on for a long time, but was proceeding now more briskly than ever, his Eminence wished me to set out at once for England, so that he might take the necessary measures according to what I should report on my return. He made me come into his study on the eve of my departure, and there said everything to me which he thought likely to cause me to be of use to him. Accordingly, as one always measures others by one's own standard, and as nothing affected him like avarice, he told me that this matter concerned me as much as himself, because great benefit might accrue to me through it. I must then take good care not to be deceived. He intended, continued he, to have me given the first post in the household of his niece, directly she should become Queen, from which I might imagine how greatly my interests lay in securing a throne for her.

This minister apparently thought, from his way of talking, that I was a man to be satisfied with chimeras. I knew, better than he had any idea of, how England was governed. I knew, I repeat, that even were he to succeed in his plans, it would not have been in his power to appoint any officer for his niece. The English are a little too jealous of strangers to allow such a thing. However, as it was not my own interests which made me set out, I made reply that it was unnecessary for him to hold out any rewards to me, for I was entirely devoted to him, and would before long prove it, and besides, I was born a good Frenchman, and, did it rest only with me to obtain the greatest fortune in the world amongst foreigners, I would not renounce my own country. I preferred to remain plain captain in the Guards there than colonel of Guards anywhere else, and especially in a country where the people were wont, as their history taught me, to dethrone their kings when the fancy seized them. M. le Cardinal rejoined that, if I set out with such ideas, I ran great risk of bringing back but bad news. With such sentiments I could have no great esteem for Cromwell, and should be too apt to think he was hated, because I disliked him myself. Meanwhile, he wanted to make me realise that, if all usurpers were to be hated, my King would come first. The descendants of Hugh Capet, from whom he sprang, had usurped the Crown of France from those of Charlemagne, to whom it legitimately belonged. They, in turn, had done the same thing for the Merovingians, so, according to my ideas, it was neither to the Carlovingians nor the Capetians that our Crown by right belonged. I must know, however, that what at first appeared tyrannical became just in the sequel, for time rectified all things, and so, with a little patience, a usurper and even a tyrant became a legitimate King. He would, therefore, have me like Cromwell if the English liked him,

and hate him if they hated him.   This was the touch-
stone I must make use of to discover if he reigned
over them legitimately, for on this alone did it depend
to know if his posterity should succeed him or not,
just as our kings had succeeded their fathers.

I thought this line of thought wonderful and well
worthy of him.   Nevertheless, Cromwell was not yet
a king, though he would much have liked to have been
one, and all he had been able to effect was to have
himself declared Protector of the three Kingdoms.   Be
this as it may, after having heard this speech of the
Cardinal's, I would not contradict him.   On the contrary, I assured him that I hated Cromwell less as
an individual than all his countrymen in general.   I
accordingly set out for England for the third time,
with orders not to show myself before our ambassador.
At that time[1] M. de Bordeaux, son of M. de Bordeaux,
Intendant des Finances, occupied this position.   He
was a little man, very vain, and one who was accustomed to say (so conceited was he) that there was not
a virtuous woman in the world.   All his success, however, in that country was limited to having debauched
the daughter of an officer of the late King, with whom
he kept up an intimacy, which was scandalous enough
for an ambassador.   After having married her off to
one of his relations, who was a young fool, and whose
only bravery lay in his sword, he had sent him back to
France and kept a sort of household with his wife.

---

[1] The position of the French Ambassador in London at this
time was one of great difficulty, and Hume, in his " History of the
House of Stuart," pays a tribute to his patience. In the Treaty,
which was signed after long negotiation, the Protector's name
was inserted before the French King's in that copy which remained
in England. See " Thurloe," vol. vi, p. 116.

He drank and ate with her, and all the difference there was between his way of life and that he might have led with a wife was that they did not live together. The Cardinal knew of this fine life, which made respectable folks talk, for they did not think, and they were quite right, that it at all suited a man in his position. However, much did his Eminence care for that, provided he did not ask for any money for his salary. He had adopted the course of giving none to some ambassadors, and would tell them, when they asked for it, that they did not deserve what he did for them, for there were many people in the Kingdom who would consider themselves too lucky to be spending all their money, provided they occupied such a position as the one he had bestowed upon them. Their name, he added, would go down in history, instead of which it would have remained enveloped in darkness and dust, unless he had been good enough to bring it forth.

He was right to speak in this way of M. de Bordeaux, who was a nobody, and whose father had founded the fortunes of his house. But, as he was wont to say the same about people of distinction and rank like M. d'Argenson, who was Ambassador at Venice, it was easy to perceive that it was avarice alone which inspired such speeches. Nevertheless, as nothing is so pernicious as an evil example, it happened that M. de Brienne, who was not a conjuror, though he occupied a position which required unusual gifts (since it lay with him to speak and write letters to the ambassadors), it happened, I repeat, that he formed such a poor estimate of M. d'Argenson, though a more capable man than himself, that on his death several packets of letters from that Excellency were found amongst his papers which he had never troubled to open! This was how the King was served at that time. There was as minister a man who did not even pay ambassadors, who ought, nevertheless, to be paid more highly and more regularly than others, since, whatever their stipend may be, none escape ruining themselves in that kind of position. This, I repeat, is how the affairs of the King were conducted! A minister of such a kind, and a Secretary of State for Foreign Affairs so neglectful as not to open the despatches of ambassadors. It is, as it were, incredible; so much so that it seems a kind of miracle how the Kingdom, with so many formidable enemies without, and servants of this sort within, has been able to preserve itself in the glorious position in which we see it at this day.

Be this as it may, M. de Bordeaux being a man of this kind, I could easily have avoided him, since I should only have had to keep away from where his mistress (in whose house he was every hour and minute) lived, had it not been that, when one least expects them, unavoidable things happen. Some days after setting foot in England, I went in the evening to a merchant's, who sold Indian stuffs. I wanted to buy a dress for a lady of Paris, to whom I had promised to send one from England. My weakness and lack of discretion had been the cause of the promise. As I was fond of her, and from my disposition could never do without a mistress, she had pressed me so hard to say where I was going, after I had told her that I should be away for a month or more mayhap, that, after having at first tried to keep my destination secret, I had not eventually been able to help telling her. She had then begged me to send her this dress, and, as

I have always been a man of my word, I believe that
it was the day after my arrival that I went to the
merchant's I have mentioned. On my entry there was
no one of importance in the shop, but a moment later
I perceived a magnificently dressed lady of great beauty
make her appearance. She was, besides, of very considerable height indeed, so much so that it rather
spoiled than improved her. However, as, when a face
is pleasing, nothing else matters to one, I delayed my
bargaining, so as to have the pleasure of looking longer
at her. She asked for the material for an entire dress,
and, judging from the livery of her servant, which was
very fine, and the respect paid her by the merchant,
that she must be a person of rank, I fell in love with
her in a moment.

The fact of the lady's continuing to ask for finer
stuffs, none of those shown her proving rich enough,
gave so much employment to the shopmen, that I was
not much pressed to buy what I was bargaining for. I
could thus look at her at my ease, and falling more
and more in love every minute, my eyes were so fixed
upon her, that she had no trouble in divining what was
passing in my heart. This made her eye me the more
attentively, and though I was not dressed to advantage,
she nevertheless thought me well made, as she herself
told me some days later. She at once concluded that
I was a foreigner and even a Frenchman, and having a
moment later whispered in the shopwoman's ear, told
her to find out from me. I could never have guessed
she was saying this, for she had taken good care to
turn her eyes away from me first and cast them elsewhere. She even told the woman to act discreetly so
that I might suspect nothing. The shopwoman, who

did not belie the reputation which nearly all her
countrywomen have of being very shrewd, exactly
followed her instructions, indeed, so cleverly did she
proceed, that one would have had to have been very
sharp to detect her intention. She begged my pardon
for not attending to me as quickly as she might have
wished, and was indeed requisite for one of her calling.
The entry of this lady was the cause; but, for two
reasons which she thoroughly relied upon, she hoped
I would forgive her. One was, that no Cavaliers like
myself would ever be annoyed at ladies being served
first, especially when as beautiful as this lady, the
other, that being a Frenchman, as she believed, I
excelled the men of all other nations in politeness and
courtesy, especially towards everyone of her sex.

If there was anything in this speech of hers to betray
her, it was at most its being made by an Englishwoman
to a Frenchman, the ladies of that country not being
too fond of us. For, whatever other people may say
about it, I for my part know that, in common with all
the men of that nation, though liking gallantry as much
as any women in the world, they are secretly jealous
of us. Nevertheless, her position of shopwoman, which
entailed her flattering everyone, having banished any
suspicions I might have had, I admitted not only that
I was a Frenchman, but further that she could serve
me in no better way than by waiting upon the lady without paying any attention to me. Nor did I forget, as
can easily be imagined without my saying so, to drop
a word about the beauty of the lady. The lady herself
then spoke, telling me that from all appearance I did
not wish to give the lie to the shopwoman about what
she had said in favour of my nation. A French,

Swedish, or Danish woman would have been more restrained in her talk, and, if possessed of the slightest knowledge of life, would have pretended not to have paid the least attention to what had been said. I say nothing of Spanish and Italian women, who are even more circumspect still and better actresses than the others. Be this as it may, her answer having given me a chance of paying her a formal compliment, my words were no more unpleasant to her than my appearance had been. I perceived this plainly enough, for she at once told me to come and help the merchant cheat her, and, when a bargain was struck, she in turn would help me to complete mine, always provided that I should first tell her for whom it was that I wanted to buy the stuff for which I was now bargaining.

I was not vexed at her curiosity, flattering myself, as I had none too bad an opinion of my own merits (in which I resembled M. de Bordeaux), that mayhap a little jealousy inspired her question. I did not however answer her frankly, declaring that the stuff was intended for a sister of mine in Gascony. The lady enquired if she was pretty, and upon my answering no and that all I would say was, that we were supposed to be so much alike that our dresses alone distinguished us, she rejoined that, if this was so, she did not pity her husband. I rejoined that my sister was unmarried and but seventeen years old, upon which she said that she must then have many lovers, and that I seemed to be forgetting a thing which was of great importance. I was about to be the cause, by further enhancing her beauty with the stuff I was going to send her, of a number of deaths in my province, and she was glad to warn me of it, lest I should be answerable to Heaven for them. I must look to it, for after her warning there would be no excuse to be found for me.

Nothing could have been more charming than this speech, especially after my having said that we were so alike. But as it was made by an Englishwoman, and the women of that nation are wont to say a number of things which other people would not say, I did not feel unduly elated, but determined to judge of my happiness or misery by what should take place later on. Meanwhile, after the lady had concluded the bargain and helped me to finish mine, as she had promised, she allowed me to extend my hand to help her get into the carriage which had brought her. I thought I should find a magnificent one at the shop door, such as the English have always had up to now, but instead of the triumphal car which I expected I found only what is called a hackney[1] coach in that country. A hackney coach is a hired carriage, not like those which we have in France, which are clean enough and which we call *carosses de remise*, but a wretched cab, such as those we see to-day on the Place du Palais Royale, or before the Église des Grands Augustins. This surprised me, for although men of rank in England do not scruple to go in these kind of vehicles, this is not the case with the ladies, who are more particular. It would have almost made me form a strange opinion of this woman, had I been in France, for, knowing that there is nothing so like a person of rank as certain courtesans, I should have half believed her to have been one. I should indeed not have known what to say, so suspicious did things look,

1 This is the earliest known mention of a hackney coach: see "Notes and Queries" for November 19th, 1898.

had I not noticed the shopman pay her unusual defer-
ence. Be this as it may, wanting to leave the lady
after having put her into the carriage, I was thoroughly
astounded by her bidding me get in with her. Having
done her bidding, she told me that she wished me to
do her a service. I thought that she was about to ask
me without ceremony for that which a woman usually
requires when very hard pressed, but it was for something quite different. She declared that she wanted
me to come and visit her father, and tell him that I had
seen her husband in France, and that he had given me
a positive assurance that he would come and join her
at the end of April. It was now January, and seeing
me completely mystified, the lady went on to say that
everyone was not like myself, who had been so polite. She
had been married against her father's will to a Frenchman, who had left her because he had found her poorer
than he had expected before marriage.

As it happened, this lady chanced to be the mistress
of M. de Bordeaux, but she took good care to make
no mention whatever of him, and I for my part was
totally ignorant that such was the case. Nevertheless,
I formed the opinion that, if the Frenchman had gone
away, it had been for some other reason than the one
she was giving. I knew that England was just as full
of horned cattle as France, and that, though there were
very fine bulls and cows there, there were other animals
besides, which were in no wise less magnificent.

This thought rather cooled my ardour. If I loved
ladies to distraction, adventuresses, amongst whom I
already included this woman, had no charm for me. I
deemed them all as crafty as the Devil, in which I was
not far wrong. I looked upon them as debauched

creatures, and as such, unworthy of the attachment of
an honourable man.   Nor was I of a disposition ever
to run the same risk for them as did one day the Duc
de Bellegarde, to avoid being found by Henri le Grand
with la belle Gabrielle, when he took the trouble to
jump out of the window into the garden of the Hotel
de Vendôme.   Women of this kind do not deserve that
people should break their necks on their account.
One can do no more for a pretty lady who has commerce only with her husband; indeed I would not jump
down a foot for any of them.   In spite of this, I am
ignorant why I draw such a distinction between the
two classes.   The woman who has but her husband
must be just the same as she who has one gallant only.
Both have but a single man, and if the matter is carefully thought over, it seems as if the one should be
blamed no more than the other by a lover, for both are
equally unfaithful.   Indeed, the woman who wants a
gallant as well as a husband seems to me the more
guilty of the two.   She has sworn fidelity before
Heaven, and is breaking her oath, whilst the other has
but sworn it in the gutter or behind her bed-curtains.
Besides, the God of Love, whom she has invoked as
witness, is quite used to see all the promises made
him broken, for the streets are chock-full of unfaithful
swains and their loves.   Be this as it may, a mistress
is less unfaithful than a wife, and so, less to be
despised.

However, to be serious—the lady having thoroughly
instructed me whilst we drove along—in due course we
reached her father's house. I found him to be a worthy
gentleman, but a little rough.   He listened to what
I had to say, and made reply that he believed my story,

because I looked as if I belonged to the family of the absent husband. I did not at first understand his meaning, and answered that I had not the honour in question. "If you are not the relative of my son-in-law," rejoined he, "you are closely related to my daughter, and, when all is said and done, that is pretty much the same thing." By this I understood him to mean that I was quite able to take the husband's place during his absence. My position now appeared somewhat difficult. He had two big boys by his side who were like regular "white rocks." Both looked as if they had sent as many English into the next world as the English had Frenchmen. I even thought that they would not have had more scruple about attacking a person from behind his back than the English sometimes had about being two against one. Mayhap I was wrong, since people must never be judged by appearances. Besides, even had the Duke of York been their patron, as Monsieur was of the French, he might not have perhaps been able, as the latter was, to save them from the hangman.

Be this as it may, seeing that I must carefully weigh my words, I told the father that I was no relative of either husband or wife, the latter of whom indeed I had met for the first time but two hours ago. He replied, as roughly as before, that that was of no consequence, for she was a good girl, and a short or long acquaintance with her made no difference. Her appetite was so keen, added he, that she would have deemed it an injustice to herself to refuse anybody. This was a thing for me to look to, for he should be sorry that I should be deceived.

The poor woman was very confused at hearing him

speak thus, and would have given a good deal to be able
to have begun matters all over again. Nevertheless, she
kept winking at me in a way I did not understand.
Indeed, I was in despair at her doing so, being afraid
of the father and sons perceiving it and picking a
quarrel with me. She said not one word however,
being apparently afraid of a thrashing, for there was
no joking with the man nor his children. They were
honourable folk and could not bear the lady's connection with the ambassador. Meanwhile, I awaited the
end of this scene with some apprehension. I was
wishing myself far away, when the brothers enquired
how I knew the husband of their sister, and according
to the instructions she had given me, I replied that I
came from the same neighbourhood and had stayed at
the same hostelry with him in Paris before setting out.
They at once began to abuse their brother-in-law, and
cautioned me against believing a word of what he might
have told me, adding, that he never spoke the truth,
and, were all Frenchmen like him, there would be no
cause for astonishment at their being hated in a
thousand places as they were. As, however, I had
never seen their brother-in-law, I cannot say whether
they spoke truth or falsehood.

They continued in the same strain for some time,
the old man occasionally joining in these attacks on
his son-in-law. Meanwhile, the lady seized the opportunity to gently withdraw. I was much astonished to
find her gone, and, had I been in France, should
certainly have thought that all this was but a plot
got up to assassinate me. However, as the English,
cruel as they may be, are not given to those kind of
things which so often happen in Paris, and which dis-

honour our nation, I was somewhat reassured, for I saw nothing in either the father or the sons to cause me to fear a trap. At length, when they had had their say without any contradiction from myself, I thought the time had come for me to depart. I was afraid of nothing except being detained, but, my apprehension proving groundless, I got into the street without further ado. Nevertheless, I was curious enough to occasionally cast a glance behind me to see if I was followed, and, perceiving a girl hurrying along with her eyes directed at me, I got into a doorway to let her pass, in case she might be looking for someone else. However, she began to slacken her speed, and, coming up to me, I awaited her with a stout heart, curious as to how all this might end.

I had not been deceived, for she had come from the lady who awaited me four paces away, and had, so the girl said, something to say to me which it would not displease me to hear. I was near saying that I had no answer to give to this, but, considering that this would be acting rudely, I bade the girl lead the way and I would follow. She stopped at a certain door and wished me to enter the house, in which she declared her mistress was awaiting me. Having, however, little desire to be once more shut up, I somewhat ungallantly told the maid to ask her mistress to come down, as a sprain prevented my going any further. At the same time, I feigned lameness, and the girl, who was none too sharp, believing my story, did as I had told her. The lady eventually appeared, and tried to make me credit that what her father had said was but caused by the effects of drink. He was, she added, constantly drunk, and when in that state had no idea what he was doing or saying, so much so that people who knew him paid no attention to his words. In short, it was not her fault that I did not attribute everything I had heard to the effects of Bacchus, but, not being so foolish as she thought, I formed my own opinion without saying anything rude to her. In the meantime, as my ardour seemed to have cooled since I had left the shop, and as I appeared to be not over eager to enter her house, she proposed to accompany me to mine. This was a choice of two evils, for, on leaving the merchants, she had had my stuff placed in her carriage by one of her lackeys, and, consequently, I was anxious to see it again. I accordingly got in, after glancing round to see if we were watched, but, observing no one, I began to think myself safe. She had previously asked me my address, so as to tell it to the coachman, who did not know a word of French, and, as I did not know one word of English, I could not understand what she said to him. This being so, as she had ordered the man to drive to her house instead of to mine, I was astounded, on getting out, to find myself in a courtyard which was quite unknown to me. The lady perceived my surprise, and told me to be reassured, saying that it was not a fine thing to tremble in a lady's presence, and she knew a thousand people who, very far from pulling such a long face as I was doing, would have thanked her a thousand times for her complacency. I made no reply to her cajoleries— indeed, I had no reply to make, finding myself shut up within four walls without any idea as to how I was to get out.

The lady would have been much upset if her lackeys had understood French, for she would not have been

pleased that they should have been witnesses of my
conduct towards her; besides, they might have repeated
it to the Ambassador. However, as she had taken care
to choose those who were new comers and dullards, so
that they might not understand, she again reproached
me a thousand times, and receiving these reproaches
coldly enough, she told me that I was unworthy of her
attentions. She was beautiful, as I have already said,
and even so beautiful that I know not if her like existed
in all England, and so, soon putting on one side delicacy
about making love to another man's mistress, it was
not my fault that I did not that moment give a proof
that I found her even more beautiful than I had done
when she had come to choose the stuff. I begged her
to dismiss her lackeys and her maid, so that I might
speak at my ease, to which she replied that my memory
must be short for me to have already forgotten that her
servants did not understand one word of French. To
this I rejoined, that it was true that they had no ears
for my words, but she must agree with me that they
had eyes to observe my actions. Love made itself
known in many ways, and after a lover had tried to
make himself understood by fine protestations, he must
have recourse to even more significant things still. This
was my case, and why I wished her people sent away.
She clearly understood my meaning, but, as this was
not what she desired, made answer that I passed too
quickly from one extreme to the other for her to take
me at my word. At first I had appeared to her all
fire, then all ice, immediately after hearing what her
father had said. She had in vain used all efforts to
warm me, though I had done everything to discourage
her. One could place little reliance on people of this

sort, and what I was proposing would on the contrary turn me into ice again; so, to be more certain of me, she must sell her favours more dearly than I thought.

True is it that nothing sharpens the appetite like difficulty; the more fuss she made, the more eager I became. She soon perceived this both from my words, and my flashing eyes. In vain I begged her to dismiss her servants that I might kiss her hand. She retorted that, were I to kiss that, I should afterwards want to kiss something else. I was unable to alter her resolve, and all I could obtain from her was a promise that we should meet again, and the assurance that patience conquered all things. We had supped together without ceremony, and I had made an excellent ragout for her, which she declared was the best she had ever tasted. I promised to soon prepare another of the same sort, for it would not be long before I would return. Indeed, I proposed to come back the next day, always providing *que la Signora ne fut pas inpedita*, as the Italian runs, that is to say, that "the lady was not prevented"; for, ever since her father's words, I entertained suspicions as to her being a Vestal. Meanwhile, whilst in bed, I received a note by an old Duenna, in which she sent me word to take care not to return and see her till further notice, for her husband had arrived a quarter of an hour after my departure, and, as he was a curious man, she had to be careful with him.

At first I thought this a pretext to get rid of me for some reason or other, but she was not lying on this occasion, though sometimes she did so, as it is easy to perceive from her story to me of her father's drunkenness. Be this as it may, being doubtful whether her note was true or not, I went to discover in the neighbourhood of her house if her husband had really returned. A neighbour, who knew some French, told me that he had and, asking me if I was thinking of entering his service, advised me against doing so, because, besides being a beggar of beggars, he was a very bad master to boot. It was not surprising that this man should take me for a servant. I was wearing a ragged suit and my hair was concealed under a wig which I had adopted as a disguise on my voyage, so as to be unrecognised, for usually I wore it as I do to-day. It was consequently easy for me to make him believe all I wished, and after some further talk I went to see the husband of my Englishwoman in the wretched clothes I was wearing, which exactly suited my part of a cook out of place. As I knew very well how to cook a ragout, I was quite ready he should take me at my word, and besides, reckoned that my new rôle would in no way interfere with the affairs of M. le Cardinal, which, as there was no great cooking to be done, I should find time to look after, whenever I might think fit.

The husband of the lady himself came to open the door when I knocked. On seeing him I was afraid that I had come too late to obtain the place, for he was of evil appearance, with hands as black as a charcoal burner's. I indeed took him for a cook, which he was much more like than a gentleman, so much so that he had to tell me who he was before I could believe he was really the master. However, after having learnt from whom I had come, he told me to go into the kitchen and prepare supper and afterwards we would discuss my wages.

It was then about four or five o'clock in the afternoon,

and I passed unrecognised by his wife's servants, who
had seen me as it were but for a minute. The lady,
on being informed that her husband had engaged a
French cook came downstairs to ask me to make
a ragout similar to the one she had eaten with me,
and having better eyes she immediately recognised
me, but being afraid of harming both of us she took
care to give no sign of recognition, but at once went
upstairs again. She was enchanted, as she afterwards
told me, at the proofs of love, which she deemed me
to be giving her, and I took good care not to destroy
her illusions, as I should have done, had I told her
that jealousy had had as much to do with my conduct .
as love. Indeed, had I been thoroughly certain of her
virtue, I should never have made any enquiries whether
her husband had really returned, as I had done. Be
this as it may, having cooked him an even better
ragout than that of the day before, the poor cuckold,
who was like a regular Sancho Pansa, told me that
whilst I made sauces like this I should be the man
for him, and at the same time promised me large
wages, apparently on the condition they should never
be paid. It was a great pity that he was not a
follower of M. le Cardinal, for like him he would
have ruined himself in promises. Never had man
such a bent for lying as he, and from what he said
he was the richest individual in the world. Everything
belonged to him—Heaven and earth, so to speak!
Nevertheless, though he had not one sou of ready
money, he was always boasting of his wealth, though
not of something else which really belonged to him.
He was fit for a straight waistcoat, and kept that
quiet, though one had but to see him to perceive
the truth.

What I had done for the lady—at least what she thought I had done—soon obtained its reward, and she accorded me what I asked the very first time I did so, declaring that a woman who could be ungrateful after my having become a cook for her sake would deserve drowning. Thus did she excuse her weakness, and as when one's own interests are concerned one is but too feeble, I thought myself lucky in occupying a position which could not be considered a great one by any disinterested person; for, to have the leavings of a second Sancho Pansa and the ambassador was not much.

The lady was, however, as one may say, a novice in love, and had never had a child. In spite of these advantages, she was, to my mind, spoilt by a fault which some, though not sensible, people consider a merit. There were certain moments when she affected to be too much carried away by love, a thing which in no wise befits, I will not say a respectable woman, but, further, a respectable mistress. Woman's distinguishing quality should be modesty. It is to guard this as well as to keep draughts away that beds have curtains, and a virtuous woman dislikes these to be drawn aside at certain moments, for daylight might seem to reproach her for lacking that delicacy which her sex demands.

Be this as it may, this lady in due course began to show signs of being about to become a mother, and at once gave me the credit of being the cause. I had my own opinion on the subject, and, without being certain of anything, felt sure that I had, at all events, done my share as well as other people. Sancho Pansa, indeed, took all the credit to himself, and, in short, this child, after being attributed by its mother to her

husband and myself, was further laid at the door of
the Ambassador, M. de Bordeaux, by her—a gift which
was at once registered by public opinion. The latter
was a man of some worth, clever and polite, besides
being generous enough when his heart was captured.
The gift of this lady in no wise displeased him, and,
indeed, his affection for his Englishwoman was considerably increased thereby. Every day he was wont
to come and visit her, and, chancing to eat one of my
ragouts, curiosity seized him to see me and learn my
history. With this object the ambassador sent a
lackey for me, but, being in no mood[1] to show my
nose to a man who might be returning to Paris at
any moment and meet me there, I feigned a headache
to escape such an unpalatable interview. Besides, I
hated him at heart as a rival, though, curiously enough,
I bore Sancho Pansa no ill-will, deeming him too con-
temptible for my notice. Mayhap I was wrong to
avoid this interview, for it was inevitable that M. de
Bordeaux should again ask to see me, for, since my
arrival, his own cook no longer came with him to
prepare his food. I had realised this, and, consequently, had an idea of cooking all his dishes so badly
that he should lose all desire to see me, but, fearing on
reflection that such a course might cause my expulsion,
I continued to please the ambassador's taste so much
(though he himself kept an excellent table), that he was
not long in paying me the compliment I dreaded.
This time I dared not make the same excuse as before,
so, deciding to play the loon, I told the lackey sent to

[1] D'Artagnan had probably secret orders from Cardinal
Mazarin to keep a close watch on the ambassador and report
what he was doing.

fetch me that I was afraid to go upstairs for fear of his
master's laughing at me.   Poor as I was, I hated being
made a laughing stock, for I came from a province
where folks were so full of pride as to often injure
their own interests.   At least, that had been my case,
for, had I not been unwilling to be jeered at, I should
still have been with the Commandeur de Jars.

The name of this officer sprang to my lips sooner
than anyone else's, because I knew that he kept a
good table and loved laughing at everyone.   My
answer, however, but increased the Ambassador's
curiosity, for he knew that this commandeur only
employed first-class servants, and he accordingly sent
for me once again.   I showed myself no more obedient
than on the other occasions, and Sancho Pansa, who
chattered as was his wont, chancing to say that my
conceit gave him no surprise (for I was a fine, well-
built fellow, and were he not certain of his wife, a
man he should not care for her to cast her eyes
upon), the ambassador, whose suspicions were perhaps
aroused by the lady blushing or by some decrease of
tenderness on her part, became very uneasy.   He
announced his intention of himself going to see me and
taking Sancho Pansa (who could refuse him nothing
as he lived at his expense) with him.   I found myself,
to my great surprise, confronted by these unwelcome
visitors.   Covered with confusion, which was only too
apparent, I answered the interrogatories put to me
by M. de Bordeaux as shortly as possible, but in
spite of this he clearly perceived from my demeanour
and appearance that I was no mere cook.   Deciding
to watch me he sent one of his men, eighteen or
nineteen years old, on the pretext of learning how

to cook a ragout after my fashion.   This youth was usually his agent when he wished to debauch some girl, which was often enough, for a wife and mistress did not satisfy his appetites.   His wife indeed had remained in Paris, where she led a very gay life, which in due course was reported to her husband by his father.   As the ambassador was a man of honour, he was much annoyed at these scandals and wrote a lecture to his lady, threatening to come to Paris unless she gave up certain friends.   She might well have done so, but, being of a perverse nature, she feigned illness and closed her door to everyone, which coming to M. de Bordeaux' ears made him so jealous that, forgetting me, he set out from London, alleging a hunting party near Dover as his excuse, and crossed the Channel without saying a word to a soul.   He arrived at his house about midnight, and, awakening the porter, who did not dare to refuse him the entry, went upstairs to his wife's room, which he found shut up.   Having aroused an old servant, who had been his nurse, he learnt from her that her mistress had twice, twenty-four hours before, bidden her adieu for a fortnight or three weeks without saying where she was going, and had given strict instructions that her sudden departure was to be kept a secret.

This was terrible news for the ambassador, for he could not go and look for his wife, for he feared that being away from his post might injure his prospects with the King or his minister, were they to hear of it. He could therefore only speak to his father on the subject and beg him to avenge his honour when the lady should return, keeping in the meanwhile silence about the matter as much for his own honour as for the ultimate success of his revenge. This being done, he at once set out on his return to London, occasionally telling himself on the way that now the only misfortune left to him would be to find himself as unlucky in the matter of his mistress as he had been with his wife. He still had suspicions about me, but, as the other affair was far more serious, one jealousy had well nigh obliterated the other.

In due course M. de Bordeaux arrived in London, and the very day of his arrival his cup was filled to the brim by the discovery of the truth of his suspicions about myself. The youth he had set to spy over me reported to him that, Sancho Pansa having got as drunk as a pig with two Englishwomen, his wife and I had been shut up in a bedroom together from eleven at night till five the next morning. Such news was not calculated to soothe the ambassador's ruffled feelings, and he determined to break all the fine mirrors and other costly furniture which he had given his mistress before her eyes, as he could not decently give the woman a castigation. However, when he appeared on the scene, the work was already half done. Madame de Bordeaux had arrived there with a companion, and had at once begun by smashing the mirrors to bits, and had then covered her husband's paramour with abuse. All this had just happened. The Englishwoman had been completely taken by surprise, for she did not know who the ambassadress, who had come simply dressed in a travelling costume, might be. Madame de Bordeaux had intended to return at once to Paris, but this the Englishwoman prevented by sending at once for a constable, which corresponds with the man we term a commissaire.

Meanwhile, she had her door guarded, declaring that, when this officer should arrive, neither the lady nor her companion should get out of his hands till they had paid the last sou for the damage they had done, and also for the affront which she had received.

The ambassador, under these circumstances, had a good deal of trouble in obtaining admission, the man at the door telling him that, two female thieves having come to rob his mistress, they had been secured whilst breaking her mirrors. M. de Bordeaux took this for truth and praised the man for his vigilance, but, on going upstairs, could not have been more astonished, had horns suddenly sprouted from his head, than he was at the sight of his wife and her companion. For some time he was speechless, but, regaining his senses, he begged the Englishwoman to counterorder the constable and he would have all the damage made good; then, being left alone with the ambassadress, he bade her give her reasons for having left Paris without his leave. In reply, she retorted that a woman had no need of such a thing, when she possessed a husband who led a life such as he did. This was why he had not brought her with him. However, news of this kind soon travelled across the sea, and, therefore, he should not be astonished at her having come in person to show her resentment and contempt.

The ambassador had been so alarmed at the reports sent him by his father that he was delighted at matters turning out in this way, so, begging the Englishwoman to hold her peace about what had occurred, he told her to say that the lady was a mistress of her husband, who had been promised marriage by him, and, having been deceived, had come to create a scandal. At the same time he sent word to Sancho Pansa not to come home that day, so as to give greater colour to this story. He knew he was to be found either at an inn or a tennis-court, as, indeed, was the case, and this husband duly betook himself to the Embassy, so as to appear to have need of some safe retreat, awaiting there the orders of the ambassador as to showing himself again. The Englishwoman's servants were much surprised at matters settling down so easily, M. de Bordeaux taking care to tell his mistress in their presence that her husband had brought all this scandal upon himself. He then, after a hasty supper, sent off his wife and her companion towards the Tower, where a frigate he had hired was ready to take them back to France under the charge of Sancho Pansa, whom he was delighted to get rid of in such a manner, for he was killing two birds with one stone. The ambassadress was much upset at being sent off after this fashion, for she was compelled to depart by her husband, who kept his face in his cloak for fear of being recognised whilst seeing her go on board the frigate.

His Excellency, having settled this matter, now had only me to deal with. The report of his spy had increased his suspicions that I was quite a different character from the one I pretended to be, but nevertheless, he was very much puzzled as to how I could have obtained a footing in the house. In the meantime, it must not be imagined that I had been neglecting my duty. Twice had I written to M. le Cardinal about those subjects which he had sent me to enquire into, and he had found my information so much in accord with that of his other informants that he sent me

word back expressing his satisfaction with my conduct
and instructing me not to return till further orders.
To tell the truth, I was becoming fatigued with the
part I had been playing at the house of the Englishwoman.   It was paying too dear a price for her favours
to have to personate a cook, though, in addition to
my expecting to please the Cardinal, the lady was wont
to embrace me in spite of my kitchen apron, and
to declare that she loved me, as I was a thousand times
better than the whole English Court.   She took care
not to say the ambassador, though she had always
denied having any relations with him like grim death
itself.   Whenever I mooted such a thing, she would
reply that he came merely as a relative and intimate
friend of Sancho Pansa.   There were many spies of
M. de Bordeaux in London, who kept him informed
about matters which were of importance to him to
know.   It must be understood that I had taken to
frequenting inns (as does everyone in England) so as
to pick up anything likely to forward my interests with
his Eminence, and, as I had the wherewithal to be
decently dressed, no one took me for the cook of
Sancho Pansa's wife.   Not that this kind of life was
to my liking; indeed, except at the time of[1] my early
loves, and in order to see my mistress, I had never
indulged in this kind of debauchery.   Indeed, I think
it ill befitting a respectable man to go and tipple the
greater part of the day, and in France it is only done
by the dregs of the populace, for if by chance other
people take to this kind of life, as sometimes happens,
they are thought worthy only of the finger of scorn.
    Be this as it may, thinking that, the less I liked it,

1 See Vol. I., p. 97.

the more praise I deserved from the Court, for whose sake I did it, I became so assiduous in my attendance as to occupy the position of one of the chief pillars of the inn I frequented. In consequence, people began to grow curious as to where I lived, and my reasons for having come to England. By way of satisfying their curiosity, I made reply that I was travelling for my own pleasure. When however I tried to give evasive answers as to where I lived, the matter became more serious, for enquiries were made as to the truth of my statements. A spy of the ambassador's in particular, was very suspicious as to my reasons for being eager for news, and watched me near Long Acre where I had told him I was living. This is a big street at the exterior of the town leading to Whitehall, which is the palace of the Kings of England. He wasted his time there, from five in the morning to five at night, which was showing a good deal more patience than I could ever have shown, though my business in England was much the same as his own. Be this as it may, coming on to our accustomed inn, he proceeded to eye me carefully, and became every moment more certain that his suspicions were correct.

I left the inn at seven that evening, and the spy would have followed me to find out where I really lived, had he been able to do so, but, as he was not prepared for this, he let me go alone, and delayed his schemes to the morrow. Meanwhile, betaking himself to the ambassador, he informed him of his discovery. M. de Bordeaux showed himself very keen about the matter, for just then M. le Prince was doing his best to get Cromwell to make a treaty against France, so, at once concluding I was one of his men, he bade him

be sure and follow me the next day, and he would provide him with an assistant to let him know what was
to be done with me.   Never dreaming of this, I went
next day as usual to the inn, and should soon have been
trapped, had I not been wont to always look behind me
on going out.   I consequently had no difficulty in perceiving that I was followed, and having tried in vain to
baffle my pursuer, I thought it best to go straight up to
him.   The man was rather taken aback at this, but,
being an impudent fellow, kept on his way, stopping
only in a doorway to observe my movements.   However, coming within three paces of him, I taxed him
with having followed me for a quarter of an hour past,
and demanded what the meaning of such conduct
might be?   He retorted with much insolence, that I
then wished to stop him walking in the street, which I
could not do, since the King of England, who alone
could forbid it, allowed everyone in the town to take as
many turns in it as they liked.   His answer seemed to
me to deserve only punishment, and at once drawing
my sword, he fled to escape my rage, not having as
much courage as chatter about him.   He ran well
enough, and, as far as I could see in the lantern light,
was a spare man and not at all fat, so though a good
enough runner myself, I forbore to pursue him. Indeed,
I did not wish to do so, my sole desire being to avoid
him.

After this, I lost sight of the man who had been so
terrified at my wanting to attack him, that following
me further was the last thing he dreamt of.   My path
was therefore clear to return to my Englishwoman who
would have liked me to spend all the afternoon with
her, being of opinion that, as her husband was out and

the ambassador looking after his despatches, I was
wrong to waste such precious time. But, if his
Excellency had business to do, I had mine just as well
as he, so I told her plainly that the nights were long
enough without my giving up the days too. Indeed,
I passed most of my time with her, and I had found
means to frustrate the intentions of the ambassador by
making his spy drunk every evening, for he was devoted
to wine and was too poor to buy it himself, for in
England it is very expensive. Nevertheless, as one
must be very cautious when meddling with one's
neighbour's wife, I made this apprentice believe that
the wine cost me nothing, in order that my generosity
might not arouse his suspicions, telling him that I had
found means to open the cellar door of the ambassador,
which much delighted him, for he appeared to be afraid
of my money coming to an end. Being calmed by the
idea that we were drinking at his Excellency's expense,
he could not prevent himself telling me, whilst in his
cups, that the ambassador was jealous of me and had
sent him to the Englishwoman's house much more on
that account than to learn how to cook my ragout.
He omitted, however, to add that he had told M. de
Bordeaux of having on one occasion seen me enter his
mistress's chamber, and that I had passed the night
there. Had he done so, I should have taken certain
precautions which in my ignorance I failed to do, and
so escaped something which happened to me a few
days later.

Meanwhile, as I felt afraid of thanking him for his
information, lest when his senses should have returned
he might take advantage of it, I pretended not to be
able to believe what he had said, declaring that Heaven

was no further from earth than the suspicion of the
ambassador from the truth, and his reply should have
put me on my guard, had I been as wise as I ought to
have been.   He rejoined that whatever I said would
not alter his opinion, and when I tried to make him
explain his meaning, (perceiving that he had said too
much, which might some day get him into trouble with
his Excellency) this man feigned not to know what he
was saying, so as to make me think that drunkenness
rather than truth had caused him to talk as he had
done, but in spite of this he was not so drunk as I
imagined.

The ambassador was much surprised at the report
given by the man he had deputed to watch me, and
was angry with him for not having followed me further.
Questioning the spy, he discovered from his description
of my appearance, that I was undoubtedly the individual who was passing as a cook in his mistress's
house, but wishing to make certain of it, he sent at
supper-time to the Englishwoman to beg her to send
her cook to him for but a quarter of an hour.   Both
she and I were much disturbed at this summons, but
after consulting together we decided that the best
thing for me to do was to obey it and go.   One of my
reasons for taking such a course was, that I feared
being sent away in case of disobedience, which indeed
would not have mattered to me much, but my liaison
with this woman had made me more eager to stay
than I ought to have been, and so I accordingly
dressed quickly and set out for the Embassy.   The
ambassador had concealed his spy in a place where
he could not be seen (a thing which I could not
possibly have any idea of) and had given him orders

to at once come out of his ambuscade, should I prove to be the man who was wanted, and accuse me there and then of having told him that I intended poisoning his Excellency. No sooner therefore had I entered the room than the spy came out of his hiding place.

My surprise was extreme, for as the ambassador had given as an excuse when sending for me that he wanted the recipe of my ragout (which was a ragout peculiar to my own province) for his wife, I had some idea that such was really the case. He had, however, merely said this so as to be able to dismiss me without arousing my suspicions, should he have wrongly suspected me. Perceiving however that I was the man he expected, he told me, after ringing a bell which stood on a bureau near him, that I had then but taken up my abode at the Englishwoman's to poison him. This he said before his spy had opened his mouth, fearing perhaps, after what that individual had said, that rage might carry me away and cause me to forget the respect I owed to the ambassador of my King, or perhaps he may have trembled at the thought of the accusation he was making. Be this as it may, before I could reply, most of his servants entered the room armed in different ways, and headed by his écuyer with a pistol in one hand and a sword in the other. Seeing how matters lay, I said that such a deed as this must redound but little to his honour when it should have become known. He might have me assassinated if he liked, but such a piece of cowardice would sully his fame and mayhap I should be revenged after my death more dearly than he thought.

My words made M. de Bordeaux more certain than ever that I was an agent of M. le Prince and that I

meant that it was he who would exact vengeance for
my blood, so the interests of the State increasing the
ill-will which he already bore me by reason of his
jealousy, I should have been unfailingly lost, had I
not possessed so good a patron saint as I did. His
Excellency again accused me before his servants of
having wanted to poison him, and, referring to his
spy as to whether such was not the case, the man
with unparallelled effrontery declared that it was, adding
that other witnesses could corroborate his statements,
and that I had much better confess my guilt and
implore the mercy of the ambassador, for perhaps
his anxiety to conceal the defects of our nation might
prevent his pushing matters to the last extremity.
In short, this insolent fellow, talking as if I were a
real criminal, threw me into such a rage that had it
not been that in no pass whatsoever is it befitting
to show one's anger, I do not know what I might not
have done. Be this as it may, the ambassador, who
wanted to ruin me, because not only was he jealous,
but believed me to be a spy, having produced another
witness just as shameless as the first one, I was
completely dumfounded as to what to think of such
villainy.

The ambassador then caused me to be shut up in a
room and there kept under observation until he should
have written to M. le Cardinal and received an answer.
He then wrote to his Eminence, telling him he had
seized a Frenchman—a spy of M. le Prince—who had
introduced himself, disguised as a cook, into a household where he was wont to visit, adding a great many
more fantastic details. The Cardinal, who had no
mean opinion of him, consequently sent back word

to have me conveyed, bound hand and foot, to Boulogne, there to be handed over to the Maréchal d'Aumont, who would hold me in safe keeping till such time as men should arrive to conduct me to the Bastille. Meanwhile, he was to take good care that Cromwell should not hear of a prisoner being seized, or that he was to be sent to France, for his nation was so jealous of its privileges that, without fail, he would take exception to his having dared lay hands on my person. He should, therefore, whilst despatching me from London by night, not only have me manacled hand and foot, but also have me gagged till the ship was reached.

This was the terrible sentence pronounced by his Eminence against me, and the ambassador, urged both by reasons of State and jealousy, took all possible care to see it carried out. He sent two relays of carriages on the road which had to be traversed, so as to ensure greater safety and speed. These were posted in the country, and not in a town or village, lest I might occasion some disturbance and rouse the inhabitants. I was gagged only with great difficulty, but, my feet and hands being put in irons, I was forced to submit to my fate. About one in the morning I was placed in a carriage, and, three men entering it, the blinds were drawn down to prevent my being observed. Taken to a place of embarcation, I was carried on board ship with a guard of six men with muskets pointed at my head, which, however, somewhat decreased my fears, for I deemed that I should not have been brought so far if I was to be shot; much more did I fear being thrown overboard, but, far from this being the case, no sooner had we made a quarter of a league than my gag was removed. I had already been fed two or three times on the road, which should have reassured me, for one does not feed a man who is to be stabbed or thrown into the sea. Nevertheless, I did not think myself safe till we were in sight of Boulogne, but this took a long time, for, though as a rule it is but a passage of five or six hours, in our case it was one of four whole days, and we were near perishing on the way. A storm arose two hours after raising anchor and drove us far out of our course, which enabled the men sent by M. le Cardinal to reach Boulogne before I did. They presented their credentials to M. le Maréchal d'Aumont, who had been informed what to do, and declared himself ready to hand me over directly I should have landed. I had hoped to be taken at once before the Maréchal, or the Lieutenant de Roi, if he were away, but my escort, having come to fetch me at the landing place, at once thrust me into a hired carriage which they had brought with them in order to conceal me from the people of Boulogne, who were then somewhat rebellious, and might have attempted a rescue. My captors paid no heed whatever to my entreaties to take me before the maréchal, which, indeed, I might have caused them to do, had I let out who I was, in which case I should have been treated as no spy, but as a man of some consequence. Fearing, however, lest my speaking out might displease his Eminence, I allowed myself to be taken where my escort pleased, without breathing a syllable as to my identity.

Seven or eight days after, we reached the Bastille about four or five o'clock in the afternoon, and I began to laugh to myself at the thought of my being taken there. I pictured the governor's surprise (for I was known to him) when I should be delivered into his hands, knowing that I should only have to whisper a word in his ear to receive quite a different reception from that which my guards expected. However, the governor proved to be away, and so I was taken before an underling of his, who was a stranger to me, and I, therefore, determined to keep my secret till his return, which I thought would be that evening. He stayed, however, at St. Germain, where he had gone, till the next day, and dressing for the King's levee, before returning to Paris, the Commandeur de Souvrai sent him word to join him in a hunting party with M. le Premier. The governor, who was passionately fond of hunting, gave up his idea of going to pay his court to the King, and at once changing his dress, started off. The stag led the hunt near to Mantes, and his horse falling, this governor broke his left arm. The accident delayed his return, and gave me more time than I expected to bore myself in. I had been thrown into a dungeon where my clothes became every night wringing wet with damp, though I kept a fire burning all day. I had besides, a sorry bed which was half a foot too short for me.

Three weeks elapsed before the governor returned to Paris, for he had at first been treated by a village surgeon whose work had to be done over again. Meanwhile, all my entreaties to communicate with him were scoffed at by my gaoler. I also asked in vain for a confessor in spite of my feigning illness, and my attempts to obtain an interview with the governor's substitute proved in no way more successful. At last, in despair, I begged the man who was wont to bring me food, and who was one of the men who are called by the name of Porte-clef in the Bastille, to all events tell the governor that I was a gentleman of the Court. He promised to do so, but instead of faithfully carrying my message, sent word to him that I had lost my head, and was trying to pass for a great lord; adding, that I had even erected a canopy in my room made of my bed clothes, under which I would sit and show off my madness. It was true that I had erected something of the kind, but it had been only as a protection against the wind which blew in exactly upon me. The governor, who was quite accustomed to see most of his prisoners go mad, thought that this was my case, and consequently paid no further attention.

Meanwhile, M. le Cardinal was writing to me in London about some instructions he wished to give me, and was much puzzled at receiving no reply. He did not dare to ask news of me from M. de Bordeaux, for he had sent me to England without giving him any information as to my coming. This being so, he had recourse to a banker, whom he was wont to employ in that country, and the latter, having made every enquiry, sent word back to his Eminence that I had disappeared a month ago and given rise to much uneasiness as to my fate. The Cardinal was more puzzled at this than ever, and ordered the banker to make further search, which he did with no better success than before. At this time Treville was beginning to lower his tone, and chancing to be discussing matters which concerned his post with his Eminence, he was asked by him if he had heard any news of me, to which he replied that he thought I had returned to my own province. Besmaux, in answer to the same question, declared that I was just the man to have joined the Carthusians, for I had often said they were the happiest people in the world, and in consequence of this statement the Cardinal had all the Carthusian monasteries in the kingdom written to, but naturally obtained no news of my whereabouts. Under these circumstances he might perhaps have disposed of my post, had he not thought fit to wait yet a little longer.

The Englishwoman, mystified at my disappearance, had meanwhile kept asking for news of me from M. de Bordeaux, who maliciously pretended to have sent me back to her house. Thinking, therefore, that I had become weary of her and reflecting that a dozen lovers could be found for one who was lost, she easily consoled herself for what she believed to be my fickleness. When the ambassador perceived that his mistress bore my absence with such indifference, he began to fear he had made a mistake and that I was innocent. He accordingly wrote to M. le Cardinal to ask him whether the prisoner he had sent over had proved guilty or not, so as to be able to take the requisite measures to guard against the plots of the Prince de Condé.

His Eminence had been so busy that he had forgotten all about the prisoner, but this letter jogging his memory, he gave orders for the lieutenant-criminel to come and interrogate me. There was then no lieutenant-général of police, as there is to-day. I was delighted beyond measure, when this magistrate announced what he had come for, and he, in turn, was astounded at perceiving who the prisoner was. He knew me to be no spy of M. le Prince, but yet, carrying out the forms of his office, and proceeding with his questions, all the answer he could obtain from me was that I had been tricked, and would beg him to tell the Cardinal of my plight. The lieutenant-criminel went straight from the Bastille to the Palais Mazarin, and saw M. le Cardinal, who at once asked if the prisoner should be hung or broken on the wheel? The officer replied that there was nothing to be made of M. d'Artagnan, for he would answer no questions. At first his Eminence could not realise that I was the prisoner sent over from England, but having at last done so, he immediately despatched a courier to that country to enquire the grounds on which the ambassador had accused me of being a spy of M. le Prince. My name was not as well known as that of M. le Prince, nor the Vicomte de Turenne, nor many others of like merit, but still, as, when one is a captain in the Guards, one is in some way beginning to distinguish oneself, M. de Bordeaux had heard enough about me to know who I was, and was, therefore, much astonished when he heard whom he had caused to be arrested. He sent excuses to M. le Cardinal, saying that being ignorant of my presence in London, my avidity for news, together with the fact of my having personated a cook at the house of a lady whom he frequently visited, together with other circumstances which had come to his knowledge, had caused him to believe me to be acting thus for love of M. le Prince, and, therefore, he had deemed that both prudence and his duty demanded my being made a prisoner.

M. le Cardinal, who was the most suspicious man in the world, thought my masquerade such a bad joke as to suddenly lose more than half the good opinion he had up to then had of me, and he began to be somewhat suspicious as to whether I had not really been won over by the Prince. His Eminence knew nothing of the part which love had played in my disguise, nor of the relations of M. de Bordeaux with the Englishwoman, so telling the lieutenant-criminel to return the next day, he instructed him to continue my interrogation and inform me, were I still to refuse to answer, that I should be treated[1] like a dumb man. I was also to be told that the Cardinal would be delighted for me to justify myself, but were I by chance to be found guilty, less mercy would be shown to me than to anyone else, since ingratitude, as well as treachery, must then be laid to my charge. I had been five weeks in prison, but long as these weeks had been, they seemed to me shorter than the twenty-four hours which elapsed before the lieutenant-criminel returned to question me, and I was totally at a loss to divine the reason of his being so long—I was so disturbed at this that I could eat nothing, and indeed I must really have appeared a madman to my gaoler. The only consolation I could give myself was that M. le Cardinal had gone to Vincennes, and so had not been able to be found.

At last, after this terrible twenty-four hours, the Porte-clef, came to say that the lieutenant-criminel was waiting for me with his clerk in the hall of the governor, a piece of news which alarmed me beyond measure, indeed, I felt a shock just as if all the blood in my veins had rushed to my heart. It was the mention of the clerk being with the officer that disturbed me, for I knew what this meant! The lieutenant-criminel received me in a very grave fashion, and

1 Meaning that torture would be resorted to.

having made me sit opposite to him, set forth that
when a man was once in the hands of justice matters
moved none too quickly, and he must justify himself to
get out of them.   I had been painted as black as coal,
and before being thought white as snow, I must give
certain proofs of my innocence.   He had been deputed
by M. le Cardinal to interrogate me and make a report
to him, and I must therefore answer his questions.
This I declined to do, being unwilling to be treated as
a malefactor when I had but done my duty.   Eventually, after much threatening on his part and much
firmness on mine, I bethought me of asking for an
interview with Navailles, adding that I would answer
any questions put to me by him, and if his Eminence,
after that, were still to believe me guilty, I would
willingly submit to be tried, though I did not imagine
that matters would ever come to such a pass, unless it
was a crime to have made love to the mistress of the
ambassador !

The lieutenant-criminel, through whose hands all
criminals who were to be hung or broken on the wheel
were wont to pass, was so experienced in distinguishing
the innocent from the guilty as to hardly ever be
deceived.   Forming a just estimate of me, he returned
to M. le Cardinal, and told him that it was his opinion
that my present plight arose from the jealousy of
M. de Bordeaux, who had wished to rid himself of a
rival.   The Cardinal, who now began to have serious
doubts as to my guilt, sent Navailles to see me at the
Bastille, and, when he appeared, I told him everything
as to my adventures in England, protesting that, in
future, I would confine myself to the strict duties of
my post, or withdraw altogether from the Court, for I

felt terribly bitter against the Cardinal. Navailles, having counselled me to be calm, returned to his Eminence thoroughly sure of my innocence, and, having convinced him of it also, an order was sent to the Governor of the Bastille to give me my liberty. I do not know which of us was the more confused, the Cardinal or myself, when I went to his house to thank him. If I was afraid of being looked upon as a criminal for having lain nearly six weeks in the Bastille, he, for his part, feared my reproaches, for he knew he had been in the wrong. I described to him my doings in England, and, our interview having passed without allusion to my misfortunes, he told Navailles, when I had gone, that he was completely satisfied with my conduct. Some days later I received an order for two thousand crowns, alleged as a reward for my secret services to the State. Had I been over scrupulous, I might have refused this money, for it was not indeed the State which I had served, but the Cardinal. Be this as it may, having gone to thank his Eminence, he took the opportunity of saying that my imprisonment had not arisen from any wish of his own, having been caused solely by the denunciation of M. de Bordeaux. His Eminence added that he had to be careful not to show any undue favour to his servants for fear of a public outcry. These excuses, together with the two thousand crowns (which seemed to me most important of all), entirely calmed my resentment, and, having made a suitable reply, we became once more upon the very best of terms.

The campaign of 1655 was now about to commence, and I spent part of my money in an outfit, and kept the rest to entertain my friends with. Unlike the

people of my province, who are, as a rule, stingy,
I liked to be hospitable, being wont to declare that
money was made to be used, and I would as soon have
none at all as keep it at the bottom of a coffer, as
many people did.   M. le Cardinal was glad to see me
of such a disposition, though not of it himself.   Our
army set out for Hainaut, and suddenly attacked
Landrecies.   M. le Cardinal came to Guise with the
King, so as to be able to issue his orders.   The army
was that year commanded by the Vicomte de Turenne
and the Maréchal de la Ferté, his Eminence having
adopted the plan of having two generals to an army,
so as they might act as a check on one another in the
way of treachery.   Landrecies was in due course captured, the Vicomte de Turenne giving proof of the
very highest generalship.   I acted as a hostage whilst
negotiations were being carried on for the surrender of
the town, and, when these had been signed, Navailles
advised me to ask for the governorship, which I should
not have done of my own accord, for it was a most
important position.   His Eminence very politely expressed his regret at not being able to comply with my
wishes, citing many officers senior to myself, who
would raise strong objections to my obtaining such a
reward, and, at the same time, advised me to be more
moderate in my demands in future.   After the capitu-
lation of Landrecies, the King held a review of the
army, remaining on horseback from four in the morning
till eight at night, taking even his food on horseback ;
everyone admired his determination.   His Majesty
afterwards returned to Guise.   La Capelle was now
attacked by our troops, but, after two or three furious
combats, we abandoned the siege of that city.   We

then, after some further fighting, drove the enemy to take shelter under the cannon of Condé; and the Château de Bossu having been captured by our forces, the King was installed in it. As his Majesty was followed by a large suite, much forage was wanted for their horses; and this had to be obtained from under the gates of Valenciennes, our supplies having given out. Foraging was dangerous work, and the parties which engaged in it were always commanded by lieutenant-généraux, some of whom were none too clever officers.

Bussi Rabutin did not however include himself amongst this latter class. Never had man such a good opinion of himself, and because he was successful with the ladies, he wanted to be so in military matters, for which he had in reality but little bent. Everyone wished him to meet with some reverse, so as he might be humiliated, for there was nobody secure against his tongue. It was not long before this desire was gratified. Having been ordered to go on a foraging party, Bussi set out with a certain number of squadrons, and being lured into an ambuscade by the enemy, who executing a clever manœuvre devised by the Duc de Bournonville, Governor of Valenciennes, at first pretended to retreat, the body of horsemen under his command was totally routed and forced to fly. Nor was he one of the last to do so, and, in fact, it was he himself who brought news of the defeat, though he tried to make light of it. This reverse was a great mortification for him, and for some time he behaved more wisely, but as when people are used to anything, they speedily return to their vomit, not only did he recommence being more slanderous than ever, but

further employed his pen, which was just as biting as
his tongue.   He composed his "Histoire amoureuse
des Gaules," a small book quite full of slanders, with
which he mingled some truth to make it appear more
true.   Nevertheless, he kept this book quiet for some
time, fearing lest it might prejudice his chances of
becoming a Maréchal de France, which he arrogantly
aspired to be.   Indeed, I have heard one of his friends
say, that so afraid was he on this score, that the book
would never have been published, had he obtained the
honour he coveted, but perceiving that the peace of the
Pyrenees which was concluded some years later, had
prevented all chance of his obtaining what he wished,
Bussi was enchanted to produce it from his study, so
as to revenge himself on a minister with whom he was
dissatisfied.   Apparently, he was of opinion that he
deserved this honour as much as others, amongst
whom it is true there were men no more worthy than
himself, but had it been given to everybody who did
not deserve it, there would have been more Maréchaux
de France than soldiers, for officers at that time were
far from thoroughly doing their duty.   For one who
did it, there were a thousand who thought only of
pleasure.   Not that this was the fault of the King, for
during the whole of the siege of Condé, he continued
to be seen on horseback from morning till night, just
as after the taking of Landrecies.

Condé, the siege of which had begun in the early
days of August, held out till the eighteenth of that
month, and we next besieged Saint Guillain, which
made but a feeble resistance.   After the capture of this
town, the King and his whole Court returned to Paris.
The Cardinal then recommenced his negotiations with
M. de Treville, who, as I have before said, was show-

ing himself more tractable; but, nevertheless, his
pretensions were very great, and his Eminence had
as yet come to no arrangement with him. In the
meanwhile, he had given a regiment of cavalry to his
nephew, which was to bear his name; however, the
young man was so proud, that he scorned the post
given to him, just as he would have thought the
Crown itself too insignificant a thing! His uncle
was infuriated at his behaviour, for he was very
desirous of making him into a great man. The
Cardinal would sometimes tell me with tears in his
eyes, of his unhappiness at perceiving after all he
had done for his family, that not one member of
it was able to sustain its lustre. He lamented his
nephew who had been killed at the combat of St.
Antoine, saying, that he was quite a different kind of
man from his brother. Nevertheless, his Eminence had
yet another nephew; the younger brother of these two
gave some signs of being like the eldest, but this boy
was too young for the Cardinal to rely much upon his
future, in which he was not wrong, for he was killed
some time later. Being at school at the college of
Clermont, his friends tossed him in a blanket, and
tossed him so well, that they threw him against the
ceiling. Hitting his head, he fell back into the blanket
covered with blood, and being afterwards trepanned,
died a day or two later, to the great grief of his uncle
who, nevertheless, still continued to amass all the
wealth he could lay hands on. Meanwhile, his
Eminence married one of his nieces to the eldest son
of the Duc de Modène, knowing that there were still
enough left to make a Queen of England out of,
which was still an idea of his.

His only trouble was as to which to choose—his

Britannic Majesty or Cromwell, and one of the reasons for his having sent me to England, had been to see whether Charles II. had any chance of recovering his crown. I had reported my opinion on my return. I believed that the English were much opposed to the King's restoration. Cromwell, to strengthen his position, had made them think that Charles II. had become a Catholic, owing to the persuasion of the Queen, his mother. This was enough to make them hate him more bitterly than ever, since this religion was unutterably hateful to them. Not that they could say, that the Catholics had ever done them any great harm, on the contrary, they were the sufferers since Queen Elizabeth had made Protestantism supreme in her Kingdom, but if they could not reproach them in that respect, the English were yet afraid of the yoke of the Popes. The more they examined their policy, the more they concluded that their sole end was the subjection of everyone under the guise of religion.

The Cardinal, on my reports, gave up all thoughts of the King of England, and turned his entire attention to Cromwell, though to me it seemed that he had no more to hope for from him than from the other. Religion constituted a great obstacle, but in any case, his Eminence instructed M. de Bordeaux to make an alliance with the Protector in the name of the King his master. For a long time past, our ambassador had been trying to make such a treaty, so as to prevent an alliance between England and Spain, which the Spaniards eagerly desired. Cromwell was much more inclined to make a treaty with us, and as matters appeared to be progressing well in this direction, the

Cardinal formed the idea of once more sending me to England, not secretly as before, but to deal with the Protector directly, and urge on the alliance. I was delighted at the thought of revenging myself on Bordeaux, and was calculating on embracing his mistress under his very nose, but his Eminence deeming that, after what had happened, he would make the ambassador his mortal enemy were he to send me, despatched Marsac in my place. The latter was a very simple man, and the dullest and least capable Gascon I have ever seen, and indeed, he acquitted himself of this mission so ill, that on his return, his Eminence abandoned all hopes of succeeding in his plans. He might just as well have sent a child as a man like this. The Cardinal speaking of him to me, said he was so good a man, that he had become a complete fool. My reply was, that Marsac might be said to be no richer in intellect than in manners. As a matter of fact, he was like a pig jobber, and without his sword, might have been taken for one just come from selling his stock at a fair. For this reason, as he knew he would look no better in a rich dress, he spent no money on his clothes, but was always so simply dressed that one clearly perceived that he took no delight in the vanities of the world.

However, to leave this poor man, who has for some time been rotting in the tomb, I must mention that M. le Cardinal, always eager for gain, now took it into his head to substitute a new copper coin for the " denier " which then circulated in France. He declared that there was not sufficient small coin in the country, but a governor of a province, who was a very clever man, hearing of this, played him a trick which his Eminence did not forget for some time. Being called upon to pay the minister one hundred thousand crowns, he collected all the small money in his province, and placing it in carts, sent it to Paris with a letter stating that, there being only small coins in his district, he was obliged to send the sum in this form, though he had wasted much time in endeavouring to obtain larger pieces. The Cardinal was much astonished at seeing a number of carts entering his courtyard, but clearly understood that which this governor meant to express, which was that he was wrong to try and pretend that there was any lack of small coins.

Cromwell, whilst negotiating the treaty which I have spoken of, had wished it to be kept secret till such time as he should have drawn some money from the English Parliament on certain specious pretexts. However, as everything is liable to be discovered, the Spaniards were informed of what was going on by the wife of Major-General Lambert, the great friend of Cromwell. She hid herself one day in her husband's room to learn what Bordeaux came there so often for, and she was the more curious because Cromwell himself took part in these conferences. Nevertheless, she, as well as her husband, was a pensioner of France, which should have prevented her from disclosing our secrets. However, being in possession of such an important one as this, she thought she would make something out of it; and, having entered into communication with the Spanish Ambassador, the latter deemed her information so valuable that he readily agreed to her stipulations. He at once went *incognito* to see the Speaker of the Lower House, who was a staunch partisan of the King, his master, and told him what was going on. The Speaker, in return, advised the Spaniard to continue trying to make his treaty without taking notice of anything else, and, further, to notify to the Parliament the conditions he was proposing, so as to make clear how advantageous they were to England. The ambassador followed this advice, and, further, had his proposals printed, so as to make them known in the whole City of London, and then all over the entire Kingdom. Hiring some men, he told them to go and distribute these pamphlets all over the town. Probably it had all been arranged with the Speaker. Be this as it may, one of these men having cried the contents of his pamphlets right under the windows of Cromwell's room, the latter listened to what he was saying, and, no sooner had he done so, than he immediately ordered the arrest of the crier, and, after extracting the name of the person who had instigated him to do this, had him conveyed to Newgate and strangled the next evening without further trial. His companions no sooner heard of this than they fled in all directions, and no longer dared sell their wares, except in secret.

The Spanish Ambassador received his own particular correction the first time he returned to Whitehall, but going, as it were, double or quits, he complained to the Parliament of the way the Protector had behaved in the matter, and though it was largely composed of Cromwell's creatures, there was a party in it which began to protest against what was going on. Indeed, this agitation went so far that there was a kind of rebellion in the City of London, which retarded the execution of the treaty, which the Protector had made with his Majesty, and made the Cardinal clearly see that his great schemes were still a long way off realisation. He, consequently, determined not to again refuse any good match for his nieces on account of imaginary hopes.

The campaign of Flanders having ended after the taking of St. Guillain, the King returned to Paris, and M. le Cardinal, to keep his Majesty amused whilst he filled his purse, gave a magnificent ball, the marriage of one of his nieces with the Duc de Modène serving as a pretext. The position of his Eminence was now more assured than ever, and the King, as it were, saw only with his eyes, which was natural enough, considering that the Queen-mother perpetually sang his praises. She was, nevertheless, much pained at the war with Spain, though it was now forty years since she had left her country, and did not fail to attempt to make the minister conclude a peace, which for his own reasons he was unwilling to do. He declared that it would be very unwise to draw back now that matters were proceeding so well, and, besides, the French nation wanted occupation, and the nobility required something to do, to that extent that did they not find it outside the kingdom they would soon look for it within.

The winter having thus passed with many entertainments, the Cardinal held a great council of war in the month of March to know what the King's arms in Flanders were to do in the next campaign. The siege of Valenciennes had already been decided on, and great preparations made for it. The enemy had taken measures to oppose us, and it was a question whether we ought not to attack Dunkerque instead, so as to carry out the conditions of the treaty with the Protector. However, Cromwell had more to do at home than people thought, and could not consequently keep his word. The complaints of the Spanish Ambassador had aroused the English people from its indifference, and it appeared so outraged at his having looked after his own private interests in preference to those of the public, as never to forgive him for it. In short, everyone in England cried out for a war with France, instead of approving of the treaty. All Cromwell had done had been to declare that he understood what he was doing better than the people themselves, but they were so much struck by the offers of Calais and Boulogne, with which the Spanish Ambassador tempted them, as to appear deaf to everything else. The Cardinal, therefore, could not rely upon the treaty, and, in consequence of this, held the council of war which I have mentioned. It was there resolved, on the advice of the Maréchal de la Ferté and other generals, to push on with the campaign; the Vicomte de Turenne alone strongly recommending that matters should be thoroughly considered before an advance was made. In due course, Valenciennes was besieged and the resistance we encountered there was of a very formidable kind. After some slight successes, which were due to the cleverness of the governor, who was the Comte de Hennin, the Prince de Condé, the Comte de Fuensaldagne and Don Juan d'Autriche advanced to the attack. These three commanders were, indeed, formidable opponents. Perceiving that the position held by M. de Turenne was defended in a manner which showed that everything was in order, they turned their attention to the lines of the Maréchal de la Ferté, who, impetuously

declining an offer of assistance made by the Vicomte
de Turenne, paid dearly for his folly, for his position was
easily carried, only our regiment and the regiment of
marine offering any serious resistance. The Maréchal
de la Ferté disdained to take refuge in the camp of
M. de Turenne, and was made prisoner, together with
three lieutenant-généraux, to wit, MM. les Comtes de
Gadagne d'Estreés and de Grandpré. Besides this, a
number of distinguished persons fell on this occasion
into the hands of the enemy. I was not so particular
as the maréchal had been, and saved myself by the
dike. Meanwhile, M. de Turenne, forgetting all
rancorous thoughts as to the way in which he had
been treated, gave orders to the regiments of Rambures
and de la Feuil to advance to the attack, but the
bogginess of the ground caused by the breaking of the
dike forced them to retreat—the soldiers sinking in
the mud at every step, and it was all the general could
do to keep order amongst his troops. He now sought
to reassure the army, and displayed the greatest coolness and composure.

It is extraordinary why we were not hard pressed
after our defeat by the enemy, instead of being merely
harassed by two or three squadrons, which were easily
kept at bay by the two thousand horse, with which the
Vicomte de Turenne covered our retreat. Indeed,
to such an extent were our soldiers overcome by terror
that the rustle of the smallest leaf aroused them.
A hare, for instance, chancing to be started under the
hoofs of the cavalry, the advance guard no sooner
heard some musket shots, which were fired at this
poor animal, than they became quite as alarmed as
if the enemy were already upon them.

Having learnt that an attack was contemplated upon Condé, he sent eight hundred horsemen to that town by a circuitous route, each with a sack of corn on his horse, for it was but ill-supplied with provisions, and was full of fugitives from our army who were starving. After depositing the corn, these horsemen returned; but it would have been better had they stayed in the place of the stragglers who filled the city. Condé, nevertheless, made a vigorous resistance under the lieutenant-général, who was its commander—Passage by name, a good soldier, whose only fault was a hankering to be thought of a great family. Finally, however, it surrendered on honourable terms, and so M. de Turenne found himself in a more difficult pass than ever. Nevertheless, after a pretended retreat towards France, he made direct for la Capelle, which he besieged. This city was held by the Comte de Chamilly for the Prince de Condé, who hearing of its siege, at once sent the son of Chamilly to help his father, and to reassure him. He, therefore, in spite of having but a small garrison, declined all proposals for surrender, and made a much better resistance than might have been anticipated. Meanwhile, the Spaniards on the urgent appeal of M. le Prince, abandoned besieging Saint Guillain and went to the relief of la Capelle, but they were much chagrined on the way to learn that the city in question had capitulated.

The whole of France which had deemed itself lost, or at least in great danger after the defeat of Valenciennes, admired the conduct of the Vicomte de Turenne, who had set everything right; indeed, he had done a good deal, for, if we had lost Condé, we had recaptured la Capelle. For the latter town had

been captured during our civil wars, and since then we
had been unable to retake it, though from no lack of
wishing to do so. The King came to the camp to
show his army his satisfaction at what it had done,
but while he paid us all these compliments, he reserved
some special ones for the Vicomte, who assuredly
deserved them. His Majesty remained in the camp
for some days, until a convoy destined for Landrecies
had been prepared. He selected that route to return
to France, and our regiment went ahead to reach
Compiègne, where I was to be quartered. Some time
afterwards, I returned to the Court where such
magnificence prevailed, that it was very easy to see
that it was no longer suffering from the misery which
had been its lot during the civil war.

END OF PART II

Milton Keynes UK
Ingram Content Group UK Ltd.
UKHW022014160823
426999UK00004B/70